Drugs, Alcohol and Sport

The use of alcohol and drugs seems contradictory to the popular ideal of sport as a healthy moral and physical pursuit, and yet it has been present in sports culture since clubs first became the focus for competitive games and social gatherings. Charting the changing patterns of the use of drugs and alcohol since the nineteenth century, this is a critical history that relates substance consumption and regulation to social relations of power: sports men and women almost revelling in their deviance and leaving the moral agonising to their supposed 'superiors'. In addition, certain substances have become at various times the focus of heightened controversy, raising questions about the symbolism of the body in sport, its uses and behaviours and associated perceptions. These questions are tackled here in a lively discussion on the social construction of drug and alcohol use, ideal as a catalyst for debate or as an informed introduction to the hottest topic in sport today.

This book was previously published as a special issue of *Sport in History*.

Paul Dimeo lectures in Sports Studies at the University of Stirling.

Drugs, Alcohol and Sport

Edited by
Paul Dimeo

Routledge
Taylor & Francis Group
LONDON AND NEW YORK

First published 2006 by Routledge
2 Park Square, Milton Park, Abingdon, Oxon, OX14 4RN

Simultaneously published in the USA and Canada
by Routledge
270 Madison Ave, New York, NY 10016

Routledge is an imprint of the Taylor & Francis Group, an informa business

Typeset in Frutiger and Minion by Datapage International Ltd., Dublin, Ireland.
Printed and bound in Great Britain by Antony Rowe Ltd., Chippenham,
Wiltshire

British Library Cataloguing in Publication Data
A catalogue record for this book is available from the British Library

Library of Congress Cataloging in Publication Data
A catalog record for this book has been requested

ISBN10 0-415-40016-3
ISBN13 978-0-415-40016-9

Contents

Introduction

Paul Dimeo

To borrow a phrase from Jeff Hill, there is a certain 'unevenness of coverage' [1] in the history of drug use in sport. If we begin by considering that drug use can include alcohol, recreational drugs and performance-enhancing drugs, then it is clear that most of the analysis and debate has been skewed towards the last of these, with some recent studies on the first and almost none on the second. Another consideration is one of time-frames: most of the alcohol studies are rooted in early modern periods, while the 'doping' studies tend to focus on the post-war period of policy, regulation and scandal. Which leads to a third difference, that of subject matter. Alcohol studies tend to focus on individuals who had sporting careers blighted by addiction, on the contributions made by members of the alcohol industries or on spectator consumption. Doping studies tend to focus on the formalities of ethics, punishment, rationales for legalization/liberalization and moments of scandal.

It should be acknowledged, though, that in the case of performance-enhancing drugs we are dealing with a highly politicized environment. William Taylor expressed his exasperation with the field in which he worked as pioneer, educator, scientist and writer: 'I have learned that when medicine, sports, and politics collide, it is not a pretty sight.' [2] As a result, the fascination of doping use and anti-doping legislation has been the dilemmas resulting from the mismatch of ethics, science and governance. A story different to that of alcohol where intervention has been limited, despite numerous cases over the best part of two centuries to suggest that the health and moral benefits of sport can be undermined by alcohol use. This history is not nearly so political.

There is a form of hypocrisy in the diverse ways in which alcohol and other drugs have been treated. The late American comedian Bill Hicks mocked this tendency in wider society by pointing out that 'It's OK to *drink* your drug' because it can be taxed. What he then argued was that alcohol 'kills more people than crack, coke and heroin each year', and that alcohol is most likely to be the drug causing anti-social or violent behaviour among spectators at public events. [3] It is rare to find such a strenuous attack on the 'social acceptability' of alcohol – for this, and several other similar reversals of mainstream opinion, Hicks was considered a maverick and marginalized from developing his career through popular media outlets.

He does have a point, though. If sports authorities are so obsessed with protecting the health of participants that they ban a range of drugs that might be used for performance, why is the widespread consumption of alcohol by spectators actively encouraged? And why has so little been done to protect sportsmen and -women from addiction problems during and after their careers? Yet, paradoxically, recent British football players who have admitted alcohol addiction have been treated with offers of rehabilitation and counselling rather than purely with moral disgust. Alcohol therefore is part of the environment; abuse is a failure of self-control.

Something similar might be said for doping drugs. Modern sport involves socializing individual performers from as early in their lives as possible to be more driven than any of their peers to succeed. Stimulant drugs are part of their environment: on offer through various forms of 'underground' networks, from local gyms to cycling teams to research laboratories. Such drugs are the extension of the logic to succeed, and the logic to seek out external techniques for improvement. Not taking them is a test of self-control. The significant difference between 'dopers' and alcohol 'abusers' is the determination of the authorities to catch, humiliate and punish offenders. While this is a crucial point and has ramifications for policy analysis, it suggests that the problem may not just be with how sport is regulated but with the essence of sport and the pressure put on performers.

The contributions to this special issue each in their own way push forward our understanding of drug use in sport. It is now becoming more acceptable to face the reality that sports participants will at times choose to contravene moral opinion and to take health risks in their desire to win. There has also been a fuller discussion of the notions of health and fair play – the classic twin pillars of anti-doping. However, there is still a need for good histories of certain social processes: the optimistic sense of progress of the inter-war period; the gradual emergence of anti-doping ethics in the 1950s and 1960s; the eventual emergence of anti-doping policy and science; the struggles to consolidate and harmonize policy. There is also a need for a critical interrogation of anti-doping: not as a movement or a campaign but as a loosely connected series of individuals with their own subtle but possibly pernicious agendas. Finally, we need to know more about the history of science as a social and cultural construction – something that sports historians have shied away from. The changing perception and use of alcohol as stimulant shows that scientific knowledge is not static or culturally neutral.

If there is an overarching theme it is health – or rather the connection between health, performance and ethics. This collection aims to open up the debates on what we know about drugs, what myths are passed off as facts, and leads us to ask critical questions about the values and logic of sport itself.

Acknowledgements

I would like to thank Joyce Kay and Jacqui Baird for their help with this collection.

Notes

[1]   Jeff Hill, 'Introduction: sport and politics', *Journal of Contemporary History*, 38 (3) (July 2003), p. 355.
[2]   William N. Taylor, *Macho medicine: a history of the anabolic steroid epidemic* (Jefferson, NC, 1991), p. 93.
[3]   Bill Hicks, *Love all the people: letters, lyrics and routines* (London, 2004), pp. 59–60.

The Sons of Lush: Tom Wills, Alcohol and the Colonial Cricketer

Gregory M. de Moore

Alcohol, cricket and the colonial era

The temperance movement was a potent force for social and moral reform in nineteenth-century Australia. There were four principles of temperance teaching: that alcohol was not a natural substance, that is, it was man-made and not God given; that alcohol was a poison; that it was produced through decomposition; and that it was not a food. [4]

The temperance voice was strident and unbending. It gave political weight to the stories of wreckage and despair from alcohol abuse. It wedded alcohol to madness, poverty, criminality and corruption of the hereditary line. Its language was unforgiving, obsessive and histrionic. Like an expanse of reclaimed land, men were hoped to be redeemable and made arable once again. Overzealous, the extreme temperance view became an easy target for its enemies in politics, the licensed victuallers and brewing industries. [5]

Reports of excessive drinking in the colonies were daily fare for newspapers and periodicals. It was seen as a barometer of moral health. Despite the apparent widespread drinking in colonial and English cricket, the game was portrayed as a saviour for those who might otherwise be seduced by alcohol, sloth and sin. As described by the general newspaper *Sydney Mail* in 1862,

> the habits that cricket renders imperatively necessary are those of studied and continued temperance. No man who has not such habits can long preserve that accuracy of eye and that prompt decision that are indispensable to the cricketer. But needful as these habits admittedly are in England, they are very much more so here. In order to preserve health it is well known that exercise is necessary but this climate is peculiarly enervating, and naturally indisposes to the taking of necessary exercise, therefore to promote the disposition to take exercise it is essential that some interest and enjoyment should be mingled with it. Now there is no game that gives this interest and enjoyment in a higher degree than does the game of cricket. It promotes a wholesome exercise and furnishes an innocent means of enjoyment. [6]

A similar theme was expressed in specialist sporting papers:

> The cadaverous cheek, the sunken eye, the attenuated limbs will quickly vanish, and give place to the bright glow, the cheerful glance, and the sinewy form of robust health. Content will mantle every countenance, and dissipation be banished. The pot-houses of the towns and villages will no longer be inundated with swarms of sottish drunkards, expending their last hard-earned penny in the purchase of maddening liquors; spouting obscenity with inflamed and haggard looks and phrenzied gestures; or endeavouring in their infuriated state to cut, maim, and mangle each other's bodies, until conveyed by the constabulary to a place of safety for the night, and next morning condemned by a magistrate to expiate their folly by months of incarceration. Encourage, we repeat, those manly pastimes, and you will have no cause to repent of a course so politic and commendable but agree with us in opinion that such sports are the germs of sound

morality and permanent happiness – of national prosperity, and of national honor. [7]

To define the extent of drinking, its effect upon players, and the role of entrepreneurial publicans requires the accumulation of flints of evidence. Most of this evidence derives from newspapers and constitutes a strong argument that alcohol was an inseparable part of colonial cricket. The rituals of drink were as integral to the composition of cricket as any piece of physical apparatus. There is evidence of drinking before, during and after matches. Important occasions such as intercolonial matches were festooned with dinners, balls and lunchtime banquets. Less formal drinking took place in the cricketers' tent on the ground during the course of a game.

The more formal occasions fulfilled a number of functions. They provided sustenance for the players as well as a public exhibition of courtesy to visiting teams. The offerings of liquor and food were not trivial but were itemized tokens of an elaborate ritual. Alcohol symbolized celebration, camaraderie and leisure. Invited guests and players sat down to their banquet as toasts and speeches were made. Guests could and often did include governors, key sporting and political personnel. When the governor of Victoria trumpeted that no one ever saw an intemperate cricketer in Victoria there were jubilant assents. [8] Speeches were not confined to the subject of cricket. This was a forum for pontificating about the links between masculinity, nationalism, sport and heroism. These rituals exemplified the double standards of sporting attitudes to drink. Dignitaries, administrators and players could drink their fill at lunch breaks while extolling the virtues of manliness and athleticism.

Tom Wills

Tom Wills was born in Australia in 1835. He committed suicide in 1880 while in the throes of alcohol withdrawal. He was the first hero of Australian Rules football and the greatest colonial cricketer of his generation. [9]

Although the most brilliant of the brilliant, his career was marked by controversy. He was the first cricketer to be called for throwing during intercolonial matches. The blueprint for his cricket career was set when his father, in 1850, despatched him to Rugby School in the English Midlands. The years he spent in England, first at Rugby, then travelling the country as a gentleman cricketer, shaped his life's trajectory. He returned to the colony of Victoria in December 1856 with the accoutrements of the well-appointed amateur cricketer. He returned to dominate colonial cricket as Victoria's captain. He was one of a coterie of young men who played cricket and football and drank, as they lived, for pleasure. Many of these men, including Wills, died well before old age. [10]

In 1861, at the beckoning of his father he was summoned from Victoria to the family property of Cullinlaringo in Queensland. On 17 October 1861, his father, along with eighteen other settlers, was killed in conflict with the local Aboriginal people. Intriguingly, and despite this traumatic event, he later coached an Aboriginal cricket team from western Victoria. Captained by Wills, they played on Boxing Day 1866 at the Melbourne Cricket Ground to the applause of 10,000 spectators. [11]

Wills left a trail of letters in public and private through which much of his life can be reassembled. This article examines the Australian colonial period during his lifetime. The personal and developmental factors that shaped Wills's drinking are mentioned in passing only. Rather, in this article, Wills, as the foremost athlete of his day and as a man who died from the consequences of alcoholism, is used as a centrepiece around which to discuss and illustrate the place of drinking in colonial cricket, how it was reported and its impact on health.

During his cricket career, Wills rubbed shoulders with the significant Australian and English players of his day. But he gradually fell from being a gentleman amateur to the status of the more ambivalently regarded professional cricketer. By the end of his life, he was an alcoholic, living on the outskirts of Melbourne. He committed suicide, puncturing his heart with a pair of scissors while in a state of frenzied delirium. [12] His death from the consequences of alcohol abuse was the most famous and tragic of the era. Tom Wills's drinking was severe, but was typical of many sportsmen of the day. He, more than any other Australian, exemplifies the period of Australian cricket from the early matches between colonies in the late 1850s until the beginning of regular Test cricket.

Drinking and the intercolonial player

> Tom got drunk the other day when he was playing in a match in Melbourne and he kept himself on bowling all the time with his slows. He had a short clay pipe in his mouth and was kicking up a fine to do and making the people laugh. [13]

Organized colonial sport was a seductive and welcoming place for those who wished to drink, and like-minded males from late adolescence, with little constraint, were likely to drink and drink heavily. It was a narrow world of players, administrators and admirers; time was plentiful and players sufficiently idle for recreational drinking. Explicit documentation of intoxication on the sports field, however, was uncommon. More commonly there was the insinuation of intoxication, but even when descriptions were candid, individual players were rarely named. This applied to Tom Wills as much as to any other individual during his playing lifetime.

There are numerous examples of former players who recalled drunkenness on the cricket field, beginning with the first match between New South Wales (NSW) and Victoria in 1856. Josiah Hammersley played cricket for the colony of Victoria before taking on a career as a sports journalist in Melbourne. English by birth, his sense of superiority led him to patronize and taunt his colonial peers. He rapidly became the dominant voice in cricket journalism in Victoria and remained so for nearly two decades. He recalled how a profligate and cocky Victorian team lost to NSW: 'Nor can we forget our dismay at being beaten on our own ground when we reckoned victory a certainty, and were inclined rather to look with disdain on our opponents, who wisely slept when others feasted and danced, and preferred their Spartan broth to turkey and champagne.' [14]

In 1883, in a series of reflective articles, Hammersley recalled a conversation in Melbourne with a member of the Victorian cricket team from that first intercolonial game of 1856. It was a game which was notable for the effect of alcohol upon the players in the field. Vital catches were dropped. Hammersley records: 'It was a curious match, and Captain Hotham told me that many of the Melbourne players were "suffering a recovery" the last day, and it looks as if some of the New South Wales were also.' [15]

The second intercolonial game between the two colonies, and the first in which Wills played, took place in 1857. Responding to criticism of another Victorian loss, it marked a rare occasion when Wills defended his players from taunts of drunkenness. He wrote:

> It is stated that some six or seven of the eleven, when they appeared on the ground, were not able to stand; in fact, that they were intoxicated. Now I really do not see what good people do themselves or any one else by bringing forward such uncalled for and most ungentlemanly reports, to say the least of it. Now I have played in as many matches as any one in the colony, and know, or ought to know, what cricket is; and I will say I scarcely ever saw an eleven conduct themselves with such propriety as did the Victorians on this occasion. [16]

There are scattered but consistent accusations that intercolonial cricket teams indulged in drinking throughout the 1860s and 1870s. In 1861, a querulous correspondent to *Bells Life Victoria* repeated accusations that the Victorian cricket team was in a state of chronic intoxication. Two years later, the same correspondent wrote that the Victorians needed to swear off their liquor before going to Sydney to play in the intercolonial match. [17]

The earliest unequivocal evidence we have for Tom Wills being drunk on the sporting field is 1865. The description quoted earlier was penned by his adoring brother Egbert, then a young schoolboy at Scotch College, Melbourne. Egbert casually recalled a recent club cricket match in Melbourne where Tom, drunk, created havoc. The crowd reaction was not one of condemnation but of mirth as he played up to their expectations. The pantomime unfolded as he puffed on his small clay pipe and self-indulgently tossed down his innocuous slow balls. [18]

In the 1866 intercolonial, in which Wills did not play, William Greaves and Sam Cosstick, who were professionals with the Melbourne Cricket Club (MCC) were accused of misbehaviour and intoxication during the match in Sydney: 'one of our principal bowlers was out dissipating until four o'clock on the first morning of the match! . . . [O]ther bowlers were never to be found in their hotel, and turned up on match morning evidently very seedy and in need of rest and sleep. [19] Both continued to play with the Melbourne Cricket Club despite their 'spreeing'. [20]

Though less lurid in their language, the archives of the nineteenth century reveal bad behaviour and drunkenness similar to today's newspaper articles on contemporary sportsmen. In 1868, a champion amateur cricketer, John Conway, and another player were brought before the MCC for misbehaviour after a cricket match. They were chastised for drunkenness and lewd behaviour while in the company of women who were taking a buggy trip between Melbourne and Ballarat. [21] On another occasion, an intoxicated Conway and the professional Sam Cosstick caused a public nuisance with 'blackguardly and disgusting' behaviour on a steamer on their way to represent Victoria in an intercolonial match. [22] The public expectations of the amateur cricketer were similar to modern calls for sportsmen to act as role models for the community:

> Passengers on board intercolonial steamers will be apt in future to regard Victorian cricketers as undesirable companions, and it is even possible that the directors of steam-boat companies may impose a higher rate of passage money or stipulate that a certain portion of their vessels shall be set apart for cricketers, so that other passengers may

avoid any possibility of annoyance. . . . We may make some allowance at times for professional players, but men who assume the positions of gentlemen should remember what is expected of them, and that it is their duty to set an example to professional players. [23]

Drinking affected players off the field as much as on it. A brazen exhibition of drunkenness by the Victorian professional Sam Cosstick never saw the light of day in the public press: instead Sam Cosstick was hauled up before a Melbourne Cricket Club committee for his customary misbehaviour. He was accused by the pavilion-keeper of being insensibly drunk and lying unconscious near the bar. Tom Wills was called in as a witness, not coincidentally, by Cosstick. Maintaining a strict policy of evasion and camaraderie with a fellow professional, Wills's testimony was farcical and despite evidence to the contrary he refused to condemn Cosstick. An exasperated and frustrated committee dismissed Wills:

> Mr Wills was questioned on the subject at Cosstick's request and was also invited to say anything he wished bearing on the matter, but his evidence only went as far as supporting Cossticks' denial of having made any disturbance or said anything disrespectful of any member of the club as far as he knew also in accusing Mr Treen of having made statements at variance with the truth – it entirely failed, did not even attempt, to touch upon the principal charge and the committee after a careful and patient investigation were compelled to believe that Mr Treen's statements were in substance correct. [24]

Aboriginal cricket team

In 1866 Tom Wills captained and coached an Aboriginal cricket eleven from western Victoria. The team was later captained and coached by Charles Lawrence who arrived in Australian with H.H. Stephenson's England tour to Australia. It was Lawrence, after having usurped Wills as the Aboriginal team's leader, who took the team to England in 1868. The fear that alcohol might corrupt the team was ever present, if understated, in newspaper reports. Accusations of intemperance were few but did surface both when the team was captained by Wills and by Lawrence. A private letter that recalled the England tour makes it clear that alcohol abuse was at times a problem. [25]

There were several public incidents during the period 1866 to 1868 in which individual Aborigines were reported as intoxicated. The most notable public example on tour in England was the arrest of a player called Tiger, who was charged with assaulting a police officer in Sheffield. [26] In 1870 Bullocky, one of the more accomplished aboriginal players, was accused of intoxication on the cricket field while playing for Victoria. The language used was euphemistic and knowing in its implication of alcoholism. It is notable because reference to on-field drunkenness of any kind at any time for cricketers, Aboriginal or otherwise, was uncommon. The newspaper reporter wrote: 'Bullocky, who had not evidently the strictest regard to the centre of gravity (attributable to a cause then too apparent) missed 2 very simple catches at the most critical part of the game.' [27]

Although newspapers of the day did not highlight alcohol abuse in the Aboriginal team, the evidence suggests it was a problem in a manner not dissimilar to that of the broader cricket community. Race neither protected nor promoted its reporting in cricket. There was no suggestion that misconduct by the Aboriginal team was magnified, pounced upon or denigrated as a general rule: if anything, the team was unrealistically held up as a paragon of temperance. This was contrasted with the popular view of alcohol abuse in Aboriginal communities that had reduced individuals to live a life of squalor and humiliation. However, one aspect of the press response to the Aboriginal players was distinctive. When accusations did break through into print, such as with Tiger and Bullocky, the individuals were stereotyped as either the dissolute and vagrant Aborigine, or as exemplifying a race of weak intellect.

England tours of Australia

The England tours of the 1860s and 1870s offer a unique opportunity to scrutinize player habits. The first tour, by H.H. Stephenson in 1861, was sponsored by Spiers and Pond, the 'eminent purveyors of nobblers'. [28] (A nobbler was a common mid-nineteenth century slang term for alcohol.) Stephenson's tour and that of George Parr in 1864 saw comment on the English players' propensity to drink and their seduction into 'high living' by the locals. Commentary was often critical of local players while the English were afforded an obsequious deference:

> We have heard much of their doings in the field; and more of their performances at the festive board. They have shewn what English muscle can do; ... our colonial men have only indicated their ability to play better than their antagonists in 'heavy ballast,' and under certain unsteady conditions of hand and eye. [29]

But it was the anticipated tours by W.G. Grace in the 1870s that most clearly exposed the wanton drinking by players. Grace's journey across the colonies was charted and scrutinized. Team breakfasts in fashionable hotels were not uncommon; for example, the team breakfast menu at Tattersalls Hotel, Sydney, included game food and a wide array of alcohols. These breakfast beverages included champagne, colonial wines, hock, claret, sherry and liqueurs. [30] James Southerton, who toured with Grace, was an English professional of acute intellect and fine sensibilities, and his handwritten diaries give graphic accounts of drinking among the visiting English cricketers in the 1870s. With an ironic twist, it was Southerton the professional who was contemptible of the low life and habits of his colleagues. Drinking and debauchery were variously described in the language of the day as 'on the spree' and 'knocking about'. [31]

One of these profligate cricketers was Henry Jupp, who came to Australia twice, the first time with W.G. Grace in 1873/4. He was at centre stage of one of the most conspicuous allegations of drunkenness in cricket at that period: he was hospitalized in Adelaide with what was reported as 'delirium tremens' (DTs). Southerton nursed Jupp through the most florid of visual hallucinations and fragmented delusions. Southerton's diaries give a dramatic account of Jupp's hospitalization: Jupp exploded into delusional accusations against those around him and was 'so evidently mad' that he was taken to the Adelaide Hospital with 'the assistance of two policemen...and put...in a padded room' [32] The admission register from the hospital states that Jupp suffered from alcoholism. [33] It was later queried whether he did suffer from DTs. [34] Regardless of Jupp's precise diagnosis, he was clearly affected repeatedly by excessive alcohol use during the tour. The casual acceptance of Jupp's diagnosis of delirium tremens by Southerton and by the press tells a great deal about attitudes to, and knowledge of, alcohol consumption in sporting circles. There were no apparent repercussions for Jupp, nor was his hospitalization commented upon in detail in the press despite such a graphic and harrowing illness.

Increasing contact with England teams led to familiarity with the human frailties of the English cricketers. The colonial press found it harder to offer obsequious excuses for imperial misdemeanours and poor form on the field. The colonial press was emboldened to write about the English as they saw them:

> In the first place, they were not in a fit state to play, having partaken too freely of the generosity or mistaken kindness of the Stawellites [citizens of the Victorian town of Stawell], who were very anxious to show that their love of mother country had not diminished....The cricket ground was surrounded by tall trees, and a halo of dust raised by the vehicles. The Englishmen said that the shadows from these trees

themselves prevented them from seeing the pitch of the ball. Others give a very different reason for their dullness of vision but it is very likely that it was a little bit of both. . . . If the AEE [All England Eleven] turn teetotallers, I think I could predict a complete victory for them were they to play at Stawell again. [35]

The publican cricketer

Cricket – Brewers v. Publicans

The day was wet, down poured the rain
In torrents from the sky; . . .
And on the road each brewer spent
His coin in frequent drains,
For mere external moisture went
Against those brewers' grains
And, with a bright triumphant flush,
Their captain, Mr Staves,
Swore they should crush those sons of Lush. [36]

Publican cricketers were conspicuous figures in early colonial cricket. They were all professionals who were paid to play with prominent clubs such as the Melbourne Cricket Club and this close playing association influenced the commercial relationship between clubs and professionals. In the 1850s and 1860s the group was influential in shaping the drinking culture of cricket but, for most, their frequency of moving between hotels and the occasional conviction for breaching licensing rules suggest that this was not an easy source of income. Though Wills was not a publican, he was closely associated with almost all the principal publican cricketers in the colony of Victoria, the most prominent of whom were James Bryant, Gideon Elliot, George Marshall and William Greaves. [37] Although Wills was for much of his career an amateur, he displayed an affectionate regard for these professionals. He drank and celebrated at their hotels, sat down to post-cricket-match dinners at their tables and used their facilities to convene meetings as he contemplated the rules for football. In 1876, a writer recalled how, in 1859, Tom Wills helped formulate the early rules of Australian football at the Parade Hotel, a local watering hole near the Melbourne Cricket Ground. [38]

Young sportsmen required a venue for their social and sporting meetings. There was a natural convenience in plying the trade of drink in the midst of young male sportsmen needing a venue to meet. Publican cricketers promoted local games, provided venues for dinner and entertainment and in so doing allowed their business to infiltrate sporting clubs. Thus it was typical at the intercolonial matches for Elliot and

Bryant to have prominent advertising flags in the crowd while they were on the field bowling for Victoria. The link between sport and alcohol was reinforced through newspaper advertisements which emphasized the name of the hotel, the name of the proprietor and how the hotel catered for sporting functions. [39] There was an inherent suggestion that these establishments would attend to the particular needs of sportsmen. Additionally brewers and publicans sponsored cricket publications, games and trophies. All of this provided a pervasive culture of sponsorship, camaraderie and expectation for cricketers.

These cricketers sought to press home their commercial advantage through their association with prominent clubs by linking their playing position with favourable consideration for the provision of alcohol to players, administrators and spectators. The minute books of the MCC contain detailed information on negotiations for refreshment booths at cricket matches. For example, in 1859 J.M. Bryant was granted the tender to cater for the ground for three years

> on condition that he put up a bar subject to the approval of the committee on the ground apart from the Pavilion, and serve liquor and provide refreshments to the satisfaction of the committee. The committee to have the power to dismiss him from the office of caterer for any just complaint, without notice. [40]

The harsh conditions were typical of the manner in which professionals were treated. The MCC was protective of its capacity to earn income from alcohol sales and was high-handed towards those who disputed contractual arrangements: it sought the best commercial deal for itself.

Professionals who sought such an alliance clearly knew they bargained from a position of inferiority. This extended even to the English cricketer William Caffyn, who stayed in Australia after George Parr's 1864 tour. When contracted as a professional to the MCC it was stipulated that he was 'Not to keep a house licensed for sale of spirituous liquors at any time during the engagement'. As far as is known, this was not in response to any specific accusations of intemperance towards Caffyn but rather a more general stricture the MCC came to adopt. [41]

The dubious liaison between public houses and professional cricketers was reflected in Hammersley's musings on the Richmond CC. In doing so, he made the point that the MCC wanted clearer control over its income from alcohol and that publicans who doubled up as players were less available and fit for the task of playing cricket:

> It has suffered, like many other clubs, from want of funds; and, in consequence, the professional assistance it has been able to obtain has

generally been given in return for the privilege of selling refreshments on the ground. This is anything but satisfactory; for it is well known that a publican's business and the business of a professional cricketer do not harmonise; and that men who are continually called away to 'the bar' and who seldom get to bed before the small hours of the morning, are not generally in good trim either for a match or for practice. On the Melbourne ground the refreshment department is not in the hands of a cricketer and the professionals there engaged are in no way now connected with the 'bar trade'. [42]

It is interesting to consider to what extent the Melbourne Cricket Club chose to keep or dismiss its professionals based upon accusations of intoxication and misbehaviour. In the early 1870s, Wills was overlooked for the job of professional with the MCC: preference was given to Sam Cosstick. Several MCC players, but most notably Sam Cosstick, had a record of intoxicated and unseemly behaviour, yet despite the MCC's private condemnation of Cosstick in the minute and letter books, it did not discard him. In the end, Cosstick's form was superior to Wills and the former's selection was won most likely on these grounds. Despite its moral posturing, the Melbourne Cricket Club seemed more interested in the pragmatics of winning than refusing to employ talented players even when the club had found them guilty of repeated drunkenness.

Newspapers

Oh the champagne has been at work. [43]

There were double standards in the depiction of alcohol and sport in the newspapers, but although their attitude was at times ambiguous and contradictory, only rarely was there direct comment on the effect of alcohol on individual players. When this did occur, it was their performance rather than their morality that was commented upon, in contrast to the preoccupation on the moral depravity of alcohol abuse in the general community. For most of his career, an inquisitive press did not unduly molest Wills over accusations of drinking, nor was there preoccupation with the potential conflict between the role of alcohol in commercial sponsorship of cricket and its ill effect upon players. Apart from occasional high-toned moral edicts the press seemed to play a conveniently collusive role when it came to alcohol and sport.

Newspapers varied in how openly they criticized the practice of drinking on the field. In one of the more vociferous attacks, the *Yeoman* acknowledged that there was a place for drinking: what was criticized was its extent: 'The notorious habit of leaving the field so often for the purpose of "nobblerizing" is another evil which requires a remedy.' It further described the use of the 'nobbler' as a tactic to dislodge a 'sticker' who was a troublesome batsmen to dismiss. [44] In various guises drink was claimed to unsettle, lull or stupefy the opposition before or during a game. Apart from the general effect of drunkenness it was the impact on one's sight of the ball that was regarded as most important. As one reporter described: 'Leave the field for a "nobbler," and the chances are that, upon returning to his wicket, he will find he has lost his "sight" of the ball, and so become an easy victim.' [45]

Journals such as *Melbourne Punch* were able to poke fun with seeming impunity at the Bacchanalian pleasures of cricketers: thus references to alcohol were most typically puns, asides, hints and innuendo. There was an entire vocabulary to convey attitudes to alcohol in sport. Inventive adjectives and puns like 'nobbler', 'swiper', 'licker up' and 'swingers' were used knowingly by journalists and public alike. The terms nobbler and swipes referred to alcohol. A swiper was someone who drank alcohol; licker was a play on liquor; swingers referred to the lack of balance of an inebriated individual. [46]

Euphemisms abounded: the term 'jolly' was knowingly used in reference to intoxication. [47] Vaudevillian exchanges poked fun at what the public considered was going on with their cricketers. 'Why ought some of the Victorian Cricketers to be hard hitters? Because they are such swipers.' [48] Cartoons that caricatured drunkards were common – though rarely did these relate to sport – but there were exceptions. *Sydney Punch* drew a cartoon of dissolute sportsmen, while *Melbourne Punch* pictured a drunken husband returning home to a troubled wife at the start of the cricket season. This was a rare depiction that highlighted the role of sport in the more frequently condemned link between alcohol and domestic neglect. [49]

Verse was a medium in which scandalous descriptions of Wills and other cricketers could be made by stealth. By such means journals such as *Punch,* under the cover of humour, could skewer hypocrisy and give voice to the public imaginings about alcoholic players. This was not a luxury afforded to the more conventional newspaper descriptions where sensitivities about etiquette and legality may have deterred frank portrayals of alcohol abuse. When a New South Wales periodical wanted to lampoon Wills and Victorian cricket, it did so by the following verse:

> *I think it was stuttered the Melbournites led,*
> *And hiccuped, 'Our fellows are going ahead*
> *In spite of (hic) Wills and his "swingers".'. . .*

But I cannot wind up without hinting of pale
Bottled brandy and liquors like porter;
Ye knights of the bat with a droop in the tail,
If ye wish for the future to win without fail,
Remember when next in a match you regale,
Though the 'swells' of the senate grow gay upon ale,
'Tis wiser to stick to pure water. [50]

The word 'hic' was strategically placed next to Wills to hit its mark. It suggested his drunken state on the field in a way that conventional papers found impossible to convey. 'Swingers' referred to his wayward alcoholic lurches rather than the aerodynamic trajectory imparted to the ball. While somewhat tongue-in-cheek, there is little doubting its intent to highlight Wills and take a swipe at alcohol consumption by cricketers.

This use of verse was not restricted to Wills. In 1864, during George Parr's England tour of Australia, verse from *Melbourne Punch* had Parr giving advice to young cricketers in the colonies. No fewer than three verses were devoted to the detrimental effects of alcohol:

Aye strive to keep your mental sight
Particularly clear,
And if you want some stimulant,
Just take a 'ginger beer'.
And so defy sarcastic hints
Flung out by Mr PUNCH,
That some of you may sometimes play
Less steady after lunch.

For after six and twenty years
I've little cause to doubt,
That cool champagne and curly slows
Get many a batsman out. [51]

Teams were publicly warned not to drink to excess before games. In 1860 the NSW players were entreated to keep a 'steady eye and a sure arm' and to 'beware of the assiduous attention of friends, whose politeness might lead to unpleasant results. Quiet, healthy habits will greatly conduce to their chances of success. Let these be *strictly observed*, for then, if beaten, no fault will be fairly attributable to the eleven.' This overly polite but unmistakable warning regarding alcohol was typical of the period. [52]

Ambiguous and different attitudes to alcohol are not difficult to find in the sporting pages of the newspapers. An early NSW team was mocked over its public stance to eschew alcohol yet during the same period it was recalled how the Victorians drank beer for breakfast. [53] The abuse of alcohol by players was also a common excuse for a poor team performance and was used by journalists and public alike. Regardless of its validity, it was perceived that alcohol could determine the course of games. [54]

Alcohol as stimulant and tonic

> And who, again, does not recall the facies alcoholica – the blotched skin, the purple-red nose, the dull, protruding eye, the vacant stare of the confirmed sot?' [55]

While there was voluminous medical and lay literature on the deleterious effects of alcohol, these same effects upon sportsmen were rarely articulated and, when they were, often centred not on the serious physical and psychological damage but on the effects on performance. The broad effect on health was curiously ignored for the most part. There was no concerted push to alter athletes' pattern of drinking, and sporting clubs were silent on the matter.

Certain types of alcohol more than others were considered a hindrance to performance. James Thompson, intercolonial cricketer, co-author of the first written rules of Australian football, wit and journalist wrote: 'During a match be abstemious. A hearty dinner of all kinds of mixtures will seriously affect your sight. Avoid stimulants; the game is too exciting for calm play with many; and especially wine and beer *"induce a careless state of mind."* [56] Thompson's view that certain alcoholic drinks were more dangerous was reflected in other literature of the time. Claret and sherry were regarded as less harmful to the cricketer and boys in particular were advised to refrain from drinking other types of alcohol. [57]

The use of alcohol as a stimulant in sport was not unusual when one considers that it was used in a similar vein by the medical community to treat the sick. On a blisteringly hot Australian day in 1866, with wind and dust to parch the throat, the players went off the field 'to liquor'. After one break, Wills emerged from the tent 'like a giant refreshed with claret negus'. [58] Claret was commonly held to invigorate flagging sportsmen. The description of Wills as being refreshed after consuming claret during a cricket match was not just a turn of phrase: it was believed to possess restorative powers that enabled batsmen, refreshed, to face the bowling again.

An 1888 English text on cricket gave advice to young cricketers on drinking during a match:

> In hot weather something must be drunk, and the question is, What?
> Our experience is that beer and stout are both too heady and heavy,
> gin and ginger beer is too sticky, sweet, etc, to the palate. In our
> opinion, shandy-gaff, sherry, or claret and soda are the most thirst
> quenching, the lightest, and the cleanest to the palate. [59]

This reference further highlights that it was the effect on the batsman's
eyesight for the ball that was of most concern. Questions regarding long-
term physical health, effect upon performance other than eyesight and the
broader commercial marriage of alcohol and sport were never raised.

That beer improved players' abilities, particular those of a bowler, was a
subtext frequently repeated in the literature of the time. There seems to
have been a genuine belief, at least in some quarters, that a combination
of beer and beef was necessary for a fast bowler. This thinking was allied to
the belief that the fatness of the beer drinker was a sign of physical
robustness. Thus when the Victorian fast bowler Frank Allan lost form it
was duly noted prior to the next season that, as he had undertaken the
appropriate diet of beef and beer, the Victorians could expect an improved
performance. Although one is tempted to doubt this, the tone of the text
suggests it to be a genuinely held view:

> and as for the crack bowler [Allan], he, I should imagine, has taken a
> new lease of the game, for he has given up being a vegetarian and
> drinking cold water, and has taken to good solid beef and beer. If this
> does not more than place him on his old pre-eminence I shall be very
> much mistaken. [60]

The staple drink of the professionals' diet, by social class and probably
predilection, was beer. The evidence, meagre as it is, suggests that Wills
had a preference for beer. The importance accorded the type of alcohol
consumed was most clearly seen when the England team visited the
colonies in the 1860s and 1870s: beer was portrayed as the professionals'
drink while champagne was that of the gentleman amateur. The evidence
was that professionals and amateurs alike exhibited drunken behaviour
during the English tours of the 1860s and 1870s. Despite this egalitarian-
ism of drunkenness, it was the amateurs who staked the higher moral
ground when it came to matters of alcohol, as one contemporary paper
noted:

> The reason the [English] professionals did not attend the farewell
> dinner was through a remark heard by Humphrey. Mr Pickers-
> gill ... said second class was plenty good enough for us; at home we
> travelled third class, and were glad to get a glass of beer, consequently

we could not appreciate champagne given to us by these liberal-minded men. [61]

By early 1873 Josiah Hammersley and Tom Wills were engaged in a virulent public feud played out through an exchange of letters in the metropolitan newspapers. In a series of attacks and counterattacks Wills' fondness for colonial beer was publicized. Wills was humiliated and his drinking exposed to public criticism; he was dismissed by Hammersley as needing to take the 'pledge'. (There was a well-known temperance practice whereby those wishing to spurn their alcoholic ways were invited to sign pledge books). Hammersley wrote:

> You are played out now, the cricketing machine is rusty and useless, all respect for it is gone. You will never be captain of a Victorian Eleven again that you may be sure of.... Eschew colonial beer, and take the pledge and in time your failings may be forgotten, and only your talents as a cricketer remembered. Farewell, Tommy Wills. [62]

When Hammersley shamed Wills in his newspaper column by asking him to eschew colonial beer, this was not a vacant rebuke. It was a considered insult that took aim at Wills's colonial origins, his fall from the rank of amateur and the popular nineteenth-century view that linked colonial beer with violence, insanity and suicide. Accusations of the adulteration of beer were rife in the colony. [63] Colonial beer was synonymous in many minds with inferiority: therefore Hammersley's comments reflected a deeper war waged between colonial and imperial origins.

Physical decline and mortality

The caricature of the alcoholic was well publicized in the nineteenth-century press. Temperance language coloured the popular view of the alcoholic. Repulsive adjectives blurred medicine and morality in conveying the visual obscenities of extreme and prolonged alcohol abuse. The blood of an alcoholic was not merely abnormal it was 'depraved'. [64]

As measured by physical appearance Tom Wills's trajectory was steadily downwards. Immaculate and stylish in the late 1850s, his pictures in the 1860s reveal him coarse, unshaven and prematurely balding. His once admired apparel seems ill-fitting in the last fifteen years of his life. [65] An oil portrait from 1870 captured the beginnings of a gentle paunch and perhaps an alcoholic blush of his cheeks suggestive of early stages of physical deterioration. [66]

Physical decline, madness, hereditary taint and loss of one's moral fibre were viewed as natural consequences of drink. The link between alcohol, brain pathology and madness was regarded as incontrovertible. Pathology was thought to reside in the layered membranes that wrapped themselves intricately about the brain's contours, the vasculature of the brain and the brain substance itself. The brain was most commonly said to have undergone 'softening' or 'shrinkage'. In the lay literature emotive terms such as softening, shrinkage and congestion blended accusatory images of enfeeblement and moral responsibility for one's plight. Such was the case when Hammersley commented after Wills's death that the cricketer had suffered from softening of the brain. [67]

Many colonial cricketers died early deaths. Addiction to alcohol, tobacco and poor nutritional status was a feature of such deaths. In May 1880 Tom Wills developed a fulminant picture of delirium tremens (DTs) over the course of several days. DTs develops over forty-eight to seventy-two hours after the cessation or reduction of drinking in a person with a history of sustained heavy drinking of many years. [68] It is the most severe form of alcohol withdrawal. The nineteenth-century press was littered with references to DTs: it was caricatured with religious and demonic overtones, it was linked with frenzied, violent attempts at suicide such as cutting one's throat. On the afternoon of Sunday 2 May 1880, Wills, withdrawing from alcohol, was psychotic and frightened. Hounded by visions and persecuted by the shadows within his mind, he stabbed himself in the heart with a pair of scissors. [69]

The life of Tom Wills spanned a remarkable period of development for Australian cricket. His death came as Test cricket was born in the late 1870s. His great cricketing feats were achieved well before the first Test between England and Australia in 1877. By 1879 Wills had drifted to the outskirts of Melbourne. His intercolonial glory, the Aboriginal cricket team and the personality he forever imprinted upon Australian sport belonged to a colonial life that, by then, seemed like a distant land, quaint and old fashioned. Partly because of this and partly because he missed out on inclusion in the rich English literature of nineteenth-century cricket, Australia's first great cricketer was little recorded in contemporary texts beyond newspapers.

Acknowledgements

I would like to thank Dr Rob Hess, my PhD supervisor; Mr Tom Wills, Mr Terry Wills-Cooke and Mr Lawton Wills-Cooke for access to archival material on Tom Wills. I would also like to thank Peter Wynne-Thomas for access to the James Southerton diaries.

Notes

[1] Captain Hotham, recalling Victoria's loss in the first intercolonial cricket match in 1856, *Sydney Mail*, 6 Oct. 1883, p. 651.

[2] Governor of Victoria, 1862, quoted in W.J. Hammersley, ed., *The Victorian cricketer's guide for 1861–2* (Melbourne, 1862), p. 109.

[3] *Australasian*, 4 Feb. 1871, p. 139.

[4] Ann. M. Mitchell, 'Temperance and the liquor question in later nineteenth-century Victoria' (Master's thesis, University of Melbourne, 1966), p. 76.

[5] Stephen Garton, '"Once a drunkard always a drunkard": social reform and the problem of "habitual drunkenness" in Australia, 1880–1914', *Labour History*, 53, (Nov. 1987), pp. 38–53.

[6] *Sydney Mail*, 3 Feb. 1862, p. 5.

[7] 'The influence of manly sports upon national character', *Bells Life Sydney and Sporting Reviewer*, 1 Aug. 1857, p. 2.

[8] Hammersley, *Victorian cricketer's guide*, p. 109.

[9] Gregory M. de Moore, 'The suicide of Thomas Wentworth Wills', *Medical Journal of Australia*, 171 (1999), pp. 656–8.

[10] Ibid.; G.M. Hibbins, 'The Cambridge connection', *International Journal of the History of Sport*, 6 (2) (1989), pp. 172–92.

[11] Henry Reynolds, *An indelible stain* (Ringwood, 2001), p. 122; Terry S. Wills-Cooke, *The currency lad* (Leopold, 1998), pp. 97–122; L. Perrin, *Cullin-La-Ringo. The triumph and tragedy of Tommy Wills* (Stafford, 1998), pp. 84–93; 126–132.

[12] de Moore, 'Thomas Wentworth Wills'.

[13] Letter, Egbert Wills to his brother Horace, The Wills family archives, 15 Dec. 1865.

[14] *Australasian*, 8 July 1865, p. 4.

[15] *Sydney Mail*, 6 Oct. 1883, p. 651.

[16] *Bells Life Victoria*, 7 Feb. 1857, p. 3.

[17] *Bells Life Victoria*, 7 Dec. 1861, p. 4; *Bells Life Victoria*, 31 Jan. 1863, p. 4.

[18] Letter, Egbert Wills, 15 Dec. 1865.

[19] *Bells Life Victoria*, 5 Jan. 1867, p. 2.

[20] Letter to Wheelock from Andrew Newell, 27 Jan. 1867, Royal Historical Society of Victoria.

[21] Melbourne Cricket Club (hereafter MCC) minutes, 21 April 1868.

[22] *Australasian*, 15 Feb. 1868, p. 204.

[23] *Australasian*, 8 Feb. 1868, p. 172.

[24] Minutes of the Match and Ground Committee, MCC, 6 April 1869. The words are underlined as in the original document.

[25] Letter, R.C. Hayman to E.E. Bean, 20 Dec. 1933, Melbourne Cricket Club archives.

[26] '"Tiger" in Trouble', *Sheffield and Rotherham Independent*, 14 Aug. 1868, p. 3. See also *Sheffield Times*, 15 Aug. 1868, p. 7.

[27]   *Leader*, Melbourne, 26 March 1870, p. 9.

[28]   *Geelong Chronicle*, 19 Oct. 1861, p. 3.

[29]   *Bells Life Victoria*, 22 Feb. 1862, p. 4. See also *Argus*, Melbourne, 8 Jan. 1862, p. 4.

[30]   See breakfast menu, 22 Jan. 1874, Tattersalls Hotel, on display at the New South Wales Cricket Association.

[31]   James Southerton diaries, Trent Bridge Library. The diaries comprise five small (4 inch by 2 inch) notebooks handwritten by the professional bowler during the 1873/4 and 1876/7 tours of Australia.

[32]   Southerton Diaries.

[33]   GRG 78/49, admission register for Adelaide Hospital 1840–1900, 1874/414, State Records of South Australia.

[34]   *South Australian Register*, 25 March 1874, p. 5.

[35]   *Geelong Advertiser*, 16 Jan. 1874, p. 2.

[36]   *Illustrated Sydney News*, May 1876, p. 15. The noun 'lush' typically refers to a drunkard. Variations on this basic usage were commonly used as slang in nineteenth-century Australian newspapers.

[37]   For example, *Yeoman*, 25 April 1863, p. 468, where Greaves is cited as managing the Royal Hotel, Punt Road, Richmond.

[38]   See *Australasian*, 26 Feb. 1876, p. 269.

[39]   *Richmond Australian*, 3 Oct. 1863, frontispiece, advertisement for J.M. Bryant and the Cricketers Arms Hotel.

[40]   MCC Minutes, 28 Nov. 1859.

[41]   Handwritten contract, MCC minutes: the terms of agreement are between Thomas F. Hamilton, president of MCC and William Caffyn, professional cricketer, 23 April 1864.

[42]   *Bells Life Victoria*, 30 Jan. 1864, p. 4.

[43]   *Leader*, 25 March 1871, p. 11.

[44]   *Yeoman and Australian Acclimatiser*, 13 Sept 1862, p. 11.

[45]   Ibid.

[46]   For example, *Sydney Mail*, 6 Jan. 1866, p. 9; *Argus*, 28 June, 1860, p. 3; *Melbourne Punch*, 19 Feb. 1863, p. 240.

[47]   *Australasian*, 16 June 1866, p. 331.

[48]   *Melbourne Punch*, 14 Jan. 1864, p. 20.

[49]   *Sydney Punch*, 10 Sept. 1864, p. 124; *Melbourne Punch*, 19 Sept. 1867, p. 92.

[50]   *Sydney Punch*, 11 March 1871, p. 165.

[51]   *Melbourne Punch*, 7 Jan. 1864, p. 16.

[52]   *Sydney Morning Herald*, 27 Jan. 1860, p. 8.

[53]   For example, see *Cricket footprints on the sands of time* by F.M.Harpur, Box 305/1, State Library of Victoria. See *Australasian* 16 June 1866, pp. 331–2. for an example of ambiguous reference to the effect of alcohol.

[54]   For example, *Leader*, 25 March 1871, p. 11.

[55]   *The Cantor lectures on alcohol*, Australian Medical Pamphlets, no. 6 (1875), ch. 6, Physician Library, Sydney.

[56]   J.B. Thompson, ed., *The Victorian cricketer's guide* (Melbourne, 1859), p. 94.

[57]   Diary of Charles Lawrence, pp. 14–16, copy from Bernard Whimpress, South Australian Cricket Association, when playing cricket as a boy. See also Edmund H. Fellowes, *A history of Winchester cricket* (Winchester, 1930), pp. 95–6.

[58] *Sydney Mail*, 6 Jan. 1866, p. 7.
[59] A.G. Steel and R.H. Lyttelton, *Cricket* (London, 1888), pp. 212–13.
[60] *Leader*, 4 Sept. 1875, p.12.
[61] *Argus*, 17 March 1874, p. 4.
[62] *Australasian*, 25 Jan. 1873, p. 108.
[63] See *Argus*, 3 March 1875, p. 6; *Argus*, 10 March 1875, p. 10.
[64] *Australasian Medical Gazette*, June 1883, p. 192.
[65] *Weekly Times*, 22 Aug. 1908, pp. 19–20; *Leader*, 22 Aug. 1908, p. 29.
[66] Artist, William Handcock, Melbourne Cricket Club collection.
[67] *Sydney Mail*, 15 Sept. 1883, p. 508.
[68] Marc A. Shuckit, 'Alcohol-related disorders', in B.J. Sadock and V.A. Sadock, eds., *Kaplan and Sadock's comprehensive textbook of psychiatry*, vol. 1 (Philadelphia, PA, 2000), pp. 953–71.
[69] de Moore, 'Thomas Wentworth Wills', pp. 656–8.

Drink and the Professional Footballer in 1890s England and Ireland

Pamela Dixon & Neal Garnham

Drink played a crucial role in the lives of professional footballers at the end of the nineteenth century. It was the public house that had been the original focus for the formation of many clubs and subsequently they provided changing rooms and other facilities for players and fans. For example, the Everton club was based in the Queen's Head until the mid 1880s, and Blackburn Rovers used the Bay Horse Hotel as its base into the 1890s. [1] At least two Irish clubs, Distillery and Avoniel, owed their origins directly to the drink industry, as they grew out of distillery works teams. [2] For many early professionals the managing of a public house provided a welcome supplement to the wages they received for playing, or a necessary way of circumventing the rules regarding payments to players. Nick Ross, an England international and a stalwart of the Everton side, accepted a coaching appointment in Belfast in 1890 and with it the management of a pub in the Sandy Row area of the city. The premises later passed to Samuel Torrans, who also replaced Ross in his role at the Linfield club. [3] J.W. Robinson, the England goalkeeper, signed for both the Southampton club and the Wareham Arms pub in the summer of 1898. It was hoped the licensed premises would be 'thronged with football enthusiasts anxious to catch a glimpse' of the celebrity landlord. Competition eventually came from the nearby Kingsland Tavern, where Tom Nichol, Robinson's team mate, was the 'presiding genius'. [4] The leading English sports paper suggested in 1890 that the offering of licensed premises to professional players was the ultimate incentive to sign on, as 'the attraction of a public house is irresistible to most'. [5]

Moreover the drink industry generated much of the capital that found its way into the professional game. In Liverpool the very foundation of Liverpool FC owed its origins to a dispute between a sponsoring brewer and the already established Everton club. [6] The Middlesbrough Ironopolis club came to be referred to as 'the Brewers' by one local newspaper due to the measure of support they received from the local brewing family of Cameron. [7] In Ireland the Belfast Celtic club's flotation as a company was generously supported by the city's 'spirit merchants', seventy-four of whom purchased shares in the new venture. [8] An aggregate assessment of a sample of English companies for the period suggests that around 15 per cent of shares were purchased by individuals with links to the drink trade, though even this may be an underestimate. [9] Thus the drink industry was vital in the development of professional football, providing both facilities and funding. Alcohol, the money it generated, and the premises associated with its manufacture and consumption, were essential components in the creation of professional football in the late nineteenth century.

However the direct relationship that existed between alcohol and players is less obvious, and its nature is far less easily ascertained. The most recent consideration of the relationship between sport and alcohol has stressed the extent to which 'overindulgence' by players was apparently common in the period. [10] Such an assertion can certainly find an echo in the modern game. Personal confessions of alcoholic excess among football players seem to have begun with former England centre-forward Jimmy Greaves's revelations in the 1970s. He has subsequently been joined by, among others, fellow internationals Paul Merson, Tony Adams and Paul Gascoigne. [11] It is perhaps better to leave the continuing saga of former Manchester United and Northern Ireland star George Best to one side at this stage, pending further developments. [12]

More relevantly, the stress laid on excessive drinking by Collins and Vamplew, and its associated dangers, also resonate in some of the contemporary criticisms offered of the conduct of football professionals. The generally sympathetic J.J. Bentley noted in 1896 that many people thought that a professional footballer was 'a person beneath contempt – a vagabond who spends the whole of his time in a public house except for an hour and a half, when he is called upon to earn his wages'. [13] A decade and a half later, C.E. Sutcliffe, an official with the Football League and a man less attached to the ways of the professional, noted in a syndicated article that 'too many professionals become rash, extravagant and profligate'. [14] A magistrate and Baptist lay preacher in Sunderland simply dismissed professional footballers as 'ruffians'. [15] More than once profiles of professionals in the Belfast press were accompanied by the surprised announcement that the men were in fact teetotallers. [16] In Newcastle a group of players from a local club became known as 'the Burton Wanderers ... on account of their frequent journeys to licensed houses in search of liquid lunch from the town on the Trent'. [17] Even some of the players themselves thought that drink posed a peculiar problem for them and their comrades. John Bell of Everton suggested in 1898 that 'many a man has had a brilliant career cut short by over indulgence'. [18]

Occasionally, specific incidents occurred that seem to confirm that drink and drunkenness were distinct problems for footballers of the period. In Southampton in early 1898, John Farrell, a Scottish professional with the town's Southern League side, appeared in the borough police court on multiple charges of assault. His victims included a woman and a police sergeant. Following his side's victory over Leicester Fosse in the first round proper of the FA Cup, centre-forward Farrell 'took two or three glasses of drink' and became 'quarrelsome drunk'. A street brawl ensued. The result was fines totalling £5 12s, though one reporter thought Farrell should 'thank his lucky stars that his little adventure' did not have more serious consequences'. [19] In April 1893 Henry Boyd, a professional with West Bromwich Albion and at one time described as 'one of the most honest and straightforward of men', absconded before he was due to appear in court on similar charges, again apparently fuelled by drink. [20] Two years before this George King, a professional with the Sunderland Albion club, had been bound over to keep the peace following a charge of being drunk and disorderly in the town.[21] Fifteen months later, two players from the rival Sunderland Association club were prosecuted on similar grounds, and for assaulting a police officer. Only one was convicted however: Hugh Wilson, a Scot and the captain of the celebrated 'Team of All the Talents'. [22] Such misadventures occurred despite the fact that alcohol was now seen as a barrier to fitness, and potentially impeding footballers' training. Advice from an Irish coach in 1894 stressed that footballers should 'abstain from alcoholic beverages, [and] eat plain wholesome food'. Four years later 'drinks of an intoxicating nature' and smoking were reportedly prohibited before all important games. [23] In 1896 Newcastle's *Sporting Man* reprinted an article from the *Illustrated Sporting and Dramatic News* proclaiming that 'even a novice' was aware of the necessity of staying in condition, and that peak performance on the pitch proved more about a man's habits of temperance 'than the possession of all the Rechabite diplomas in the world'. [24]

Such reports, comments and advice deal only with the public face of the professional footballer, however. Yet even the records of the clubs and the football authorities, which were not prepared for public information or titillation, seem merely to offer corroboration of the situation, with accusations of excessive drinking and inappropriate behaviour appearing here too.

One example in which public utterances and private records seem to be in agreement can be drawn from the English Midlands. When the Aston Villa side under-performed in early 1893, one local newspaper had no qualms in highlighting what it perceived to be the problem. 'Drink,' it declared, 'has been the curse of the team'. [25] Despite subsequent 'great reforms', another commentator thought that success was only likely when 'the players [could] foreswear their public house appearances'. [26] A few months later a local magazine noted that although there had been a few departures from the club and some new signings, the team remained 'a warm lot' who not only worked together, but enjoyed socializing together as well. [27] If such reports suggest that there may have been a culture of drinking at Aston Villa, this is apparently confirmed by both the actions and the records of the club.

By late 1892 Villa had already secured a 'club house' for the players, complete with smoking, reading and billiard rooms, apparently in an attempt to provide an alternative attraction to the local pubs. [28] Subsequently a prize of one guinea was offered for a monthly billiard handicap among the players [29] However, the success of the venture was apparently limited. Damage was done to the billiard table and the fittings of the smoking room in late 1896; and by the spring of 1897 the players had gravitated away from the confines of the club house to the less salubrious surroundings of the New Inns public house, just ten minutes walk away. [30] Although it was thought that the summoning of the players to tea with the directors 'would do good' the result was just a request by the players that they should do less training. [31] Even the decisions to issue each player with a set of printed rules regarding his expected conduct, and the posting of a warning notice in the club house seemingly had little effect. [32] Eventually the club was reduced to writing to one local landlord, asking him not to serve their players. They also stipulated that one particular player would only be signed as a professional if he became 'a teetotaller' and agreed to attend regularly at work when he was not training. [33] When away from home the team seems to have indulged to an even greater extent. An end-of-season tour of Scotland and the north of England in 1896 culminated in a match against Newcastle United at St James's Park. The results were a win for Villa and a bill for £1 8s.6d. for 'wilful damage' to the hotel premises where they stayed. Although the Newcastle papers put the 'unusual lethargy' of the Villa side down to their exhausting schedule of games, the Birmingham correspondent who suggested the players had decided to 'enjoy themselves to the uttermost' may have been nearer the mark. [34] For the Villa club and team, drink certainly seems to have been something of a problem; and even the most attractive diversions could not deter some from alcoholic pursuits. [35]

In particular James Welford, the team's left back, seems to have had a peculiarly familiar relationship with strong drink. In March 1896 Welford was reported to the Villa committee for failing to attend training, possibly due to his drinking, and he failed to respond to a letter sent to him by the directors. Despite a subsequent promise 'to do better in future', at the beginning of the next season Welford and goalkeeper James Whitehouse were reported to the committee for getting drunk while on a trip to Grimsby to play a friendly match. Welford did not return to the team hotel until after midnight. He had also been drunk on a visit to Small Heath the previous week, and swore at the team's trainer the following Monday. As a result he was suspended for a week without pay. [36] Five months later, Welford was sent to Manchester for treatment to a recurring leg injury. While there he absconded from the clinic and returned drunk. The medical opinion was that he was suffering from ailments 'brought on by his own indiscretion'. Again he was rewarded with a week's suspension from the club. [37] Probably because of his indiscretions, Welford was excluded from the Villa team in the following games, much to the chagrin of the local press, who simply thought the committee had an unwarranted 'grievance' against the player. [38] At the end of the season he departed, along with two other Villa stalwarts, for Glasgow Celtic. [39]

The troubles experienced at Villa were not unique, and nor was James Welford. At Southampton at least one player was seemingly attracted to drink, and similar tactics of distraction were also tried. Following a report that John Petrie was 'drinking and neglecting his training' prior to an important cup tie, the club directors arranged a series of 'entertainments' for the players that varied from taking tea with the directors themselves to attending the local music hall. Though they may have been successful in the short term, within nine months Petrie was again being warned about his conduct, and threatened with suspension. [40] To return to the English Midlands, at the West Bromwich Albion club the players Dyer and McLeod were reported to the directors in October 1891 for 'drinking too much', which prompted the threat that the club would 'deal seriously with the matter'. The following month it was agreed to inform all the club's players that any of them found 'guilty of drunkenness' would be suspended without pay. [41] A year later McLeod and three team-mates were in trouble again, however, when the Albion directors learned that they had spent the entire night in the Waggon and Horses public house near the club's Stoney Lane ground. [42] Subsequently McLeod and a fellow player became involved in a brawl in West Bromwich High Street, apparently after leaving a pub. Although the incident did not make the local press, the Albion directors were concerned enough about matters to warn the players about their behaviour, and to ask McLeod to move out of his lodgings in licensed premises. [43] In Ireland, too, drink could cause problems for players and their clubs. The most serious example seems to have been that of A.J. Worrall, a professional with the Distillery club. He received a life ban from the game in 1901 for persistent drunkenness after his club, unable to deal with his behaviour, referred his case to the Irish Football Association, the sport's governing body in the country. [44]

For the most part, all the available sources seem to confirm the suggestions of the press that drink was a problem for some players. Exactly why this should have been so is debatable. It is certainly true that professional players had plenty of time and money to spare to indulge in the pastime of drinking. Training schedules seem to have covered no more than four days of the week, usually beginning in mid-morning, and terminating soon after noon. [45] For their limited troubles, players received comparatively handsome remuneration. In England, prior to the introduction of the maximum wage, a leading player with a First Division side might expect wages in season of up to £4 a week, if not more. [46] Henry Boyd, the battling West Bromwich forward, had been signed to the club from Burnley in 1892 at the rate of £2 10s. a week, with a signing on fee of £5. His comrade McLeod was receiving £3 a week in season, and £2 10s. during the close season. [47] A case in the Court of Appeal in 1890 revealed that the Nottingham Forest club was paying one of its leading players £4 10s. a week. [48] Even in Ireland, where wages were considerably lower, during the season a player could receive a wage in excess of five times that paid to an agricultural labourer. [49] Win bonuses could push earnings up even higher. At Southampton players were offered £8 each for a win in a third-round FA Cup tie, while at Aston Villa the complexity of the bonus system was alleged to resemble a set of engineering blueprints. [50]

The intimate connections that existed between football and alcohol may have further enhanced the temptations faced by players. As the *Birmingham Daily Mail* implied in 1893, the fact that the Aston Villa committee included a number of hoteliers and publicans, and that meetings and celebrations were often held on licensed premises, was simply putting temptation in the way of players. In Sunderland the fact that several players had been installed as landlords by their club meant that 'the process of degeneration quickly sets in, and...their temperance principles go to smash'.[51] Coupled with this was the position that players often occupied in local society. 'Treating' of players by supporters was more than once mentioned as a particular problem, along with the strength of character that was required by players to refuse the alcoholic tributes offered to them by admiring fans. [52] Yet if circumstances seem to have conspired to facilitate a greater access to alcohol for players, it is important to acknowledge that pre-existing factors made its consumption more likely.

The majority of early professional players in both England and Ireland came from the working classes. [53] Drink played an important part in working-class culture on both sides of the Irish Sea: by the mid-1870s, it has been reckoned, the average Englishman who drank consumed 103 gallons of beer each year. [54] One contemporary observer reckoned working-class men in heavy manual trades might spend between four and eight shillings a week on alcoholic drinks, which translates as between three-and-a-half and seven pints of beer a day. [55] In 1899, a parliamentary committee even ventured that 'according to a trustworthy calculation, 10 to 15 per cent of the total food of the average working man is contained in the beer he consumes'. [56] More importantly, drink and the culture of the public house became 'associated with manliness and virility ... conviviality, good fellowship, class and occupational identity'. [57] Drink and the public house lay at the centre of English working-class culture. Furthermore, patterns of consumption reflected the vagaries of working-class life. Beer might be taken regularly as a healthful beverage, but, along with spirits, it was also drunk for effect and at irregular celebrations and festivals. At these times especially, overindulgence was a possibility if not a probability.

In Ireland, from the middle of the nineteenth century the public house became 'the principal centre of male working-class recreation'. The pub played important political, economic and social roles. It was to the pub that men came to plot, to deal, or simply to sing a song. [58] Whether the stereotype of the lovable Irish drunkard is accepted or not, the fact that, for some, hard drinking became a part of Irish culture, must be acknowledged. Drink came to offer an escape 'from the stringencies of [the] Irish social structure and a puritan culture'. [59] Thus for some professional footballers overindulgence in drink was probably both a consequence of the combination of new and improved social and economic circumstances and a perpetuation of class-specific mores. More money and more leisure time simply allowed some professionals to engage in more of an established pastime: drinking.

The apparent relationship between players and drink was then mediated through institutions and a social class whose ideas of alcohol consumption differed considerably from their own. The vast majority of committeemen and directors at English and Irish football clubs came from the middle classes. [60] For the most part this group had considerably different ideas concerning alcohol consumption to their inferiors. Antagonism towards drink was rather more common here, as was the willingness to oppose its baneful influence. [61] Just as a section of the middle classes supported football, so another backed temperance. On occasion these overlapped. The extent to which the games' authorities agreed with the temperance message is perhaps best illustrated through examples from Ireland. The Irish Football Association shunned alcohol at every opportunity. Not until 1907 did the association agree that alcohol should be available at meals after international matches, overturning an earlier resolution that all such dinners should be 'temperance'. [62] The provision of bars at matches was not to be tolerated for some time yet however. [63] As one English newspaper put it, there was 'a strong tinge of the temperance question' about the Irish FA. [64]

Furthermore, the message concerning footballers and drink has generally been mediated through the press. Here too middle-class moralities predominated. [65] Additionally, relationships between clubs and individual players, and with the local press, could sometimes be difficult. At Aston Villa the committee was forced to draft a letter to one local periodical in November 1896, denying that John Reynolds, the club's English international half-back, 'had been left out of the first team for misconduct'. In fact he had been injured in training, and was suffering a decline in form. Despite this denial, the insinuations continued, and were amplified elsewhere in the local media. [66] The press had scented a good story and were reluctant to be deterred by mere facts. At Southampton, the club chairman elected to write to the *Southern Echo* in 1898 regarding its 'boycotting' of John Farrell, the club's brawling centre-forward. Farrell had expressed his unhappiness about the situation, which he deemed 'not fair'. [67] The press reacted to Farrell's misconduct by ignoring his performances on the pitch. In Sunderland the rivalry between the town's Association and Albion clubs spilled over into the local press, with journalists allegedly threatening to boycott the Albion club, and then one of their number suing it for libel at the county assizes.[68] Allegations were then made that local journalists were being pressurized by their employers to 'damn Albion with faint praise'. [69] In West Bromwich the local club's directors felt compelled to write to the *Birmingham Daily Gazette* in the spring of 1894 asking if the paper's football correspondent, who had published a series of rather scathing assessments of the team, might 'adopt a more generous-minded tone to clubs outside Birmingham'. [70]

Thus the perceived relationship between players and alcohol has invariably been interpreted through the distorting prism of middle-class opinion. The persistent opposition to players' drinking, and the enduring portrayal of the drinking habits of players as excessive, probably owes as much to middle-class preoccupations with the evils of drink as with fact. Worries about alcohol consumption by footballers may be seen as merely mirroring wider concerns regarding drunkenness in Victorian society, in both England and Ireland. [71] Additionally, some reports seem to have been liberally laced with class prejudice and scepticism about the values of professional sport. [72] As with so much within the history of sport, reality needs to be separated from rhetoric. Those tempted to look back and cast the late-Victorian professional footballer as a beer-swilling drunkard would do well to remember that opposing rhetoric could also attach itself to the game of football. In Sunderland the secretary of the local Church of England Temperance Society announced in 1896 that he would take up shares in the recently floated football club, as football had proved itself to be a powerful temperance agent in the town.[73] The club's secretary later ventured that 'temperance principles' were an essential for any young man wishing to make his way as a professional player. [74] The local Band of Hope had earlier had no qualms in applying to the regional football authorities for financial support, both directly and indirectly, through the sport. [75] In Belfast a number of observers were sure that football acted as 'a great temperance reformer', by diverting men from 'the public house and its baneful influences'. [76] Just as some sought to attach the bogey of drunkenness to football and its players, so others crowned it with the glories of temperance. Fundamentally, the rhetoric surrounding alcohol and football in this period is contradictory.

Moreover, it is essential that even where apparently detailed reports are available regarding the habits and behaviour of individuals, these are seen in context. For all the apparent failings of Aston Villa's James Welford in connection with the bottle, he went on to enjoy both a long life, and a remarkably successful career. In addition to the League Championship medal he won with Aston Villa, Weldon won a Scottish League championship with Glasgow Celtic, and an Irish Football League medal with Belfast Celtic. He died at the ripe old age of seventy-five in his adopted home city of Glasgow. [77] However Charles Athersmith, a team-mate of Welford's at Aston Villa and an apparently model professional, lived only to be thirty-eight years of age. Described at his death as 'always abstemious and well-conducted' and by a former team-mate as 'one of the best comrades a man ever had', his career after leaving Aston Villa had 'been a rather chequered one', and included running a public house near Walsall, as well as coaching at Grimsby. [78] It culminated in his death, allegedly due to a combination of drink and an old stomach injury, in his native Shropshire. The Villa club, which he had apparently left after being refused permission to keep a public house, was not represented at his funeral. [79] James Crabtree, another Villa star, and a man whose name does not appear once in the club's records for disciplinary reasons, lived only to the age of thirty-six. Although he was allegedly 'a careful man, [who] undoubtedly saved money during his professional career', he had died as the result of a scalding accident, which apparently occurred as the result of alcohol withdrawal. [80] At the inquest into his death, his widow revealed that she and their five children had left her husband two months earlier because of his drinking, and his own doctor noted his recent 'intemperate use of liquor'. [81] It is perhaps more important that, by the time of their deaths, both Crabtree and Athersmith were publicans than that they were former professional footballers. In the north-east of England similar examples emerge. John Smith, known as 'Jock', played for a number of clubs in the area, before retiring to become a bar manager in Newcastle in 1896. He died fifteen years later, apparently of a drink-related illness, aged only forty-four, and leaving a widow and five children suffering from 'financial embarrassment'. [82] Fellow Scot Johnnie

Campbell won three Football League winner's medals with Sunderland before moving on to Newcastle United in 1897. He retired from this club in 1898 to take up trade as 'a licensed victualler' in Newcastle. The 1901 census lists him as a 'hotel manager' in the west of the city; though within two years he had returned to Sunderland, becoming the manager of the Turf Hotel. It was here that he died in 1906, at the age of only thirty-six, following 'a liver complaint' and 'a severe illness'. [83] Unfortunately contemporary evidence is not available, but data from the 1960s shows 'publicans and innkeepers' to be the highest occupational risk group for cirrhosis of the liver, the classic disease of alcoholism, with a rate more than three times that of 'service, support and recreation' workers. Although both groups were considered to be high-risk ones, it was publicans who were fifteen times more likely than average to become addicted to drink, and to suffer the potentially lethal consequences. [84]

More than thirty years ago, in his ground-breaking study of drink and temperance, Brian Harrison suggested that while the alcoholic existed in all societies, 'the occasional drunkard ... abounds only in a specific historical and cultural context'. [85] It might seem at first glance that the professional footballer in the later Victorian period was a prime candidate for alcoholism, with his high wages and extensive periods of leisure. However, for the player to be successful in his given trade, or even simply to maintain his professional standing, he needed a measure of physical strength and endurance that was unlikely to be sustained alongside an extensive drinking habit. Rather, professional players were exemplary nominees for the positions of 'occasional drunkard'. Such men could control their drinking, taking alcohol when it suited them, and declining it when they chose to. Intermittently drink was taken to excess, but usually in the context of celebrations, commiserations or camaraderie. The occasional drunkard that Welford was should not be confused with the alcoholic that Crabtree became. For players, victories needed to be celebrated, the tensions of defeat needed to be eased and injuries required to be salved. The natural way for many to do this was by visiting a public house and drinking alcohol. Furthermore football had close and intimate links to the drink trade that necessitated a persistent and uneasy proximity between players and strong drink. Here perhaps is the ultimate example of the 'specific historical and cultural context' to which Harrison referred. Economic, social and cultural factors conspired to make many working-class professional footballers into 'occasional drunkards'. It was probably only when their playing days were over, and the daily demands on their minds and bodies were relieved, that the relationship between such men and drink may in some cases have become far more problematic.

Notes

[1] Tony Mason, *Association football and English society, 1863–1915* (Brighton, 1982), p. 27.
[2] *Ireland's Saturday Night*, 5 Nov. 1892.
[3] *Ulster Football and Cycling News*, 18 April 1890 and 18 Nov. 1892.
[4] *Southampton Amusements*, 4 July and 19 Sept. 1898.
[5] *Athletic News*, 7 April 1890.
[6] [J.A.H. Catton], *The rise of the leaguers from 1863–1897: a history of the Football League* (Manchester, 1897), pp. 77–9.
[7] *Northern Review*, 8 Feb. 1890.
[8] Neal Garnham, *Association football and society in pre-partition Ireland* (Belfast, 2004), pp. 59–60.
[9] Vamplew, *Play up and play the game: professional sport in Britain, 1875–1914* (Cambridge, 1988), p. 160; Neal Garnham and Andrew Jackson, 'Who invested in Victorian football clubs? The case of Newcastle-upon-Tyne', *Soccer and Society* 4 (1) (2003), p. 65.
[10] Tony Collins and Wray Vamplew, *Mud, sweat and beers: a cultural history of sport and alcohol* (Oxford, 2002), pp. 100–3.
[11] Jimmy Greaves, *This one's on me* (Newton Abbot, 1979); Tony Adams, *Addicted* (St Helens, 1998); Paul Merson, *Rock bottom* (London, 1995); Paul Gascoigne, *Gazza: my story* (London, 2004).
[12] The latest instalment in this sorry tale is George Best, *Scoring at half time* (London, 2003).
[13] J.J. Bentley, 'Professionalism in sport', in *Athletic News Football Annual* (Manchester, 1896) p. 13.
[14] *Newcastle Evening Chronicle* (football edition), 24 Sept. 1910.
[15] *Sunderland Daily Echo*, 13 Jan. 1891.
[16] See, for example, *Ireland's Saturday Night*, 31 Aug. 1901.
[17] *Northern Gossip*, 8 Feb. 1896.
[18] *Hampshire Independent, Isle of Wight and South of England Advertiser*, 5 Feb. 1898.
[19] *Advocate* [Fremantle], 5 Feb. 1898; *Hampshire Advertiser*, 2 Feb. 1898.
[20] *West Bromwich Weekly News*, 10 Dec. 1892 and 22 April 1893.
[21] *Sunderland Daily Echo*, 19 Jan. 1891.
[22] *Newcastle Evening Chronicle*, 7 April 1892. He was fined a total of £1 2s 6d.
[23] *Ulster Football and Cycling News*, 9 Nov. 1894; *Ireland's Saturday Night*, 27 Aug. 1898.
[24] *Sporting Man*, 25 April 1896.
[25] *Birmingham Daily Mail*, 30 Jan. 1893.
[26] *The Dart* [Birmingham], 3 Feb. and 3 March 1893.
[27] *Birmingham Owl*, 14 April 1893.

[28]   *Free Press* [West Bromwich], 25 Nov. 1892. For similar club houses for players at Middlesbrough and Sunderland, see *Sunderland Daily Echo*, 28 Jan. 1891 and *North-Eastern Daily Gazette*, 24 Sept. 1890.

[29]   Aston Villa Football Club Ltd, directors' meetings minute book, 10 Jan. 1896–4 Dec. 1902 (Aston Villa plc, Villa Park, Birmingham), 8 Oct. 1896.

[30]   Ibid., 29 Oct. 1896 and 4 March 1897.

[31]   Ibid., 8 and 22 Oct. 1896. It was perhaps unfortunate that the tea took place at the premises of J.T. Lee, a director of the club and a local hotelier!

[32]   Ibid., 3 Sept. 1896.

[33]   Ibid., 11 March and 13 May 1897.

[34]   Ibid., 28 April 1896; *Sporting Man*, 23 April 1896; *Dart*, 17 April 1896.

[35]   For the attempts of clubs to control the social activities of their players in a slightly later period, see Matthew Taylor, 'Work and play: the professional footballer in England c1900–c1950', *The Sports Historian*, 22 (2) (2002) pp. 26–9.

[36]   Aston Villa Football Club Ltd, directors' meetings minute book, 10 Jan. 1896–4 Dec. 1902 (Aston Villa plc, Villa Park, Birmingham), 19 and 26 March, 17 Sept. 1896.

[37]   Ibid., 17 and 24 Feb. 1897.

[38]   *Owl*, 23 April 1897; *Dart*, 21 May 1897.

[39]   William Maley, *The story of the Celtic* (Glasgow, 1939), pp. 39, 61 and 121.

[40]   Southampton Football and Athletic Company Ltd minute book, 8 July 1897–22 June 1899 (Southampton FC, Friends' Provident St Mary's Stadium, Southampton), 5 Jan. and 12 Sept. 1898.

[41]   West Bromwich Football Club Ltd [directors'] minute book, 24 June 1891–19 Nov. 1895 (West Bromwich Albion FC, The Hawthorns, West Bromwich), 27 Oct. and 24 Nov. 1891. The directors subsequently felt compelled to apologize for this action, however.

[42]   Ibid., 29 Nov. 1892.

[43]   Ibid., 18 Sept. 1894.

[44]   Irish FA committee minute book 25 Oct.1898–3 Feb.1903, Public Record Office of Northern Ireland: D/4196/A/1, pp. 265, 270–1.

[45]   For training schedules see *Ideas*, 25 Oct. 1913; *Nomad's Weekly and Belfast Critic*, 10 Oct. 1908; *Free Press* [West Bromwich], 26 Feb. 1892; W.I. Bassett, 'The day's work', in J.C. Clegg, ed., *The book of football* (London, 1906), pp. 110–13.

[46]   Mason, *Association football*, pp. 94–9.

[47]   West Bromwich Football Club Ltd [directors'] minute book, 24 June 1891–19 Nov. 1895, (West Bromwich Albion FC, The Hawthorns, West Bromwich), 1 Oct. 1892 and 2 May 1893.

[48]   *Newcastle Evening Chronicle*, 11 Aug. 1890.

[49]   Garnham, *Pre-partition Ireland*, p. 77.

[50]   Southampton Football and Athletic Company Ltd minute book, 8 July 1897–22 June 1899 (Southampton FC, Friends' Provident St Mary's Stadium, Southampton), 14 Feb. 1898; *The Owl* [Birmingham], 9 April 1897.

[51]   *Birmingham Daily Mail*, 30 Jan. 1893; *Athletic News*, 21 April 1890.

[52]   Collins and Vamplew, *Mud, sweat and beers*, pp. 102–3. See also note 14 above.

[53] Mason, *Association football*, pp. 89–91; Garnham, *Pre-partition Ireland*, pp. 67–8, 95–7.

[54] T.R. Gourvish and R.G. Wilson, *The British brewing industry, 1830–1980* (Cambridge, 1984), p. 35.

[55] Joseph Rowntree and Arthur Sherwell, *The temperance problem and social reform*, 5th edn (London, 1899), pp. 438–9.

[56] *Report of the Departmental Committee on Beer Materials* (Cd. 9171), BPP 1899 XXX, p. 10. This comment is, however, taken from the minority report.

[57] John Burnett, *Liquid pleasures: a social history of drinks in modern Britain* (London, 1999), p. 125.

[58] Elizabeth Malcolm, 'The rise of the pub: a study in the disciplining of popular culture', in J.S. Donnelly and Kerby A. Miller, eds., *Irish popular culture, 1650– 1850* (Dublin, 1998), pp. 51–2.

[59] Richard Stivers, *Hair of the dog: Irish drinking and its American stereotype*, revised edn (New York, 2000), p. 105.

[60] Steven Tischler, *Footballers and businessmen* (London, 1981), pp. 69–88; Mason, *Association football*, pp. 42–6; Vamplew, *Play up*, pp. 161–70; Garnham, *Pre-partition Ireland*, pp. 57–61.

[61] Brian Harrison, *Drink and the Victorians: the temperance question in England, 1815–1872* (London, 1971), pp. 151–62.

[62] Irish FA council minute book, 31 March 1903–2 Feb. 1909, Public Record Office of Northern Ireland: D/4196/A/2, pp. 179, 186–7.

[63] Irish FA international committee book, 27 Feb. 1909–25 Jan. 1949, 19 Feb. 1923, Public Record Office of Northern Ireland: D/4196/D/1.

[64] *The Grasshopper* [Birmingham], 21 Jan. 1895.

[65] On the sporting press see Tony Mason, 'Sporting news, 1860–1914', in Michael Harris and Alan Lee, eds., *The press and English society from the seventeenth to the nineteenth centuries* (Rutherford, NJ, 1986), pp. 168–186; Tony Mason, 'All the winners and the halftimes. . .', *The Sports Historian*, 13 (2) (1993), pp. 3–10.

[66] Aston Villa Football Club Ltd, directors' meetings minute book, 10 Jan. 1896–4 Dec.1902 (Aston Villa plc, Villa Park, Birmingham), 8 Oct. 1896, 26 Nov. 1896; *Grasshopper*, 15 Nov., 2 and 9 Dec. 1896; *Owl*, 27 Nov. 1896; *Dart*, 4 Dec. 1896.

[67] Southampton Football and Athletic Company Ltd minute book, 8 July 1897–22 June 1899, (Southampton FC, Friends' Provident St Mary's Stadium, Southampton), 24 Jan. 1898.

[68] *Athletic News*, 24 June and 1 July 1889.

[69] *Athletic News*, 10 March 1890.

[70] West Bromwich Football Club Ltd [directors'] minute book, 24 June 1891–19 Nov. 1895 (West Bromwich Albion FC, The Hawthorns, West Bromwich), 13 March 1894.

[71] For England see Harrison, Drink and the Victorians. For Ireland see Elizabeth Malcolm, *Ireland sober, Ireland free: drink and temperance in nineteenth-century Ireland* (Dublin, 1986).

[72] For comments on the linking of class prejudice and the debate surrounding professionalism in one sport, see Tony Collins, *Rugby's great split: class, culture and the origins of Rugby League football* (London, 1998), pp. 116–130.

[73]   *Sunderland Herald*, 14 July 1896. For similar views of football and drink in Sunderland see correspondence in *Sunderland Daily Echo*, 23 Oct. 1888, 17 Jan., 4 and 5 Feb. 1891.

[74]   Robert Campbell, *Football: physical, social and moral aspects* (Sunderland, 1897) p. 3.

[75]   [Northumberland and] Durham FA general minute book, 25 May 1883–13 May 1889, Tyne and Wear Archives Service S/DFA/1/1: entry for 13 May 1889; Durham FA minute book, 15 May 1889–1 Feb. 1893: Tyne and Wear Archives Service S/DFA/1/2: entry for 28 Feb. 1890.

[76]   *Ulster Football and Cycling News*, 6 Jan. 1893; *Belfast Health Journal*, March 1901; *Ireland's Saturday Night*, 13 April 1901.

[77]   *Glasgow Observer*, 24 Jan. 1945.

[78]   *Birmingham Post*, 19 Sept. 1910; *Birmingham Daily Mail*, 19 Sept. 1910; *Birmingham Despatch*, 19 Sept. 1910.

[79]   *Birmingham Gazette and Express*, 21 and 23 Sept. 1910.

[80]   *Birmingham Daily Mail*, 18 June 1908; *Birmingham Gazette and Express*, 19 June 1908.

[81]   *Birmingham Gazette and Express*, 22 June 1908.

[82]   *Newcastle Evening Chronicle*, 18 Feb. 1911.

[83]   *Sunderland Daily Echo*, 8 Jun 1906.

[84]   Martin A Plant, *Drinking careers: occupations, drinking habits, and drinking problems* (London, 1979), pp. 31–3.

[85]   Harrison, *Drink and the Victorians*, p. 21.

Alcohol and the Sportsperson: An Anomalous Alliance

Wray Vamplew

Alcohol as a sports drug

Alcohol depresses the nervous system, impairs both motor ability and judgement, reduces endurance and, as a diuretic, can disturb electrolyte balance and cause dehydration, all of which are detrimental to effective sports performance. [1] Contrast this with the view that 'strong ale' is the athlete's drink and the advice that

> with respect to liquors, they must always be taken cold; and home-brewed beer, old, but not bottled, is the best. A little red wine, however,

may be given to those who are not fond of malt liquor, but never more than half a pint after dinner. The quantity of beer, therefore, should not exceed three pints during the whole day. [2]

These two standpoints are almost two centuries apart. The former view is modern conventional wisdom based on sports science research; the latter formed part of the training regimen of Captain Robert Barclay Allardice, who gained fame in 1809 for winning a £16,000 challenge to run a thousand miles in a thousand hours. [3]

Barclay was not alone in his consumption of alcohol as an aid to strength and stamina. Another record-breaking pedestrian, Foster Powell, renowned for his walks from London to York and back in less than six days, was reported to take wine or brandy with water during his perambulations. [4] Pugilists also took advantage of alcohol. Bottle holders at prize fights were instructed by Vincent Dowling, editor of *Bell's Life in London*, that 'A bottle of brandy-and-water should be in readiness when a stimulant becomes necessary after long exertion, but this should be used with moderation; and at times, especially in wet, cold weather, about a table-spoon of neat brandy may be given – this ought to be of the best quality.' [5] Doubtless on occasions alcohol was also used to give the fighters extra 'bottom' or courage.

The use of alcohol by athletes should be seen in the context of a society in which many of the population utilized alcoholic drinks as thirst quenchers or for physical stamina. Such drinks were seen as less dangerous than water, which was both scarce and unsafe in rural areas and even more contaminated in urban centres. Moreover, it was generally believed that intoxicants imparted stamina: whenever extra energy was needed, resort was had to alcohol. [6]

Such ideas took a long time to change. At the end of the nineteenth century cricketers still turned to alcohol during a day's play and were advised that when playing on a hot day 'beer and stout are too heady and heavy' and 'gin and ginger beer are too sticky sweet' and that 'shandy-gaff, sherry, or claret and soda are the most thirst-quenching, the lightest and the cleanest to the palate'. [7] A writer in 1890 suggested to Scottish footballers that

there can be no harm in a glass or two of sound ale or a little light wine such as hock or claret at dinner. The glass of port afterwards I confess I think unnecessary as long as the training process is well borne. If, however, a man shows any sign of falling with the state known as 'overtrained', that is to say, when the reducing process is too rapid or too severe, a little port or dry champagne at meals may be found beneficial. [8]

The rowing expert R.C. Lehman noted that the Oxford boat-race crew in the 1890s were allowed a glass of draught beer or claret and water with their lunch, two glasses with their dinner and a glass of port with their dessert. Occasionally, champagne was substituted for the other drinks, but only when they had 'been doing very hard work, or when they show evident signs of being over-fatigued, and require a fillip'. [9] In the same decade H.L. Curtis suggested moderate consumption of alcohol as part of a sportsman's regime but warned against smoking and drinking coffee. [10]

Yet by 1888, in his advice to athletes, Montague Shearman leaned towards the increasing transatlantic tendency to adopt 'the system of training upon water alone, and taking no alcohol in any shape during training'. He left it to doctors to decide if alcohol was 'nutritious to any degree' but noted that it was universally acknowledged 'that it is very hard to digest, and this alone should be a strong argument against its use'. Nevertheless he accepted that if a sportsman was 'accustomed to drink beer or wine, it is a hard thing to say that the athlete should give up either and take to water if he doesn't like it'. He had seen men well trained 'upon beer, upon claret, and upon weak whisky-and-water'. However, he warned that 'any other wines . . . are bad in training, as they excite the nerves and interfere with sound and quiet sleep'. He allowed that 'if a man is getting stale, good strengthening wine may do him a world of good', though he stressed that 'as long as an athlete is not in this state, the glass or two of port, which he often recommended to take, is exceedingly likely to do harm, and can hardly do any good'. All in all, the 'general principle' should be 'the less alcohol . . . the better'. [11] Writing slightly earlier, the Reverend Beveridge was adamant that

> much liquid of any kind ought not to be imbibed by the training athlete; and there is one kind of liquid which must not be imbibed at all, namely that which is alcoholic in its nature. There is no use whatever of a man going into training if he intends at the same time to use intoxicating liquors. [12]

Beveridge was a member of the teetotal lobby which claimed that 'medical science has proved beyond a doubt the injuriousness of spirituous liquors to the human frame'. [13] This was countered by the *Licensed Trade News*, which argued that 'the whole field of physical culture is filled with the best of men doing the best of work on alcohol in moderation'. It recommended 'a good sound, wholesome glass of beer, there is nothing to come near it as a thirst quencher, a dietetic, a support and a stimulant'. [14] Alcohol producers lent support to the trade. The

1880s saw the start of advertisements professing the fitness-aiding qualities of alcohol. Grant's Morella Cherry Brandy claimed that it 'strengthened and invigorated the system', as was proved by Captain Boyton, who drank it while swimming the Straits of Dover. Indeed the gallant captain was quoted as finding it 'not only palatable and refreshing, but most effective in keeping up nerve and strength'. [15] Clearly the advice being provided for sportspersons was confusing and contradictory.

Such tensions continued. In the 1920s English cricketer Fred Root, after an arduous stint of bowling, was advised by the chairman of selectors, P.F. Warner, to utilize the brine baths at Droitwich and drink an occasional bottle of champagne. The health-giving qualities of alcohol were still being proclaimed in advertising campaigns in the inter-war years, most notably in the Brewers' Society slogan 'Beer is Best' and Guinness's explicit promotion of its product as being good for strength. [16] Nevertheless, by this time athletes were generally being advised not to consume intoxicants on any scale as they were considered detrimental to sporting performance. Viscount Knebworth's advice to aspiring boxers in the early 1930s was that

> any large consumption of alcohol is out of the question, but alcohol in moderation is a fine aid to the digestion. A glass of wine or a glass of beer with his supper does nobody any harm. . . . But no-one in training for a boxing match can afford to drink anything but a very minimum of alcoholic liquid. [17]

He was supported by Dr Alphonse Abrahams, who maintained that 'alcohol may be given as a medicine, but a healthy athlete should not require medicine, therefore alcohol is not needed for him'. However, in a portent of a modern argument for sportspersons to drink, he also declared 'the practice of giving champagne to the university boat crews serves some useful purpose in lessening the anxiety which often prevails before a race'. [18]

Sports scientists were winning the battle. By 1982 the influential American College of Sports Medicine had conducted an analysis of the effects of alcohol on physical performance and argued that it had four main adverse effects. First, the acute ingestion of alcohol deleteriously influenced many psychomotor skills in a dose-related manner, thus negatively affecting reaction time, eye-hand coordination, accuracy and balance, while in tracking tasks, such as driving, control movements lost their smoothness and precision. Second, alcohol consumption significantly influenced physiological functions crucial to physical performance such as respiratory dynamics and cardiac activity. Third, the ingestion of alcohol did not improve muscular work capacity and indeed may have decreased performance levels. Finally, because alcohol dilates the blood vessels close to the surface of the skin, it could impair temperature regulation during prolonged exercise in a cold environment. [19]

Nonetheless there are those who believe that there are sporting benefits to alcohol consumption which outweigh the negative aspects. Although generally alcohol has adverse effects on performance in sports that require fast reactions, complex decision-making and highly-skilled actions, it is considered to have a positive influence on performance where there is an advantage to be gained from its use as an anti-tremor aid, as an isometric muscular strengthener and as an anti-anxiety drug. For some individuals it is simply that small amounts of alcohol can reduce feelings of insecurity and tension and improve self-confidence. For some teams, too, the psychological and other aspects of drinking together may have positive outcomes. Tactical discussions in the bar at the end of a day's play – common among cricketers – is one example. [20] In football the great Tottenham Hotspur side of the 1960s used to meet in the back room of the Bell and Hare, just off the ground, to dissect every move of the last game and look ahead to the next. [21]

Team bonding is another example. Pat Nevin, ex-chairman of the Professional Footballers' Association, maintains that at the start of the football season this is sometimes more desired by managers than absolute fitness. [22] Teams are collections of individuals who may not necessarily get along with each other. On top of personality differences, there is the friction brought about by competition for places. Older players may be wary of newcomers, unwilling to pass on the lessons of experience for fear that they might hasten their journey down the inclined plane to sporting oblivion. The young bloods, aware that few of them will become established in the team, may not assist each other as much as the coach might desire. Alcohol is sometimes regarded as a panacea to these problems: drinking sessions are seen as a way of bringing team-mates together. These were often instigated by the older 'pros' but approved of by the club. Tony Parkes, who played for Spurs, Gillingham, Brentford, Queens Park Rangers, Fulham, West Ham, Stoke, Falkirk and Blackpool, found that drinking sessions were used at all these clubs as a forum to air grievances and give accolades. [23] In the 1980s Liverpool FC, a dominant team of the decade, used to hold social drinking sessions one Monday each month policed by the senior players. [24] Ron Atkinson, one of Britain's more successful managers in the last three decades, believed that 'drinking among team-mates ... creates dressing-room spirit'. [25] One of the new generation of British managers, David Moyes, has attributed a recent improvement in the performance of Everton to a pre-season trip to the USA where 'we trained hard but had a good time together as well. We had a few drinks and some good old-fashioned sing-songs . . . all of a sudden you lose your inhibitions and everyone understands each other that bit more'. [26]

For most participants sport is a recreational stress-reliever, but for elite athletes it can be a stress-creator, often producing severe pre-competition anxiety. Not all athletes can cope unaided with this and some have resorted to anti-anxiety drugs, including alcohol. Dr Tom Crisp, a medical officer for the British team at the Atlanta Olympic Games, believes 'that there may even be benefits [to drinking a week or so before a major competition] in terms of relaxation and social interaction. . . . I think if you look at professional sportsmen they are under a great deal of pressure, and alcohol is quite a good way of relaxing.' [27] That sherry was a useful pre-match drink was a prevalent belief in rugby in the 1950s and 1960s: at noon on match days Jeff Butterfield, an England rugby union back, drank a pint pot of raw eggs and sherry and as late as 1989 rugby league player Andrew Ettingshausen noted that a sherry bottle was passed around the Leeds dressing room before matches. [28] The communal whisky bottle too has featured in football changing rooms prior to the game. [29] Darts players also often resort to alcohol to calm their nerves. Leighton Rees, the Welsh international darts player, reckoned that a couple of pints of beer helped steel him for a match. [30] World Champion Andy Fordham usually has fifteen bottles of lager before each game to reduce his nervousness and increase his confidence. [31]

Some sports require steady hands as well as steady nerves. The sedative effect of alcohol can be useful where a firm stance and a reduced heart rate could be important. Predominantly these are 'aiming' sports such as shooting, archery, snooker, darts and fencing. There is greater benefit where the apparatus involved puts least pressure on the arm, so darts throwers gain more than pistol shooters, who are better off than archers. [32] As the bar-room sport of darts has moved to a larger stage, the technique that has developed among the more successful players is one of regular small 'topping up' doses of alcohol so as to avoid fluctuating blood alcohol concentrations. [33] Reaction times, however, are slowed by alcohol consumption so there is no tradition of its use in aiming sports with moving targets such as clay-pigeon shooting. [34]

In horse racing, alcohol is seen as offering two specific kinds of help to jockeys. Many of them drink champagne before going into the sauna in the belief that it helps them sweat. [35] Traditionally, too, the French sparkling wine has been used to keep down their weight. In the early nineteenth century Frank Butler, the first Triple Crown winner, followed a diet of champagne to help restrict his weight to eight stone seven pounds. [36] Later in that century, Fred Archer, champion jockey for thirteen successive seasons, allegedly breakfasted on a diet of castor oil, a biscuit and a small glass of champagne for the bulk of his racing life. [37] In more modern times, Lester Piggott, champion on eleven occasions, also used champagne in this way, but with the occasional gin and tonic as a change. [38] Although nutrition research indicates that as alcohol contains calories drinking can impair any weight reduction programme even if food intake is reduced, the very small amounts that jockeys take can be seen simply as a psychologically satisfying alternative to food. [39]

Sporting culture and alcohol abuse

British sportspeople exist within a society in which, subject to age limits, alcohol is a socially accepted drug that has become engrained in leisure activities. Like other members of society, sportspersons use alcohol for relaxation, to relieve stress and for convivial recreational purposes. Historically, some sports organizations such as the Royal Caledonian Hunt Club were in effect drinking clubs, more concerned with the quality of the wine than that of the horses. [40] Amateur sports teams have a long tradition of treating each other to refreshments, alcoholic or otherwise, after a match. That so many early football and cricket clubs were attached to public houses by sponsorship, changing rooms or ground provision both encouraged and facilitated this. [41] Possibly, of course, this treating was a means of paying supposedly amateur players. Significantly the move into professionalism in football in the late nineteenth century undermined the alcoholic reciprocity between clubs, though Dumbarton, for one, elected to continue the after-match socials whenever the opposing team was agreeable, as they felt 'that it would be a pity should it ever be considered necessary – on account of the demands of professionalism, or for any other reason – to eliminate every source of relaxation and enjoyment from the life of the football player, and reduce the game to a mere sordid pursuit'. [42] County cricketer Fred Root noted that there were plenty of 'thirst-quenching opportunities' in police cricket matches in the 1920s. [43]

The bar has in fact become a major source of revenue for many sports clubs. From the outset of Leamington Rugby Club in 1926 there was a bar. Initially simply a table from which bottles of beer were sold, by the late 1990s it generated gross profits of £66,000, roughly six times the amount raised from members' subscriptions. [44] Golf clubs, too, have benefited from the laxer licensing laws applied to membership clubs compared to public houses. [45] At the Goring and Streatley Golf Club, bar takings produced six per cent of the club's revenue in 1938, a proportion that had risen to eleven per cent by 1994. [46] The increased importance of bar profits has of course provided sports clubs with an incentive to encourage members and players to drink.

Sportspeople know that drinking can be both bad for their health and inimical to sporting performance. Yet teetotallers are probably in a minority in British sport. [47] Many of the sportspersons who drink are well aware of the negative influence that alcohol can have on their sporting functions, but often those involved are not concerned with achieving their best possible performance. They are participating for fun, aiming to win but not at the sacrifice of the social side of their chosen sport or club. Sunday league football with teams such as Real Ale Madrid and PSV Hangover whose matches end before opening time are a prime example. [48] Similarly Justin Langer, the Australian Test cricketer, has observed that English league cricket is a place 'to learn more about enjoying a pint of beer and having a few laughs' than to develop the skills to become a contender for the first class game. [49] Stewart has argued that drinking is almost a membership norm in many amateur sports, and Reilly has identified rugby, squash and water polo as sports where there is such a social convention, together with peer-group pressure to drink alcohol after training and at both matches and club functions. [50]

Sociologists Dunning and Waddington have identified a Dionysian/ Epicurean element in sport in which masculinity is demonstrated by a combination of sporting physicality and an ability to drink copious amounts of alcohol. [51] Yet drinking beyond moderate consumption levels is not just a male prerogative. A recent report in Britain has shown that young women are now more likely to binge-drink than their male counterparts. [52] This is becoming reflected in sport, where there is some evidence that women are following where men have staggered. Female footballers and rugby union players at both recreational and elite level have developed a drinking culture with some associated misbehaviour. Additionally, a recent study has shown that athletic initiation ceremonies at British universities have been normalized, and for both men and women involve excessive consumption of alcohol. [53]

Some elite sportspersons are yet to be persuaded that the case against moderate drinking has been established. It is less publicized than that against excessive imbibing and the evidence suggests that reasonable consumption has neither beneficial nor detrimental effects on physical performance and that light drinking even on the night before competition will not significantly diminish performance the following morning. [54] In any case, with their physical prowess and fitness, young athletes in particular can see themselves as immune from the addictive and adverse effects of alcohol. Certainly sportsmen can disguise the level of their alcohol consumption because of their physical fitness. [55] In the mid-nineteenth century, 'Stonehenge', a writer on rural sports, cited instances of young men drinking one to two gallons of strong ale a day for many months 'without any great injury'. It was, he added, 'astonishing what quantities of intoxicating drinks may be imbibed without much injury, provided that a corresponding amount of exercise is taken'. [56] In team sports the adverse effects of drinking may not be as obvious as in, say, marathon running or other endurance events. Australian rugby league player Ken Thornett recalled that on occasions when playing in England in the early 1950s he had 'drunk seven or eight pints of Tetley's bitter on a Friday night and played well enough the next day'. [57] Confessed alcoholic Jimmy Greaves, the England football international, noted that 'people would see me competing at sport and never believe that they were watching somebody who within the past forty-eight hours had knocked back two bottles of vodka and a couple of gallons of beer'. [58] Paul Merson of Arsenal and England was able to win the Young Player of the Year award in 1989 despite long late-night drinking sessions. [59]

One problem at the elite level is that fans have always been willing to buy drinks for their heroes. In the early 1880s a commentator on golf felt that 'treating' of professionals was too common. [60] A decade later, county cricket administrators complained about the public buying drinks for their cricketing champions, one of the down sides of players remaining close to their communities. [61] Indeed the Yorkshire chairman claimed that the 'demon drink' had cost his side the county championship and the Warwickshire secretary appealed to the public not to treat the county's professionals. [62] Bill Appleyard of Newcastle United FC, in *Thomson's Weekly News* in February 1902, and John Cameron, one-time secretary of the Players' Union writing in *Spalding's Football Annual* four years later, both felt that treating by admirers was a great temptation to footballers. [63]

Sportspersons sometimes abuse alcohol. Populist press exposés of alcohol-fuelled misdemeanours by modern footballers provide a seemingly endless catalogue of hotel smashing, sexual impropriety and drunken driving. [64] Historically perhaps this has always been the case, but possibly the media used to be less intrusive. However, there is some suggestion that misbehaviour by inebriated footballers is nothing new. In 1883 the *Scottish Athletic Journal* criticized the 'high jinks in hotels by football teams [that] are becoming such a nuisance that something must be done to put an end to the gross misconduct which goes on'. [65] Five years earlier two Queens Park players had been fined 20 shillings each for disorderly conduct after a victorious match in Nottingham. [66] Indeed trips south of the border, usually taken at New Year or Easter, allegedly often resulted in 'drunken orgies'. [67] At the end of the century it was claimed that 'nearly every club in Glasgow had had from time to time difficulties with its players because of the intemperance by which they are beset'. [68] Then there was the Heart of Midlothian goalkeeper who let in seven goals when in 'a peculiar condition'. [69] Things were no better in England. Writing in 1909, Jimmy Wilson of Preston North End noted that 'we all know the bugbear of a footballer's career is alcohol . . . perhaps it is not generally known to how great an extent such a state of affairs does exist. One has only to make his way to one or two well-known hotels to see it for themselves.' [70] H.G. Norris of Fulham maintained that players 'are not always fit to undergo ninety minutes of strenuous football on Saturdays, due to indiscretions committed during the previous week, the greatest and most frequent cause being drink'. [71] For many years some footballers out on the town, free of partner and with money in their pockets, have done stupid things under the influence of alcohol. But then so have many other young men. Their antics, however, generally go unreported, so it is hard to establish whether the relationship of footballers with alcohol is particularly unique.

Alcohol was an integral part of another sport. Most golf clubs sought to develop the 'nineteenth hole' within their clubhouse. Not only could this offer members a social refuge, but bar takings could contribute to club coffers. Professionals, however, were excluded from the clubhouse except when acting as steward: thus most golf professionals did their drinking away from the course. According to one observer there was 'one serious evil which has almost invariably accompanied . . . professional golf. I refer to the almost universal drunkenness with which it is attended.' [72] That some professionals had a reputation for over-imbibing is also reflected in a novel by golf writer Horace Hutchinson. [73] The professionals referred to in both instances seem to be those whose employment was irregular and to whom a windfall gain might well be spent on celebratory drink. As the popularity of golf increased, so did job prospects for the club professional. Even tournament players whose earnings could fluctuate wildly had their club retainer to fall back upon. Moreover, the growth in the number of tournaments enlarged the possibility of making some money from competitive play. That said, a reading of golf club histories does suggest that several club professionals continued to risk their careers by drinking. Employed as club professional, greenkeeper and caddie superintendent, Ramsay Hunter of Royal St George's was demoted to greenkeeper in 1899 because of his drinking and was then sacked for repeating the offence. [74] Sidney Humphries had cause to thank the Muskerry committee for only reprimanding him when he 'neglected his work through drinking and associating with bad characters'. He 'promised to abstain entirely from drink in the future' but had soon turned back to the bottle and was given notice. [75]

Nevertheless it may be that footballers have always had more opportunity than most professional sportsmen to indulge in drinking. Unlike golfers, who had to spend most of their time on course maintenance and playing with club members, and cricketers, who often had a full day's play several times a week with travel to follow, professional footballers have always had time on their hands. The training regimes operated by many clubs demanded attendance at the ground for only a few hours a day. Indeed a typical pre-1914 training programme would involve nothing at all on Monday; on other days a 10.00 a.m. arrival time was followed by a brisk five-mile walk unless the weather was inclement, when there might be skipping or Indian club and punchball work. [76] Little changed over the century. As Mick Quinn, footballer turned racehorse trainer, noted 'footballers have time to kill. Time to go to the bookies, pub or snooker club. They have the afternoon and whole night.' [77] The situation has been accentuated in more modern times with the abolition of wage restraint and the spiralling of earnings. Football manager Ron Atkinson recalls some hard drinkers in the immediate pre-Second World War period, but he is also of the view that there has been a change in the past couple of generations of players, with some 'wild drinking' by young star players whom he has seen 'at certain football functions quite literally drinking themselves into oblivion'. [78] Long-serving manager Bobby Robson has also seen 'booze as one of the major evils of the game. And its influence has become more widespread now there is big money to be earned.' [79] Mark Bennett of the charity Alcohol Concern puts it clearly: 'When you get young men earning enormous sums of money, with enormous amounts of free time and a heavy drinking culture, you have some key indications for an alcohol problem.' [80]

Sporting pressure and alcoholism

Modern footballers Tony Adams, Paul Gascoigne and Paul Merson have publicly acknowledged their alcoholism. [81] Predecessors shared their affliction. Albert Johanneson, the first black player to appear in a Wembley cup final, died aged fifty-five of alcohol-related causes. Former Irish and Scottish internationalists George Best and Jim Baxter both had transplants because of the damage that alcohol had done to their livers. [82] Jimmy Greaves of England eventually beat the booze, but at one point in his life he found himself 'in the early hours of a frosty winter's morning...ransacking the dustbin...for empty vodka bottles', and finished up 'kneeling by the side of the dustbin draining the last drops out of the bottles'. [83]

It is not just in football that alcoholism has found victims. To take contrasting examples: in horse racing, leading flat and jump riders Steve Cauthen (twice champion jockey), Walter Swinburn and Timmy Murphy (jailed for a drink-related assault) and in snooker, world champion Alex Higgins and title contender Jimmy White have all acknowledged drink problems. [84] Nor is the issue one just of modern times. Pugilist Henry Pearce, the 'Game Chicken', made 'too free with his constitution' and 'in company with sporting men frequently he poured down copious libations at the shrine of Bacchus' so that 'his health was impaired'. [85] It is also clear that in Victorian horse racing Bill Scott, winner of nine St Legers, and George Fordham, fourteen times champion jockey, were alcoholics, as were Tommy Loates, champion in three seasons towards the end of the century, and Bernard Dillon, the Derby-winning rider in 1910. [86]

Whether professional sportsmen have a greater tendency towards alcoholism than other occupational groups is conjectural given the inadequate statistical information. However there are features of a career in sport that could encourage its emergence in those participants genetically or otherwise predisposed towards the addiction. [87] In some sports there are job-specific issues. In professional football, there is an expectation that players will turn out even when injured and in pain. [88] In cricket there is the monotony of what could until recently be a six- or seven-day-a-week job. [89] In horse racing the low weights required can cause problems as the effects of alcohol are often aggravated by the lack of food: indeed nutrition expert Professor Michael Lean suggests that 'alcoholism is a probable effect of being starved'. [90] More generally, in most sports there are problems associated with the pressures of performance, constant job insecurity and retirement at an early age.

There is no place to hide on the sports field. Every time they play, sportspersons are subject to public and professional appraisal; and often their performance depends not just on themselves but on their team-mates and on the opposition. [91] Jimmy Greaves drank heavily when he played for Spurs in the 1960s 'to help relieve the pressures of big-time football'. [92] Pat Nevin argues that when off-form players are booed by the crowd, castigated in the media, and have their families harassed by fans 'one of the reasons why players turn to a few drinks is to cope with [this] stress'. [93] Cricket is a team game within which the individual is often isolated, worrying about his own form even in the midst of team success: as is clear from David Frith's study of cricketing suicides, some could not handle the pressure of perpetual uncertainty and turned to drink. [94]

Indeed insecurity is the hallmark of a career in professional sport. It stems from many sources including fear of injury, loss of form, threats to jobs from newcomers and the inevitable short shelf-life of professional sportsmen. Every day the professional faces the possibility of no work tomorrow: losing in a tight finish, dropping an important catch or being injured in a tackle can all lead to non-selection. Historically too there was, and for some players still is, the annual trauma of contract renewal. Writing in the 1930s, English professional cricketer Fred Root remarked on the 'extreme anxiety' among young players brought about by counties often delaying their announcements on future engagements until the middle of winter. [95] Most jockeys, even today, do not have retainers and have to compete for mounts in a vastly oversupplied labour market. [96] In many cases the professional has no control over his own destiny: a new manager or coach can lead to redundancy. Seniority offers no security: there are always rivals for their position and the decision as to the relative abilities of the old hand and the newcomer is a subjective one made by others.

Then there is the question of retirement, often involuntary and generally at an early age relative to conventional retirees. For some it comes even earlier than expected because of the socially-sanctioned violence on the field which can cause career-ending damage. Even in non-contact sports there can be serious industrial injuries. Jockey Club statistics show that a rider can expect a fall every fourteen rides over jumps and hurdles and an injury every eighty. [97] It is paradoxical that professional sportspersons must be fit to pursue their occupation but injuries often occur simply because they are playing sport. All sportsmen, of course, have built-in obsolescence. Sport is a physical activity and eventually experience no longer compensates for ageing bodies. Once their athletic peak is passed, many find themselves on a slide to obscurity. Some find it difficult to adjust to a life cut off from their previous mainline activity, an atypical lifestyle of training and competition. Few life experiences can offer the intensity and excitement of sporting competition, and for some alcohol may replace this stimulation; for others drink might be part of self-medication during the pain of the transition period. Michael Caulfield, former executive manager of the Jockeys' Association, has suggested that the real alcohol problem among jockeys emerges after their retirement when income, status and ego all decline. [98] Greaves says that his 'real drinking' started only after he quit League football and realized that at thirty-one he had done so prematurely and 'in my frustration at having let the good times go, I turned to the bottle'. [99] Hughie Gallacher, Scottish goal-scoring genius, also could not cope with leaving football, drank heavily, lost his wife and eventually, in 1957, when facing an assault charge, threw himself under a train. [100] Cricketer John Sullivan, a Lancashire player in the early 1970s, 'couldn't accept that part of my life was over' and took to heavy drinking. [101] A century before, alcoholism took its toll on several Victorian cricketers when they retired including William Barnes, J.T. Brown, Tom Emmett, William Lockwood, and Bobby Peel. [102] One of the most tragic examples of this syndrome was former world flyweight boxing champion Benny Lynch who, before his drink-related death in 1946, was known to invite Glaswegian pub customers to punch him in the face for the price of a drink. [103] Nevertheless it must be stressed that in these and other cases it is not clear what can be attributed to sport and what to the personality of the individuals concerned.

Breaking the nexus?

Although those sports bound by International Olympic Committee regulations prohibit alcohol as a performance-enhancing drug, it is the performance-debilitating effects and social consequences of alcohol that concern most sports authorities. Some have introduced compulsory drug tests which look for both performance-enhancing and recreational substances, but, apart from the Jockey Club regulations, where safety is a major issue, none of these include alcohol. [104] As alcohol is a legal recreational drug, its prohibition, except for safety reasons as in occupational restrictions on pilots and train drivers, may infringe human rights. However, most sports have a clause in their disciplinary codes on 'bringing the game into disrepute' which, if enforced, could lead to punishment after misbehaviour and thus possibly have a deterrent effect. In recent years, although the Football Association has taken a firm line against drug offenders, it has adopted a less strict position in respect of alcohol abusers, especially where this has been due to diagnosed alcoholism. It has recognized that this is a disease rather than a moral failing. Paul Merson, who publicly confessed his addiction to alcohol and drugs, was ordered to spend six weeks in a rehabilitation clinic but no other punishment was imposed. [105] Some people regarded this as excessively lenient, but, as the association's media officer pointed out, it acknowledged that drinking on this scale was an illness and 'players are human beings with real feelings'. [106]

In the late nineteenth century Montague Sherman argued that rigid rules need not be imposed on sportsmen as, unless they have self-discipline with regard to diet and drink, they 'will never be any account as an athlete'. [107] Nevertheless, most clubs believed that another form of discipline was required. When the chairman was a committed teetotaller, as was Charles Clegg at Sheffield Wednesday, strict policies were enforced. No Wednesday player was allowed to work or even live in a public house, and indeed club captain, F.H. Crawshaw was dismissed when he became a publican. [108] Wednesday also disciplined some of its players for excessive drinking which had adversely affected their match performance; and when one of them was also found guilty in the magistrates' court of drunk and disorderly behaviour, the club imposed a month's suspension and shortly afterwards put him on the transfer list. [109] In contrast to the Sheffield team, most football clubs had directors with links to the alcohol industry, but they too adopted a crime and punishment approach with fines and suspensions being used as deterrents. [110] English international Stephen Bloomer was fined and suspended several times by Derby County for insobriety and neglect of training. [111] Aston Villa's board employed a private investigator to look into allegations of drunkenness and associated misconduct by the club's players and Heart of Midlothian, among others, disciplined several players for drunkenness while travelling or training. [112] This occurred in rugby too. Wakefield Trinity expelled two of its players for going out drinking the night before a shock defeat in the Yorkshire Cup semi-final. [113] Such disciplinary policies prevailed for many years, but although clubs often set rules to regulate a player's off-field activities, these, apart from a late-night curfew, could be lax and leave much to a player's discretion. [114]

In more recent times Arsenal, for one, appear to have adopted a disciplinary approach tempered with sympathy when a problem became acute. Paul Merson was fined, suspended and sent home from an overseas tour for his alcohol-related misbehaviour, though the club chairman claimed that the board never contemplated dismissing him. Finally when he sought treatment, the club stood by him, and continued to pay his wages while he was hospitalised. [115] In 1991 Aston Villa paid for Paul McGrath to enter a detoxification clinic. [116] Many managers, especially those who utilize drinking sessions for team bonding purposes, adopt the philosophy of Ron Atkinson, who maintained that 'as long as an individual didn't betray his club with bad social behaviour because of drink, and always performed to his potential on match day, then limited quantities of liquor at the appropriate time were acceptable'. [117] On the other hand Arsène Wenger, the French manager of Arsenal, employer of both Adams and Merson, cleaned up his club by not allowing players to drink at all as a group. [118]

At the international level James Cowan, captain and centre-half of Scotland, played against England in 1898 when inebriated and was never chosen again by the national selectors. One Scottish committee member maintained that 'after Cowan, we shall see that teams are under the care of the trainer from the Friday until the match'. [119] However, by the 1960s even the England manager and strict disciplinarian Alf Ramsay was prepared to allow his squad to drink providing that it was in the team's hotel. [120] The current manager, Sven Goran Eriksson, has adopted a similar policy but has stated that 'if you play for England you don't need to drink wine or beer'. [121]

As Sherman stated over a century ago, the real key is self-discipline. In football the players' union is helping its members avoid the perils of alcohol. Until recently the Professional Footballers' Association never focused on the issue of alcohol abuse, but has always been prepared to help players if they needed to go into clinics or hospitals for rehabilitation. [122] Now the association has stepped in to try to change dressing-room culture, something that it felt had altered little from the 1970s. [123] At senior level, the old pros still had the attitude that you could always sweat out last night's booze at training, and that 'the beginner is only too apt to be led by the old stagers' remains as true today as in 1906 when the union secretary wrote the comment. [124] The opportunity to rectify the situation came with the establishment, by most professional clubs, of academies for young players. Finance was obtained from Adidas to develop an educational programme to coach players for life rather than just for football. The efficacy of the scheme has yet to be evaluated, but doubtless it will be aided by the influx of foreign players into British football with their more temperate habits. [125] In other sports, players have lessened their intake of alcohol voluntarily. In cricket there has been a decline in drinking after the game and many players stick to non-alcoholic drinks. [126] One impact of professionalism on rugby union has been for the elite player to abandon the membership norm of the amateur version of the sport and reduce alcohol consumption to a level deemed consistent with professional playing performance. [127] Training is no longer a 'social gathering' and the transformation in post-match drinking is epitomized by the Scottish international dressing room which used to receive a keg of the sponsor's beer but now waits two hours before the players touch alcohol. [128] It is ironic that the money brought into sport by sponsorship from the alcohol industry may have resulted in a more responsible attitude to drinking by sportspersons who have become more 'professional'.

Conclusion

Britain is a society with an alcohol problem. The British Medical Association says that the drinking habits of adolescents are creating a health time-bomb; random breath tests are being introduced into the Army, where alcohol abuse is costing £100 million a year and is responsible for seventy per cent of courts martial; there has been an expansion in female binge-drinking in the sixteen-to-twenty-four age group; and it is estimated that alcohol-induced sick leave, unemployment and premature death is costing the country £3.3 billion a year. [129] In such an external environment it is unsurprising that sport should itself face issues associated with alcohol.

The relationship between alcohol and sporting performance has changed over the past century. Traditionally, alcohol was seen as an aid to strength, stamina and courage. But today, apart from a few sports that require a steady hand for aiming, such as darts, shooting or archery, alcohol is no longer regarded as a performance-enhancing drug. Concern now centres on how drinking by sportspersons affects their non-sporting behaviour. Alcohol consumption in sport has now become a social rather than a sporting issue. Here there are tensions. The main one is simply the anomalous association between an activity generally seen as being good for you and one that is not. However, there are other contradictions. Sponsors want to see their products consumed at post-match ceremonies, but coaches want their athletes to restrict alcohol intake, especially when rehydration is necessary. Managers want their players to behave, but are reluctant to discipline those who might win them a title. Some prohibit their players from consuming alcohol, but others believe that drinking together helps bond a team and thus institutionalize binge-drinking. Clubs overtly criticize players who let the club down, but at the same time often market their own brands of wine and beer. Players know that drinking alcohol might adversely affect their performance yet they find that their employers are tolerant of a drinking culture, a continuation into professional ranks of a long-established amateur tradition. [130]

Acknowledgements

This article is an extended version of part of a keynote address to the 'Sport and Alcohol: Understanding the Mix' conference, held at Massey University, Palmerston North, New Zealand, February 2005. The author is grateful to the Leverhulme Trust who funded a research project on the relationship between sport and alcohol, some results of which were published in Tony Collins and Wray Vamplew, *Mud, sweat and beers: a cultural history of sport and alcohol* (Oxford, 2002).

Notes

[1]   For a full discussion see Robert D. Stainback, *Alcohol and sport* (Champaign, IL, 1997), pp. 49–63 and Thomas Reilly, 'Alcohol, anti-anxiety drugs and sport', in David R. Mottram, ed., *Drugs in sport* (London, 1996), pp. 144–72.

[2]   An Operator, *Selections from the Fancy* (Boston, MA, 1972: orig. pub. 1828), pp. 78–82.

[3]   Peter Radford, *The celebrated Captain Barclay* (London, 2001).

[4]   *Say's Weekly Journal*, 6 Oct. 1787.

[5]   Vincent Dowling, *Fistiana, or oracle of the ring* (London, 1868), p. 143.

[6]   Brian Harrison, *Drink and the Victorians* (Keele, 1994 edn), pp. 38–40.

[7]   A.G. Steel and R.H. Lyttelton, *Cricket* (London, 1893), pp. 212–3.

[8]   Medicus, 'Football from a medical point of view', *Scottish Football Annual 1889–90*, pp. 27–32.

[9]   R.C. Lehman, *Rowing* (London, 1898), pp. 115–17.

[10] H.L. Curtis, *Principles of training for amateur athletics* (London, 1892).

[11] Montague Shearman, *Athletics and football* (London, 1888), pp. 171–4.

[12] *Scottish Athletic Journal*, 13 Oct. 1882.

[13] John Weir, *Drink, religion and Scottish football* (Renfrew, 1992).

[14] *Licensed Trade News*, 27 Aug. 1910.

[15] *Scottish Athletic Journal*, 1 Dec. 1885.

[16] Jim Davies, *The book of Guinness advertising* (London, 1998), pp. 7, 16.

[17] Viscount Knebworth, *Boxing* (London, 1931), p. 194.

[18] Alphonse Abrahams in *The Practitioner*, quoted in *The British Deaf Sportsman* 6 (1) (April–June 1935).

[19] Stainback, *Alcohol and sport*, pp. 49–63.

[20] Simon Hughes, professional cricketer, quoted in Duncan Stewart, 'Alcohol, the ethical dilemma' (MA thesis, Warwick, 1997), p. 33.

[21] Jimmy Greaves, *This one's on me* (Newton Abbot, 1979), p. 10.

[22] Quoted in Stewart, 'Alcohol, the ethical dilemma', p. 49.

[23] Ibid., p. 34.

[24] 'Real lives: Jan Molby', *Total Sport*, 17 Nov. 1999, p. 28.

[25] Ron Atkinson, *Big Ron: a different ball game* (London, 1998), p. 95.

[26] *Daily Telegraph*, 16 Oct. 2004.

[27] Quoted in Stewart, 'Alcohol, the ethical dilemma', p. 46.

[28] *Guardian*, 21 Feb. 1997; *Rugby League Week* [Sydney], 16 June 1999, p. 6.

[29] Reilly, 'Alcohol, anti-anxiety drugs and sport', p. 147; Stewart, 'Alcohol, the ethical dilemma', p. 73.

[30] Peter Arnold, *Darts* (London, 1984), p. 66.

[31] *Sunday Telegraph Magazine*, 21 March 2004, p.29.

[32] Reilly, 'Alcohol, anti-anxiety drugs and sport', p. 156.

[33] Ibid., p. 155.

[34] Ibid., p. 158.

[35] Mark Johnston, racehorse trainer, Radio 5, 4 June 1998. See also Wray Vamplew and Joyce Kay, *Encyclopedia of British horseracing* (London, 2005), pp. 11–12.

[36] Michael Tanner and Gerry Cranham, *Great jockeys of the flat* (Enfield, 1992), p. 46.

[37] John Welcome, *Fred Archer: a complete study* (London, 1990), p. 29.

[38] Lester Piggott, *Lester* (London, 1995), pp. 16, 38.

[39] Steve Wootton, *Nutrition for sport* (London, 1989), p. 113.

[40] Joyce Kay, 'From coarse to course: the first fifty years of the Royal Caledonian Hunt, 1777–1826', *Review of Scottish Culture*, 13 (2000–01), pp. 30–39.

[41] On the Scottish football situation see Weir, *Drink, religion and Scottish football*.

[42] *Scottish Sport*, 4 Sept. 1893, quoted in Weir, *Drink, religion and Scottish football*, fn 23.

[43] Fred Root, *A cricket pro's lot* (London, 1937), p. 23.

[44] Stewart, 'Alcohol, the ethical dilemma', p. 13.

[45] B.T., 'The licensing Act 1902 and golf clubs', *Golf Illustrated*, 25 March 1910, p.11.

[46] *Goring and Streatley golf club: the first hundred years, 1895–1995* (Goring, 1995), p. 109.

[47] Stewart, 'Alcohol, the ethical dilemma', p. 29.

[48] See Pete May, *Sunday muddy Sunday* (London, 1998).

[49] *Independent on Sunday*, 1 July 1999.

[50] Reilly, 'Alcohol, anti-anxiety drugs and sport', p. 153.

[51] Eric Dunning and Ivan Waddington, 'Sport as a drug and drugs in sport', *International Review for the Sociology of Sport*, 38 (3) (2003), p. 356.

[52] *Daily Telegraph*, 15 Dec. 2004.

[53] Pete Davies, *I lost my heart to the Belles* (London, 1997); J. Macbeth, *Women's football in Scotland: an interpretive study* (PhD. thesis, Stirling, 2004); Alison Carle and John Nauright, 'Crossing the line: women playing rugby union' in Timothy J.L. Chandler and John Nauright, eds., *Making the rugby world* (London, 1999), pp. 128–48; Dunning and Waddington, 'Sport as a drug', pp. 356–7.

[54] Stainback, *Alcohol and sport*, p. 67; Wootton, *Nutrition for sport*, p. 159.

[55] See comments of Dr Gordon Morse of Cloud House, a Wiltshire residential addiction centre. *Daily Telegraph*, 13 Oct. 1998.

[56] 'Stonehenge', *Manual of British rural sports* (London, 1857), p. 445.

[57] Ken Thornett (with Tom Easton), *Tackling rugby* (Melbourne, 1965), p. 121.

[58] Greaves, *This one's on me*, p. 77.

[59] Paul Merson (with Harry Harris), *Rock bottom* (Bloomsbury, 1995), p. 37.

[60] Letter from 'Scratch Medal', *The Field*, Oct. 1881. I am grateful to Peter N. Lewis, director of the British Golf Museum for this reference.

[61] Minutes of Lancashire CCC, 31 Jan. 1890; Minutes of Leicester CCC, 11 June 1894.

[62] *Cricket*, IX (1890), p. 93; Leslie Duckworth, *The story of Warwickshire cricket* (London, 1974), p. 49.

[63] I am grateful to John Harding, historian of the PFA, for these references.

[64] For surveys see Russ Williams, *Football Babylon* (London, 1990); Denis Campbell, Pete May and Andrew Shields, *The lad done bad* (Harmondsworth, 1996); and Andrew Shields, 'Some people are on the piss', *Total Sport*, Dec. 1996, pp. 94–102.

[65] *Scottish Athletic Journal*, 30 March 1883. Cited in Weir, *Drink, religion and Scottish football*.

[66] *North British Daily Mail*, 22 Jan. 1878.

[67] *Scottish Athletic Journal*, 26 Aug. 1885.

[68] *Scottish Sport*, 8 April 1898.

[69] Minutes of Heart of Midlothian FC, 28 Nov.1902.

[70] *Weekly News*, 24 April 1909.

[71] *Temperance Herald*, Feb. 1909.

[72] Letter from 'Scratch Medal', *The Field*, Oct. 1881.

[73] Horace Hutchinson, *Bert Edward the golf caddie* (London, 1903).

[74] Gerald Watts, *Royal St Georges* (Sandwich, 1996), p. 201.

[75] Minutes of Muskerry Golf Club, 10 April, 29 June and 4 Dec. 1911.

[76] W.I. Bassett, 'The day's work' in *The book of football* (London, 1906), pp. 110–13.

[77] *Observer*, 6 Sept. 1998.

[78] Atkinson, *Big Ron*, p. 94, p. 97.

[79] *Independent on Sunday*, 10 Sept. 1995.

[80] *Daily Telegraph*, 13 Oct. 1998.

[81] Tony Adams (with Ian Ridley), *Addicted* (London, 1998); Paul Gascoigne (with Hunter Davies), *Gazza* (London, 2004); Merson, *Rock bottom*.

[82] *Daily Telegraph*, 13 Oct. 1998.

[83] Greaves, *This one's on me*, p. 2.

[84] Wray Vamplew, 'Still crazy after all those years: continuity in a changing labour market for professional jockeys', *British Journal of Contemporary History*, 14 (2) (2000), p. 144; *Guardian*, 6 Dec. 2004; Bill Borrows, *The Hurricane* (London, 2003); Tony Rushmer, 'Cue Jimmy', *Total Sport* (April 1999), pp. 57–61.

[85] John Ford, *Boxiana* (London, 1976), p. 85.

[86] For allegations of alcoholism see Roger Mortimer, Richard Onslow and Peter Willett, *Biographical encyclopedia of British flat racing* (London, 1978), pp. 174, 219; Frances Collingwood, 'The tragedy of Thomas Loates', *The British Racehorse*, Oct. 1967, pp. 427–8.

[87] According to Stephen Stephens, director of the Addictions Unit at Marchmont Priory Hospital, Southampton, 'the fact is that we don't really know why some people become addicts and others don't' (quoted in Merson, *Rock bottom*, p. 2). Henri Begleiter, an American researcher, estimates that genes perhaps account for 40–60 per cent of the risk of alcoholism: *New Scientist*, 27 Nov. 1999, pp. 39–43.

[88] Martin Roderick, Ivan Waddington and Graham Parker, 'Playing hurt: managing injuries in English professional football', *International Review of Sports Sociology* 35 (2) (2000), pp. 165–180.

[89] Peter Roebuck, *It never rains... a cricketer's lot* (London, 1984), passim.

[90] Jocelyn Targett, 'Slim chance', *Sunday Telegraph Magazine*, 29 Nov. 1998.

[91] For an account of such pressures across a range of elite sports see Angela Patmore, *Sportsmen under stress* (London, 1986). For a historical view see Wray Vamplew, *Pay up and play the game* (Cambridge, 2004 edn), pp. 217–32. For a specific case study of footballer Stan Collymore, see Stephen Wagg, '"With his money I could afford to be depressed": markets, masculinity and mental distress in the English football press', *Football Studies* 3 (2) (2000), pp. 67–87.

[92] Greaves, *This one's on me*, p. 5.

[93] Quoted in Stewart, 'Alcohol, the ethical dilemma', p. 46.

[94] David Frith, *By his own hand: a study of cricket's suicides* (London, 1991).

[95] Root, *A cricket pro's lot*, p. 170.

[96] Vamplew, 'Still crazy', p. 115.

[97] Based on information supplied by Jockey Club chief medical officer, Dr Michael Turner.

[98] Interview, 2 June 1999.

[99] Jimmy Greaves, *Greavsie* (London, 2003), 218.

[100] Tony Rennick, 'Hard times' in Richard Cox, Dave Russell and Wray Vamplew, eds., *Encyclopedia of British football* (London, 2002), pp. 171–2.

[101] Frith, *By his own hand*, p. 8.

[102] Keith Sandiford, *Cricket and the Victorians* (Aldershot, 1994), p. 104.

[103] Rudolph Kenna and Ian Sutherland, *The bevy: the story of Glasgow and drink* (Glasgow, 2000), p.88.

[104] Jockey Club, *Protocol and rules for the testing of riders for banned substances* (London, 1994).

[105] *Guardian*, 19 Sept., 1 Nov. 1996.

[106] 'My sporting life: Clare Tomlinson', *Total Sport*, March 1999, p. 36.

[107] Shearman, *Athletics and football*, p. 173.

[108] Minutes of Sheffield Wednesday FC, 5 Oct.1898, 19 Feb. 1908.

[109] Minutes of Sheffield Wednesday FC, 23 Feb. 1898, 5 Feb., 2 April 1902.

[110] Vamplew, *Pay Up*, pp. 161–170.

[111] Tony Mason, '"Our Stephen and Our Harold": Edwardian Footballers as Local Heroes' in Richard Holt, J.A. Mangan and Pierre Lanfranchi, eds., *European Heroes* (London, 1996), pp. 80–81.

[112] Matthew Taylor, '"Proud Preston": a history of the Football League, 1900–1939 (PhD. thesis, De Montfort, 1997), p. 208; Minutes of Heart of Midlothian FC, 21 Oct. 1895, 19 Nov. 1910.

[113] *Yorkshire Post*, 25 April 1889.

[114] John Moynihan, *The soccer syndrome* (London, 1966), pp. 139–41: interview with Archie Andrews, left-half for Crystal Palace and Queen's Park Rangers in the 1950s.

[115] Merson, *Rock bottom*, pp. 32, 37, 44, 84–5.

[116] Campbell, May and Shields, *The lad done bad*, p. 141.

[117] Atkinson, *Big Ron*, p. 95.

[118] *Mail on Sunday*, 19 Sept. 2004.

[119] Weir, *Drink, religion and Scottish football*, fn 60.

[120] Greaves, *This one's on me*, p. 50.

[121] *Daily Telegraph*, 5 Feb. 2001.

[122] Letter from Gordon Taylor, chief executive, PFA, 15 March 1999.

[123] Interview with Micky Burns, PFA, 5 May 1999.

[124] John Cameron in *Spalding's Football Guide*, 1906.

[125] Interview with Billy Brown, assistant manager at Kilmarnock, 13 Dec. 2004.

[126] Simon Hughes quoted in Stewart, 'Alcohol, the ethical dilemma', p. 39.

[127] Stewart, 'Alcohol, the ethical dilemma', pp. 38–45, 58.

[128] Ibid., p. 106; Scott Hastings, Scottish rugby union player, Radio 5, 4 June 1998.

[129] *Sunday Telegraph*, 14 March 2004; *Daily Telegraph*, 30 July 2004; *Daily Telegraph*, 11 May 2000.

[130] Paul Weaver, 'Slaves to the corporate rhythm', *Guardian*, 27 July 1999.

From Fixed Capacities to Performance-Enhancement: The Paradigm Shift in the Science of 'Training' and the Use of Performance-Enhancing Substances

Rob Beamish & Ian Ritchie

'Would you still take the drug?'

In *Death in the locker room*, Bob Goldman cited Dr Gabe Mirkin's poll of more than a hundred top runners whom he asked 'If I could give you a pill that would make you an Olympic champion – and also kill you in a year – would you take it?' More than half said yes. Goldman asked 198 world-class athletes a similar question: 'If I had a magic drug that was so fantastic that if you took it once you would win every competition you would enter, from the Olympic decathlon to Mr Universe, for the next five years, but it had one minor drawback – it would kill you five years after you took it – would you still take the drug?' [1] Again, more than half said yes.

There are four points to note about those polls. First, the data are largely meaningless, especially Goldman's, because his claim about the magic drug was too unreal to take seriously. In Mirkin's case, if athletes were offered pills to take as the question was asked and half did, then the data might mean something. But those are minor points.

More important is Goldman's rhetorical strategy. Discounting his extreme scenario – 'it can be argued that it is only because the athletes knew there is no such magic medicine that they indicated their willingness to commit Olympic *hara-kiri*', and faced with a 'real-world magic medicine, they would have second thoughts' – Goldman presents one that appears, in contrast, very creditable. 'Perhaps this argument [that faced with a real medicine the athletes would have second thoughts] is correct', Goldman wrote, 'but the evidence suggests otherwise': 'The evidence suggests that athletes will take anything or do anything to their bodies to win, with no assurance of winning, and in apparent disregard for their lives beyond Olympia, or sometimes beyond the next major competition.' [2] Dismissing the obviously fantastic to make a different, more important thesis appear completely credible is an effective strategy.

Goldman wrote *Death in the locker room* to argue that steroids and other performance-enhancing substances kill athletes. His key claim is that even without any guarantees of success, athletes will do anything to win. Well before he presents any real, systematic evidence, Goldman's rhetorical strategy seems to prove his central thesis. With the second claim established, the first one becomes plausible and that question – or one like it – is all one has to refer to when demonstrating the power of anabolic steroids and the hold they have over athletes. [3]

Of greater importance, Goldman's 'study' is referred to time and again in discussions about performance-enhancing substances. Though merely a rhetorical device, a paraphrase of Goldman's question is frequently used to demonstrate that athletes will do anything to win. [4] As rhetoric, it is effective; as analysis, it is a serious impediment to the debate about the use of performance-enhancing substances in sport.

The most serious outcome of Goldman strategy is how it shapes the public's, sport policy makers' and journalists' understanding of why and how athletes use performance-enhancing substances. 'Would you still take the drug?' indicates that performance-enhancing substances are 'magic bullets' that athletes simply take and results – both positive and ominous – follow without fail. Substance use is completely removed from the social and historical context within which it occurs.

On the social side, the Goldman claim ignores the close relationship between athletes and coaches. In fact, it implies a manipulative one where coaches, focused only on results, offer athletes substances they know little about except that they are effective and dangerous. The claim brackets the totality of athletes' life experiences and their sophisticated knowledge about every aspect of their sport as they progress through its increasingly demanding and competitive levels. Athletes and coaches do not naïvely use performance-enhancing substances and practices as they strive to be the world's best.

Important as the social context is, it rests on a more fundamental foundation – the particular, historically situated understanding of the ontology of human performance. This primary foundation is the focus of this paper – the core, deeply seated, powerfully influential ontology that frames athletes' and coaches' decisions about the use of performance-enhancing substances in the modern era.

Simply knowing that there is an important historical context under-lying the use of performance-enhancing substances is not enough to dispel the Goldman claim and others like it. A more profound analysis is required if athletes, coaches, and policy-makers are to fully address the use of various performance-enhancing substances and practices in modern sport. To that end, this paper focuses on the fundamentally important paradigm shift that took place during the middle part of the twentieth century regarding the notion of 'training' and the ontology of human performance. Based on a different ontological conception of human performance, the paradigm shift we discuss changed how coaches and athletes thought about 'training' as well as the way they understood performance and performance-enhancement. Those changes completely altered athletes' and coaches' approach to performance-enhancing sub-stances (and other practices). Any meaningful debate about performance-enhancing substances must address the ontological bases for the science that produces them and the practices which lead to their use.

The development of 'training' in sport

The application of science to progressive training methods in sport is a recent development. While scientists in the nineteenth and early twentieth centuries studied athletes, they did not do so to enhance or boost performance capacity. [5] Scientific discourse was contoured by the law of the conservation of energy (the first law of thermodynamics). Moreover, in accordance with the conception of science at that time and the concomitant belief that scientific laws applied universally, the laws of one area were applied to others; this was especially true of the laws of basic physics which were seen as among the purest of scientific discoveries. As a result, the first law of thermodynamics was applied to the scientific understanding of many realms, including how the human body operated.

In the 1830s and 1840s several European researchers – most notably Julius Robert von Mayer, James Prescott Joule and Hermann von Helmholtz – worked simultaneously on theoretical aspects of the doctrine. [6] The first law states that energy can be transferred from one system to another but it cannot be created or destroyed. The total amount of energy in the universe is constant. Einstein's theory of relativity – $E = MC^2$ – describes the relationship between energy and matter precisely and indicates that energy (E) is equal to matter (M) times the square of a constant (C). The equation demonstrates that energy and matter are interchangeable and, if the quantity of matter in the universe is constant then the quantity of energy is also fixed. [7]

While the conservation of energy applied directly to non-organic matter was instrumental in the development of machines, its proponents applied it to the human organism, comparing its biological and physiological functions to non-living systems such as mechanical engines. [8] 'As the power to work is without question the most important of the products of animal life', Mayer wrote in the 1850s, 'the mechanical equivalent of heat is in the very nature of things destined to be the foundation for the edifice of a scientific physiology'. [9] So while the doctrine's widespread influence included physics and the understanding of mechanical systems, it grew to encompass the study of living organisms, including an emerging body of work in human physiology. [10] The doctrine was extended to the understanding of human activity in social and institutional life, including physical education settings. [11] As a result, scientific studies of the human body in motion were part of a general scientific world view premised on the first law of thermodynamics.

The term 'training' existed in the late nineteenth and early twentieth centuries and coaches and athletes approached it within the premises of the first law. Training was synonymous with 'drill' – the repetition of skills to refine technique, improve coordination, and enhance precision and execution. Training was not designed to systematically increase physical power, speed, endurance, and agility through specific, targeted programmes. [12] The scientific community and the sports world alike believed those attributes were fixed and, like a well-oiled machine, could only improve through greater precision and coordination. Thus even though the legend of six-time Olympic champion Milo of Crotona was known, the sociocultural conditions conducive to the application of modern training's basic principles (working against progressive resistance, over short intervals, for a long period of time) did not exist before the Second World War. [13]

While Pierre de Coubertin began to launch his modern Olympic project, athletic training manuals indicated that the principles of training 'differ but slightly from those of judicious living'. Both 'require the same close study and proper interpretation of the laws of health, and such an application of them as will produce temperate habits and a high degree of mental and bodily vigour'. [14] In 1889, Montague Shearman's *Athletics and football* stated that 'there is no reason why an athlete who desires to get fit should lead other than a natural life'. [15]

At the end of the nineteenth century, research observations emerged that would eventually challenge the 'fixed capacity' approach to the human body and lead to a new ontological conception of how the human functioned and performed. Working with cadavers, C. Hirsch (1899) noted a direct relationship between body musculature and heart size. Three years later Schieffer, and then H. Dietlen and F. Moritz (1908), noted that habitual cyclists had larger hearts than occasional and non-cyclists. [16] In 1905, W. Roux reported in *The mechanics of development* that increases in muscle size, strength and endurance were an effect of chronic exertion. This led to his theory of 'hypertrophy through activity' and 'atrophy through inactivity'. [17]

Although these early studies identified changes in the human body due to exercise, they were insufficient to cause a paradigm shift in physiology away from the first law of thermodynamics and were certainly too obscure to have any impact upon training practices in sport. Coaches and athletes were preoccupied with 'tapping the hereditary potential of the human or animal organism rather than artificially manipulating the organism itself'. [18] In the sport literature of the period, attention centred on the biologically endowed, natural-born runner, jumper or thrower and entire sections of books were dedicated to the suitability and significance of particular body types for specific athletic events.

Based on the law of the conservation of energy, training followed the 'natural method'. Actively advocated by France's Georges Hébert, the technique required athletes to get fully in touch with their natural movements through drill and practice while emphasizing a continuous pace and eliminating unnecessary movements. While 'natural' in optimizing the natural talents of a given runner, the emphasis on pace, economy of movement and the use of clock time reflected something very unnatural, but the contradiction is only an apparent one. The 'natural method' was completely consistent with the first law of thermodynamics – a natural law. In addition, because the first law was a scientific law and applied to all instances of movement, Hébert's technique used the same principles that Frank and Lillian Gilbreth employed in their famous 'time and motion studies' in the workplace during that period as well as Fredrick Winslow Taylor's principles of scientific management. [19] Clock time, pace and efficiency of movements simply maximized natural capacities.

Taylor's principles maximized workers' output by reducing their movements to individual components and then optimizing the execution of each component. [20] Performance improved through increased precision and better technique – not increased performance capacity. Similarly, time and motion studies, whether in the workplace or on the track, optimized a given work capacity; they did not try to expand it by developing an untapped 'potential' capacity. Track and field coaches and industrial managers were working from the same set of assumptions about human performance and sought increased efficiencies rather than expanded capacities.

Finnish distance runner Hannes Kolehmainen was among the earliest beneficiaries of Hébert's technique. Kolehmainen trained at a specific tempo to determine the best running speed for his particular physique and style. At the 1912 Olympic Games, he won three gold medals including a victory over world record holder Jean Bouin in the 5,000 metres. Kolehmainen, followed by Paavo Nurmi and Ville Ritola, began the era of the 'Flying Finns'. Focusing on the style that best fit their physiques, positioning on the track, and emphasizing a continuous speed, Ritola and Nurmi, who ran with a stopwatch in his hand, dominated distance events throughout the 1920s. [21] Industrial efficiency – the conservation of energy – was the basic paradigm in athletic training in the early twentieth century.

Towards a paradigm shift in understanding human performance

While physicists, physiologists and coaches worked within the paradigm established by the law of the conservation of energy, anatomists, physiologists and laboratory researchers in other disciplines began to undermine the paradigm with respect to human performance. During the inter-war period, European researchers began to build a scientific body of knowledge concerning human physiology which inevitably recorded observations related to exercise, human anatomy and physiology. Britain's Nobel Prize-winning physiologist Archibald Hill – 'a giant in the field of exercise physiology' – probably had a more profound impact than usually recognized. [22] Hill's demanding experiments in muscle fatigue, lactic acid formation and oxygen debt required subjects who could push themselves to the extreme. As a result, Hill used athletes in his research because they could tolerate his demanding experiments. [23] Two results emerged. First, the results suggested that the conservation of energy thesis, as it was understood in connection with physiology, was suspect; and second, one could not miss the potential application of Hill's research in muscle physiology to sport. Both of these contributed to the use of a newly developing paradigm in physiology and an emergent sport science.

In a similar manner, research into questions of basic physiology led scientists such as S. Hoogerwert, W.W. Siebert, L. Pikhala, Arthur Steinhaus, A. Vannotti, H. Pfister, T. Petrén, T. Sjöstrand and B. Sylvén to develop an experimentally based body of knowledge concerning physiological responses to exercise which was progressively linked more and more closely to athletic performance. [24] For example, in 1930 Pikhala noted that athletic success required different physical 'properties' – physical power, strength and speed – and he argued that they could be developed during training if there was a variation between activity and rest and a focus on intensity in practice sessions rather than simply just volume, and if work was narrowed to specific goals. In the inter-war period, Pikhala had articulated the essential components of progressive resistance training for athletic development. [25]

E.H. Christensen's work complemented Pikhala's as he found that regular training with a standard workload resulted in lowering the heart rate required to work at a fixed load. Further training, however, did not modify the response unless the load was increased in subsequent training sessions. When that was done, the original workload could be performed at an even lower heart rate than before. Christensen also established that physiological adaptation took place at a given load and to gain further improvements one had to increase the training intensity. [26]

In North America, leading-edge research in human performance was centred in the Harvard Fatigue Laboratory, which was established in 1927 and operated until shortly after the Second World War. Elton Mayo, one of the leaders in the 'human factors' direction of the Harvard Business School, was a co-founder of the laboratory with Lawrence (L.J.)

Henderson. The relationship between the laboratory and sport is interesting because the lab's 'human factors' approach to industrial relations stemmed directly from the Gilbreths' time and motion studies and Taylor's principles of scientific management. As noted earlier, time and motion studies and scientific management had begun to exert an indirect influence on athletic training in the 1920s. [27] Archibald Hill was also influential in the development of the laboratory; his studies inspired many of the scientists who would later go on to found the lab. [28]

The Fatigue Lab's collaborative research programme involved physiologists, biochemists, psychologists, biologists, physicians, sociologists and anthropologists. The collaborative approach allowed investigators to study the effects and interrelation of the human body's many systems. Most important, research centred on 'man's adaptation to his environment ... not only his normal, everyday and working environments, but his adaptation to unusual stresses, such as athletic competition, exposure to strange environments and war'. [29] The Fatigue Lab focused on the physiochemical properties and behaviour of blood – at rest, work and altitude – and pioneered many aspects of exercise physiology and the study of physiological responses to altitude. In studies of fitness level, for example, the laboratory reached the same conclusions as Christensen regarding fitness, workload, and the improvement of maximum oxygen carrying capacity (or $VO_{2\ MAX}$). [30] The laboratory's study of lactic acid and exercise and the mechanisms and importance for actively removing it from the muscle were decades ahead of their application in athletic training. [31]

The inclusion of athletes in the lab's protocols was completely fortuitous. Although general fitness was of interest (the lab developed the well-known Harvard Step Test as a simple, inexpensive and efficient means of assessing general fitness), much of the laboratory's exploratory research was conducted on the lab workers themselves, and a number of them happened to be athletes of various levels and abilities. As a result, the discovery of differences among normal, trained and well-trained subjects occurred by chance rather than design. Nevertheless, despite the differences they discovered and the laboratory's particular interest in fitness, none of the research was directed towards enhancing athletic performance, even though the discoveries made in the areas of blood chemistry in exercise, aerobic and anaerobic work capacity, diet and physiological adaptation to physical work at altitude would all be used to enhance world-class athletic performance once applied sports physiologists had embraced the mid-twentieth century paradigm shift in human performance. [32]

Discoveries in Europe and North America during the first few decades of the twentieth century initiated a slight, but nevertheless tremendously significant, paradigm shift in understanding the human body. Rather than thinking about it as a vessel with fixed, inherited traits and capacities, scientists began to conceive of the body as an adapting organism that responded to its environment. Walter Cannon's *The wisdom of the body* (1932) presented one of the early, full-length statements of how the body seeks physiological stability and when it is altered 'then the various physiological arrangements which serve to restore the normal state when it has been disturbed' are bought into play. [33] The notion that the body could use a complex set of physiological processes to maintain its homeostatic condition in the face of significant external changes and pressures suggested that it might be possible to develop its physiological work capacity. The body, Cannon's work suggested, was not a fixed physiological entity and did not strictly follow the first law of thermo-dynamics as previously assumed.

The science/applied science lag

Although medical researchers continued to study human physiology through the 1930s and 1940s, there was a significant lag between the development of new knowledge in universities' and institutes' laboratories and its application in industry or the field of sport. Part of the reason was the inevitable and perpetual gulf that exists between theory and practice. A second major impediment was the philosophical approach that dominated sport in the 1930s and 1940s. This was the era of nascent commercialism in sport and the apogee of amateur athletics' emphasis on character development and education through sport. As a result, outcome and performance enhancement were of distinctly secondary importance. Finally, there was an irrefutable reality within the realm of sport itself that Ernst Jokl criticized even as late as 1958. 'Lord Kelvin's dictum', Jokl chided in 'The Future of Athletics',

> unequivocally accepted by the natural sciences as long ago as during the last quarter of the nineteenth century, viz. 'that no science can flourish without theory', *has made no impression whatever on physical training*. The latter remains one of the few disciplines of education whose affairs are still conducted without the benefit of theoretical concepts. [34]

A random survey of books on athletics in the late 1940s and early 1950s shows the basis and accuracy of Jokl's critique of physical education in general, and athletic training in particular. *Physical conditioning: exercises for sports and healthful living*, a 1942 publication in the Barnes Sports Library, is a good example of how even though the basic principles of an emerging physiology of exercise were recognized by proponents of athletic training, they were applied in a highly circumscribed manner. [35] Like Pikhala, George Stafford and Ray Duncan defined fitness as those 'qualities best represented by strength, power, speed, skill and endurance for the task, plus proper enthusiasm (mental equilibrium, morale, and mind-set)'. [36] But unlike Pikhala or Christensen, there is no discussion of intensity in training sessions and variations between activity and rest although there is some attention to specificity (a concept understood through the study of Olympic athletes as early as 1929). [37] For Stafford and Duncan, the main guiding principle for athletic training is 'you learn to do anything whatsoever by *doing it*'. [38] Thus athletes who ran the 440 were instructed to train at distances of 350 to 500 yards. In other sports it was recommended that practices should last about the duration of an actual competition 'and accomplish about the same amount of work at the same speed'. [39]

Chapter 4 of this text, 'Sports Conditioning', presents specific conditioning activities for a number of sports ranging alphabetically from basketball and boxing, through football and gymnastics, to track and weightlifting. The most striking feature of these 'conditioning' exercises is that high-school athletes today would think they were simply warm-up callisthenics. *Physical conditioning* recommends athletes follow these exercises throughout a four-week period with their duration reducing from fifteen minutes in the first week to only five minutes in week four. [40] Stafford and Duncan do not, in any way, draw upon Pikhala, Christensen, Steinhaus or the Fatigue Laboratory's insights and their recommendations do not remotely approach contemporary regimes of training and conditioning. *Physical conditioning* does not direct athletes to long-term development through progressive resistance and varied intervals of work and rest. It does not indicate that a regime of exercises that is as sport-specific as possible, which is carefully designed to build power, strength, speed, agility, coordination, quickness, flexibility, local muscular endurance and cardiovascular aerobic capacity is the most proficient and useful approach to enhancing athletic performance. In fact, Stafford and Duncan's text does not suggest, or even imply, the two most basic principles of contemporary training and conditioning – the 'overload principle' and the 'principle of specificity' even though Steinhaus, for example, had discussed exercise specificity, overload training, cardiac output, blood composition, vital capacity and exercise metabolism as early as 1933. [41] Stafford and Duncan do not even suggest that such a programme might be possible and desirable or that they had the knowledge basis from which they might formulate those principles or develop more elaborate training programmes.

Texts such as *Track and field athletics* (1947), *Championship technique in track and field* (1949) and the United States Naval Institute's *Track and field* (1950) also lack a sophisticated knowledge-base in exercise physiology. As a result, the general guidelines for training and conditioning do not contain the sophistication or levels of intensity that would characterize athletic training from the mid 1960s onwards. [42] Training in *Track and field athletics* reflects the pre-First World War approaches identified by Hildenbrand, where practice and drill are emphasized to refine technique, improve coordination, and enhance execution.

The main chapter on conditioning focuses on the variables that 'go to build and maintain physical and mental states which are most conducive to acceptable performance'. The chapter covers diet, elimination, exercise, weight, rest, sleep, staleness, stimulants and the use of tobacco. [43] The discussion of exercise is confined to two paragraphs which indicate that an athlete's regular daily routine is usually sufficient exercise to maintain health. When athletes must carry out manual labour, 'there exists the danger of over exercise', the authors warn. 'The ideal situation is one in which the athlete has no responsibilities requiring strenuous exercise other than the prescribed work in the event'. [44] The only discussion of physiological principles, found in the chapter 'Preliminary Season Preparations', focuses on warm-up and the development of muscle coordination. [45] While the workouts outlined in the text demonstrate a progressive workload, the principles involved in the development of the workouts are not discussed at all.

Championship technique in track and field begins by associating success in track and field with race and national histories before moving into principles of training. The 'key word in what we miscall training for track and field', Dean Cromwell and Al Wesson note, 'is moderation'. [46] The vital principle for training in track and field is preparing muscles for 'special duties'. 'No elaborate system of exercise is necessary if one will just remember that the aim is to develop muscular coordination rather than just muscle'. For Cromwell and Wesson, 'the two basic exercises that everyone should take are walking and chinning the bar'. The authors argue that people enjoy sports most when they win, which is why athletes train 'and do without a few little things like pie crust and tobacco', which is so easy to do 'that we don't need to call it training at all. It is just living a normal, moderate, regular life'. [47]

The Naval Institute's *Track and field*, 'prepared and published during WWII to provide the best standardized instruction in the sports selected to give the youth, training to be combat Naval pilots, the maximum physical and psychological benefits', emphasizes that 'the modern coach is a college graduate, versed in kinesiology, physiology, anatomy, hygiene and physics'. [48] The text presents an unsophisticated approach to training and conditioning. A distinction is made between 'core material' which focuses on 'circulatory-respiratory functions related to exercise' to promote maximal 'all-around physical condition' and 'supplementary drills and races' which are of short duration or 'acts of pure skill' that improve coordination and prepare athletes to 'meet sudden, emergency physical demands'. [49]

Despite the limited scientific information contained in training manuals through the inter-war and early post-Second World War period, athletes still sought ways to win, and they used performance-enhancing substances in many sports. Consistent with the conservation of energy, athletes used substances that maximized output on a given day rather than those that would build and expand performance capacity over time.

In this context, cycling provides an excellent case study. Unlike track and field, which was governed by the strict code of amateurism, cycling was thoroughly professionalized early on and winning was the riders' unabashed goal. Performance-enhancing substances have a long and open history in the sport. The type of substances used in the pre-Second World War period is noteworthy. Consistent with the dominant, scientific ontology of human performance, road racers from the 1800s through to the 1950s used a wide variety of 'race day' drugs – alcohol, opium, heroin, strychnine and amphetamines – to spike their performance on each particular day or to mask the pain incurred over the course of a multi-day ordeal. [50] The training and development of racers was not designed to enhance performance capacity; it simply focused on maximizing a given capacity and/or removing all sensations that would limit or inhibit the maximal use of that fixed capacity.

Although Joe Friel may not be aware of the mid-twentieth century paradigm shift in the ontology of human performance, his account of change in cycling mirrors that shift. He argues that Italian physician Francesco Conconi and his protégé Michele Ferrari initiated long-range planning and cyclists began to talk about periodization in training. It was then that cyclists began to use substances such as erythropoietin, steroids and human growth hormone rather than stimulants and analgesics. [51]

The cold war divide and the new paradigm in sport science

The Second World War and the beginning of the cold war transformed international, world-class, high-performance sport as approaches to training, the use of scientific knowledge to enhance performance and the resources directed towards the pursuit of the linear record changed dramatically. Stalwart proponents of the educative value of sport, even by the late 1950s, were yearning for the lost age of the near-mythological 'gentlemanly amateur' athlete, who had clearly faded away in the early post-war period. 'The last decade [1950s] has covered a strange period in the history of sport', Sir Roger Bannister argued, 'a far cry from what was envisaged by Baron de Coubertin'. 'It has seen the emergence of the new professionalism', he continued,

> not only in the sense of direct and indirect payment for sport, but also in devoting unlimited time and energy to sport, to the total exclusion of any other career – which has been rightly deplored. Every country seeks to enhance national prestige by physical achievements. ... Too few questions seem to be asked about the means and the motives, provided the end of national glory is achieved. [52]

But, Bannister maintained, sport would 'survive the ethical and administrative problems' that beset it because, in the last analysis, sport is an individual affair with an individual meaning – it is 'not a national or moral affair': 'We run not because our country needs fame, nor yet because we think it is doing us good, but because we enjoy it and cannot help ourselves.' [53]

The actual record of post-war sport demonstrates that the focus in Olympic and world-class sport was elsewhere. Frucht and Jokl's statistical analysis of records in world-class sport from 1948 to 1960 revealed not just continual improvement but progress at an accelerating pace. [54] The features of world-class, high-performance sport that Bannister regarded as part of 'a strange period in the history of sport' were firmly entrenched by the 1960s and they would simply expand their influence rather than retreat into the background. Two of the central reasons were the strategic political objectives that particular national leaders held and the concomitant increased allocation of resources directed to world-class sport. Scientifically assisted, high-performance *sport systems*, and not individuals, became the main agents in world-class, high-performance sport in the post-war period. [55]

Although those changes were instrumental in the changed nature of world-class sport in the post-war era, the way high-performance sport developed was premised on the underlying ontology of human performance. Two sports — weightlifting and track and field — seem to have been at the centre of the paradigm shift and, ironically, Bannister may have played a central role in the emergence of the new paradigm.

Calvin Schulman argues that by 1954 the public at large was obsessed with the pursuit of the four-minute mile. John Landy had shaved the time to 4:02. 'Two little seconds are not much', Landy said, '[b]ut when you are on the track those fifteen yards seem solid and impenetrable — like a cement wall'. 'It would take a miler of steel and imagination to break down decades of disbelief', Schulman wrote. 'It would take that special someone to summon the perfect blend of stamina and speed, with inner strength and supreme awareness of his own body, to batter down the cement wall and let the future of athletics charge into the promised land.' [56] It would actually take more — it would require a change in the approach to training and that change would, indeed, lead the 'charge into the promised land' although no one at the time recognized what that land would ultimately look like.

Efficiency alone would not make the barrier fall. In the pursuit of the four-minute barrier, Bannister, Wes Santee and Landy began to unwittingly remove a more fundamental one — the performance paradigm rooted in the conservation of energy. In pursuit of the four-minute mile, Bannister, Landy, Santee and other athletes and coaches began to use training techniques that would do more than perfect technique through drill; they began to build their performance capacities. As a result, rather than reflecting the apogee of amateurism, the 'miracle mile' is better thought of as a dramatic, 3:59.4 transition phase to the new paradigm of high-performance sport in the modern era.

With a medical degree that had followed bachelor's and master's degrees in physiology, Bannister was uniquely situated in the track world of his time; he was familiar with the experimental literature in physiology — and could well have known about the work of Pikhala, Christensen, Steinhaus, Hill and others. Irrespective of what exact literature he drew from, Bannister ran experiments on himself — including treadmill runs with oxygen enriched air — to enhance his performances; [57] used the new Swedish *fartlek* and interval training techniques that incorporated specified and very carefully planned work bouts alongside periods of rest; [58] and whenever possible, used the most advanced technology available to enhance his performances. [59] Without necessarily subscribing to the emerging ontology of human performance, Bannister's use of physiological knowledge and newly developing training techniques represents a significant incremental step towards the overturning of the old conservation of energy paradigm.

In weightlifting, Bob Hoffman – one of the most influential forces in American weightlifting in the 1940s and 50s – had assembled the most successful team of American weightlifters by recruiting widely and offering them work at the York Oil Burner company. Hoffman was not an innovator; he believed that success came when athletes with talent worked hard, kept high moral standards and lived in a congenial atmosphere. Hoffman's weightlifters' success was firmly rooted in the pre-war paradigm of human performance, which prevented him and many weightlifters from developing training techniques that would explicitly address the development of performance capacity. However, as John Fair notes, by the mid-1950s 'the course and character of American weightlifting' was changing as weightlifters began 'a deeper search for ways to alter the body's chemistry to induce more efficient muscular growth'. [60] The Soviet Union's use of testosterone in the 1952 Olympic Games, and John Ziegler's introduction of Dianabol to American weightlifters, reflected a new understanding of the ontology of human performance.

In the West, Donna Haraway argues that at the end of the Second World War there was a shift in the discourse of biochemistry from the mechanistic view of the first law of thermodynamics to one based in information theory. [61] At the molecular level, the discovery of DNA and the way its properties were understood drew upon the discourse of information theory – the body was coded, with instructions, messages, controls and feedback mechanisms which could be manipulated and maximized. Part of the reason for the paradigm shift lay in the number of biologists who were engaged in operations research during the war and their work with communications, codes and cybernetic systems led them to the new discourse. The ontology of human development and human potential shifted to the cellular level, where information was stored and could now be located and decoded to enhance performance. There was, however, a time lag between these developments in microbiology and applied sport science.

The Soviets, who had adopted a scientifically-based, instrumentally rational approach to sport in the early post-war period, made the jump from pure science to athletic performance enhancement much more quickly. [62] The reasons for the emergence of the new performance paradigm have never been fully documented but certainly one key factor was ideological. Stalin dictated that all scientific developments in the USSR must stem from the tenets of Marxism-Leninism and dialectical materialism. [63] The key text was Freidrich Engels's *Dialectics of nature* which argued that all entities – social and biological – were subject to the 'law of dialectics' and underwent continuous dialectical development and transformation. [64]

Throughout the 1920s and 1930s, Soviet geneticists argued about natural selection, species development and genetics. Within that debate, in defence of his theory of 'vernalization', the agronomist Trofim Denisovich Lysenko proffered a theory about the plasticity of the life cycle. The crucial factor determining the length of the vegetation period in a plant was not, Lysenko argued, its genetic constitution but its interaction with its environment. Because the theory was consistent with the *Dialectics of nature* and, more important Stalin's *Dialectical and historical materialism* and 'refuted' rival bourgeois and Menshevik theories, Lysenko's theory gained Stalin's support and approval. As a result, Lysenko rose to become the chief theoretician in Soviet biology.

Lysenko's chief argument was that contrary to all bourgeois theories of genetics, heredity was not determined by genes. The growth and development of all organisms depended on the laws of dialectics. Genetic endowment or heredity was largely irrelevant because organisms developed through the dialectical interaction of organism and environment – through the internalization of external conditions. Although Lysenkoism was a disaster for Soviet agriculture, its basic assumptions may well have opened the way to a new paradigm regarding the ontology of human performance. [65] Human performance capacity, within Lysenko's theory, could be altered and enhanced through the interaction of the organism with its environment. With state support, Lysenko's insights may have had a revolutionary impact on the concept of training and how the ontological foundation of human performance would be understood in the Eastern bloc during the post-war period. Irrespective of the motivation, the Soviet Union and later East Germany and other Eastern bloc countries invested heavily in the development of well-funded sport systems and put particular emphasis on the development of applied sport science.

Although interest in the scientific study of sport and exercise within North America and Europe began in the 1950s, it was not until the 1960s that the modern principles of athletic training were scientifically entrenched in the West. [66] In addition to the paradigm shift that led to the application of physiological principles to understand and enhance physical performance in athletics, there was a significant growth of institutional support for that undertaking. In Canada, for example, institutional support for sport science grew out of, and along with, the emerging emphases on applied physiology. The Canadian Medical Association in conjunction with the Canadian Association for Health,

Physical Education and Recreation established, at the Pan American Games held in Winnipeg in 1967, the Canadian Association of Sports Sciences. Renamed the Canadian Society for Exercise Physiology (CSEP), the group's goals were to 'promote and foster the growth of the highest quality research and education in exercise physiology' and 'to apply the knowledge derived from research in exercise physiology'. CSEP holds annual meetings, publishes its own journal, the *Canadian Journal of Applied Physiology* while also funding research in sport. [67] In 1970, the more exclusive Canadian Academy of Sports Medicine (CASM), open only to medical doctors, postgraduate medical trainees (residents/fellows) and medical students, was also established. CASM also hosts annual meetings, publishes a newsletter, has a fellowship programme in sports medicine and produces the *Clinical Journal of Sports Medicine*. [68]

The outcome of a paradigm shift in human performance

While the decisions individual athletes make concerning their training regimens or the use of a banned substance appear to be isolated and voluntary, in reality they take place within the context of a large, complex set of historically created and socially situated actions and relationships. Most important, and most often overlooked, is the fact that at the root of those systems and decisions is an image of the ontology of human performance. Over the course of the mid-twentieth century, for a variety of reasons (scientific, political, performance-related and accidental), a fundamentally important paradigm shift occurred in sport. Breaking away from the first law of thermodynamics over the middle years of the twentieth century, modern world-class sport now locates human performance within an ontological conception that permits and indeed promotes the continuous, scientifically assisted enhancement of athletes' performance capacities. Cycling can serve as an example of the impact this change has had upon the world of high-performance sport.

Mignon notes that during the first century of cycling (1850 to 1950–60), riders used stimulants and pain-killers to maximize their performance. [69] These substances and their intended effects were consistent with the ontology of human performance dominant at that time; they were not intended to help riders develop or expand their performance capacities, merely to allow them to use their existing capacities fully. The substances were 'home-made' and the knowledge surrounding them was passed, 'like kitchen recipes', 'from rider to rider and from *soigneur* to rider'. After the 1960s, however, systematic programmes were developed, and success in cycling, as in other high-performance sports, required highly organized, scientifically based, large and well-funded programmes of development. 'The 1960s', Mignon argues,

> saw the emergence of a new type of individual, 'the trained athlete', different psychologically and physiologically from the man in the street. There also developed medical routines specific to the sports person, with specific treatments for specific injuries, but also specific care for preparation. This went hand in hand with the development of medical staff as a necessary condition of sports preparation: bio-mechanics for exercises and massages; nutritional scientists for vitamins and complements; psychologists for personal discipline and meditation; pharmacologists for the use of different medicines on the market. This rationale could also come to encompass non-medical uses of medicine such as steroids, analgesics, stimulants or tranquil-lisers. [70]

The paradigm shift in the ontology of human performance meant more than a new way of thinking about human capacities, important as that was. The paradigm shift focused attention upon performance-enhance-ment – the scientifically informed enhancement of human athletic performance – and this required tremendous institutional support as expert knowledge, specialized materials and innovative technologies were needed to push human physical performance to its outer limits.

The focus in discussions about the use of performance-enhancing substances in sport has centred on the athletes and the alleged magic bullets they take. Those who oppose the use of specific performance-enhancing substances want to increase and improve surveillance over high-performance athletes to deter them from using substances and to catch those who do. But their focus is misdirected for two reasons. First, the overall sociocultural conditions of modern high-performance sport are central to the use of performance-enhancing substances. Without a change in the social conditions of world-class sport, the behaviour of individual athletes will remain largely unchanged. Second, and even more fundamentally important, the behaviour of today's athletes and the sociocultural conditions in which they train and compete are based upon a fundamental ontological conception of human performance. This ontology emerged from the activities of a number of different people – pure scientists, applied scientists, political leaders, sport leaders, coaches and athletes to name just a few – and is now firmly entrenched. As long as this dominant, historically established ontology of human performance exists, reformers will not be able to fundamentally change the practices that are deeply woven into every dimension of world-class high-performance sport. What has now become the status quo is much more deeply entrenched than reformers have recognized. Little will change until the ontology of human performance is thoroughly and critically examined.

Notes

[1] Bob Goldman, *Death in the locker room* (South Bend, IN, 1984), p. 32.

[2] Ibid.

[3] Goldman's evidence about the dangers of steroids and other performance-enhancing substances is very one-sided and misleading; cf Ray Tricker and David Cook, *Athletes at risk: drugs and sports* (Dubuque, IA, 1990) or William Taylor, *Anabolic steroids and the athlete*, 2nd edn (Jefferson, NC, 2002) for more balanced discussions.

[4] Goldman's actual question is not used because it is too fantastic and would, in isolation, undermine the credibility of the argument. Relying on the apparent truth value of Goldman's second claim, a paraphrased question closer to Mirkin's is used to make the argument.

[5] John Hoberman, *Mortal engines: the science of performance and the dehumanization of sport* (New York, 1992).

[6] Thomas S. Kuhn, 'Energy conservation as an example of simultaneous discovery', in Marshall Clagett, ed., *Critical problems in the history of science* (Madison, WI, 1962), pp. 321–56.

[7] See Yehuda Elkana, *The discovery of the conservation of energy* (Cambridge, MA, 1974); Kuhn, 'Energy conservation'; Cynthia Eagle Russett, *Sexual science: the Victorian construction of womanhood* (Cambridge, MA, 1989), pp. 106–7.

[8] See Russett, *Sexual science*, pp. 108–16.

[9] Cited in ibid., p. 107.

[10] Written in 1748, Julien de la Mettrie's *L'homme machine* was reissued in 1912 because it resonated with the scientific understanding of the human being at the time; see Julien de la Mettrie, *Man a machine* (La Salle, IL, 1912).

[11] Regarding physical education, see Paul Atkinson, 'The feminist physique: physical education and the medicalization of women's education', in J.A. Mangan and Roberta J. Park, eds., *From 'fair sex' to feminism: sport and the socialization of women in the industrial and post-industrial eras* (London, 1987), pp. 38–57. The doctrine was even used to understand the relationship between the mind and soul and the body's mysterious 'vital forces' of instinctual, physical drives. See Kenneth L. Caneva, *Robert Mayer and the conservation of energy* (Princeton, NJ, 1993), pp. 79–125.

[12] Eberhard Hildenbrandt, 'Milon, Marx und Muskelpille – Anmerkungen zur Kulturgeschichte des sportlichen Trainings' ['Milo, Marx, and muscle pills – observations on the cultural history of training in sport'], in Hartmut Gabler and Ulrich Göhner, *Für einen bessern Sport* ['For a better sport'] (Tübingen, 1990), p. 264.

[13] On Milo of Crotona, see Edward Gardiner, *Athletics of the ancient world* (Oxford, 1955), p. 6.

[14] See F. Hoole: *The science and art of training. A handbook for athletes* (London, 1888), p. 3, cited in Arnd Krüger, 'Viele Wege führen nach Olympia. Die

Veränderungen in den Trainingssystemen für Mittel- und Langstreckenläfer (1850–1997)' ['Many paths lead to Olympia: the changes in training systems for middle and long distance runners (1850–1997)'], in Norbert Gissel, ed., *Sportliche Leistung im Wandel* ['Athletic performance in transition'] (Hamburg, 1998), p. 50.

[15] Montague Shearman, *Athletics and football* (London, 1889), p. 7.

[16] Cited in Arthur Steinhaus, 'Chronic effects of exercise', *Physiological Reviews*, 13 (103) (1933), p. 110.

[17] Ibid., p. 104.

[18] Hoberman, *Mortal Engines*, p. 98; see also Hildenbrandt, 'Milon, Marx und Muskelpille'.

[19] See Frederick Taylor, *The principles of scientific management* (New York, 1911); Frank Gilbreth, *Motion study* (New York, 1911); and Frank Gilbreth and Lillian Gilbreth, *Applied motion study* (New York, 1917).

[20] Taylor, *Principles of scientific management*, pp. 43–74. See also Daniel Bell, 'Work and its discontents: the cult of efficiency in America', in *The end of ideology* (Glenco, IL, 1960), pp. 223–36.

[21] See Krüger, 'Viele Wege führen nach Olympia', p. 50.

[22] George A. Brooks, Thomas D. Fahey and Kenneth M. Baldwin, *Exercise physiology: human bioenergetics and its applications*, 4th edn (Boston, MA, 2005), p. 10.

[23] See Archibald Hill, 'The revolution in muscle physiology', *Physiological Reviews* 12 (1932), pp. 54–66 and Alison Wrynn, 'The grand tour: American exercise science and sports medicine encounters the world, 1926–1966', *International Sports Studies*, 24 (2) (2002), p. 8.

[24] See, for example, S. Hoogerwert, 'Elektrokardiographische Untersuchungen der Amsterdamer Olympiakämpfer' ['Electrocardiographic studies of the Amsterdam Olympic competitors'], *Arbeitsphysiologie* [Physiology of Work], 2 (1929), pp. 60–2; W.W. Siebert, 'Untersuchungen über Hypertrophie des Skelettmuskels' ['Studies on the hypertrophy of skeletal muscle'], *Zeitschrift der Klinische Medizin* [Journal of Clinical Medicine], 109 (1929), pp. 350–2; A. Vannotti and H. Pfister, 'Untersuchungen zum Studium des Trainertseins' ['Investigations on studies of being trained'], *Arbeitsphysiologie* [Physiology of Work], 7 (1934), pp. 153–5; and T. Petrén, T. Sjöstrand and B. Sylvén, 'Der Einfluss der Trainings auf die Haftigkeit der Capilaren in Herz- und Skelettmuskulatur' ['The influence of training on the absorption of capillaries in the heart and skeletal musculature'], *Arbeitsphysiologie* [Physiology of Work], 9 (1936), pp. 342–4.

[25] See L. Pikhala, 'Allgemeine Richtlinien für das athletische Training' ['General rules for athletic training'], in C. Krümel, ed., *Athletik: Ein Handbuch der lebenswichtigen Leibesübengen* [Athletics: A handbook of essential physical exercises] (Munich, 1930), pp. 185–90.

[26] See E.H. Christensen, 'Beiträge zur Physiologie schwerer körperlicher Arbeit' ['Contributions to the physiology of heavier physical work'], *Arbeitsphysiologie* [Physiology of Work], 4 (1931), p. 453.

[27] See Steven Horvath and Elizabeth Horvath, *The Harvard Fatigue Laboratory: its history and contributions* (Englewood Cliffs, NJ, 1973), pp. 18–24, 74–9.

[28] Brooks, Fahey and Baldwin, *Exercise physiology*, pp. 10–11.

[29]   Horvath and Horvath, *The Harvard Fatigue Laboratory*, p. 3; see also pp. 52, 106–7.

[30]   See ibid., p. 116.

[31]   See ibid., p. 112.

[32]   See ibid., pp. 104–22; see also pp. 122–6 for a bibliography of laboratory papers published on exercise.

[33]   Walter Cannon, *The wisdom of the body* (New York, 1932), p. 25, see also pp. 19–26.

[34]   Cited in Wrynn, 'The Grand Tour', p. 7 (emphasis added).

[35]   George Stafford and Ray Duncan, *Physical conditioning: exercises for sports and healthful living* (New York, 1942).

[36]   Ibid., p. 2.

[37]   See Steinhaus, 'Chronic effects of exercise', p. 104.

[38]   Stafford and Duncan, *Physical conditioning*, p. 11 (emphasis in original).

[39]   Ibid., pp. 11–12.

[40]   Ibid., p. 15.

[41]   See Steinhaus, 'Chronic effects of exercise', pp. 103–40.

[42]   George Bresnahan and W.W. Tuttle, *Track and field athletics*, 2nd edn (St Louis, MO, 1947); Dean Cromwell and Al Wesson, *Championship technique in track and field*, Olympic Games edn (Toronto, 1949); and V-Five Association of America, *Track and field*, revised edn (Annapolis, MD, 1950).

[43]   Bresnahan and Tuttle, *Track and field athletics*, p. 21.

[44]   Ibid., p. 31.

[45]   Ibid., pp. 38–51.

[46]   Cromwell and Wesson, *Championship technique*, p. 14; see also pp. 3–14.

[47]   Ibid., pp. 21, 24, 28.

[48]   V-Five Association of America, *Track and field*, pp. ix, 6.

[49]   Ibid., pp. 8–9; see also 'Basis of conditioning', ibid., pp. 14–7.

[50]   See Benjamin Brewer, 'Commercialization in professional cycling 1950–2001: institutional transformations and the rationalization of "doping"', *Sociology of Sport Journal*, 19 (3) (2002), pp. 294–5; Patrick Mignon, 'The Tour de France and the doping issue,' in H. Dauncey and G. Hare, eds., *The Tour de France, 1903–2003* (London, 2003), pp. 229–32, 241–3.

[51]   Joe Friel, *The cyclist's training bible* (Berkeley, CA, 1996), pp. 16–18.

[52]   Roger Bannister, 'The meaning of athletic performance', in Ernst Jokl and Emanuel Simon, eds., *International research in sport and physical education* (Springfield, IL, 1964), pp. 71–2.

[53]   Ibid., pp. 72–3.

[54]   Adolf Henning Frucht and Ernst Jokl, 'The future of athletic records', in Jokl and Simon, *International Research*, p. 436.

[55]   Rob Beamish and Ian Ritchie, 'From chivalrous "brothers-in-arms" to the eligible athlete: changed principles and the IOC's banned substance list', *International Review for the Sociology of Sport*, 39 (4) (2004), pp. 359, 361–3, 365.

[56]   Calvin Shulman, 'Middle-distance specialists committed to chasing that elusive dream', *The Times* (London), 4 May 2004, online at http://www.timesonline.co.uk/article/0,13849-1097363,00.html.

[57]   John Bale, *Roger Bannister and the four-minute mile* (London and New York, 2004), pp. 54–5, 112–3.

[58]   Ibid., pp. 23–4, 53–5, 75–6.

[59]   Ibid., p. 76.

[60]   John Fair, 'Bob Hoffman, the York Barbell Company, and the golden age of American weightlifting, 1945–1960', *Journal of Sport History* 14 (2) (1987), p. 180.

[61]   Donna Haraway, 'The biological enterprise: sex, mind and profit from human engineering to sociobiology,' *Radical History Review*, summer 1979, pp. 206–37.

[62]   Beamish and Ritchie, 'From chivalrous "brothers-in-arms"', pp. 359–60.

[63]   Joseph Stalin, *Dialectical and historical materialism* (London, 1943).

[64]   Friedrich Engels, *Dialectics of nature* (New York, 1940).

[65]   See Trofim Lysenko, *Heredity and its variability* (New York, 1946) and Helena Sheehan, *Marxism and the philosophy of science: a critical history* (Atlantic Highlands, NJ, 1985).

[66]   See Per-Olaf Åstrand and Kaare Rodahl, *Textbook of work physiology* (Toronto, 1970), esp. pp. 375–430; and Albert Taylor, *The scientific aspects of sports training* (Springfield, IL, 1975), esp. pp. ix, 5–45.

[67]   See the Canadian Society for Exercise Physiology website at http://www.csep.ca.

[68]   See http://www.casm-acms.org. On the scientific approach to physical education, see Donald MacIntosh and David Whitson, *The game planners: transforming Canada's sport system* (Montreal and Kingston, 1990), pp. 114–19.

[69]   Mignon, 'The Tour de France', p. 232.

[70]   Ibid., p. 233.

Anabolic Steroid and Stimulant Use in North American Sport between 1850 and 1980

Charles E. Yesalis & Michael S. Bahrke

Anabolic steroids: development and medical background

The age of scientific organotherapy began on 1 June 1889, when the seventy-two-year-old Charles Edouard Brown-Sequard, a prominent physiologist and neurologist, addressed the Society of Biology in Paris. In his talk (and a paper published shortly after), Brown-Sequard reported how over a three-week period he had self-administered ten subcutaneous injections that contained 'first, blood of the testicular veins; secondly, semen; and thirdly, juice extracted from a testicle ... from a dog or guinea pig'. [1] He enthusiastically described 'radical' changes in his health including significant improvements in physical and mental energy. One month after the last injection he 'experienced almost a complete return of the state of weakness'. [2] While today most experts believe that the 'rejuvenation' experienced by Brown-Sequard was the result of the placebo effect, he was correct not only in his rudimentary understanding of testicular function but also about the potential value of hormonal replacement or supplementation therapy. Because of this, he is considered the father of modern endocrinology.

Brown-Sequard offered free samples of his *liquide testiculaire* to physicians willing to test them. In addition, various laboratories, including some in the United States such as the New York Pasteur Institute, began preparing the extract for use. [3] This began a rise in experiments not only in France but throughout the Western world employing testicular extracts to rejuvenate as well as treat a wide variety of diseases. [4] The 'fountain of youth' had been found – once again – and a cult-like following arose. [5] Numerous similar accounts of rejuvenation soon followed and continued until the early 1920s. Ironically, these uncontrolled studies and bold claims also stimulated important research in clinical endocrinology.

The 'athleticizing' of testicular extracts came quickly after Brown-Sequard's initial report. In 1894 Oskar Zoth and Fritz Pregl assessed the effects of the extracts on muscular strength. [6] Although Zoth concluded that these 'orchitic' extracts improved muscular strength, it is highly unlikely they had any therapeutic or ergogenic effect beyond the power of suggestion. [7] Nevertheless, Zoth in a 1896 paper provides a chilling prophecy of the use of anabolic hormones in sport in the 20th century when he states in the final sentence: 'The training of athletes offers an opportunity for further research in this area and for a practical assessment of our experimental results.' [8]

From medical use to use in sports

In 1912, another form of glandular therapy arrived with the transplantation of animal and human testicular material into patients with testicular dysfunction. [9] As with the injection of extracts, the purposes of these transplants was curative and restorative. The practitioners of these procedures believed, incorrectly, that these testicular transplants would survive in the recipient and would function. Many respected surgeons around the world performed these transplants through the 1920s and published case reports of favourable findings in well-respected medical journals, including *Endocrinology* and the *Journal of the American Medical Association*. [10] However, in the mid-1920s, serious concern arose in the medical community regarding these overt claims of rejuvenation. [11] As a result an international committee was appointed to evaluate these claims and concluded that they were unfounded. [12] The practice had disappeared by 1935, when scientists isolated, chemically characterized and synthesized the hormone testosterone and elucidated the basic nature of its anabolic effects. [13] Shortly thereafter, both oral and injectable preparations of testosterone were available to the medical community. While there is no record of systematic use of testicular transplants or the injection of testicular extracts by athletes, these procedures likely helped lay the foundation for the subsequent use of testosterone as an ergogenic aid.

It has been rumoured that some German athletes were given testosterone in preparation for the 1936 Berlin Olympics. [14] Although the effects of other drugs on the physiology of human performance are well-documented in the German medical literature, no mention of the use of testosterone as an ergogenic aid has been noted during that period. [15] Moreover, Hoberman contends:

> It is likely that public anti-doping sentiment after 1933 was related to Nazi strictures against the self-serving, individualistic, record-breaking athlete and the abstract ideal of performance. It is also consistent with Nazi rhetoric about sportsmanship, e.g., the importance of the 'noble contest' and the 'chivalric' attitude of the German athlete

Wade [16] has alleged that during the Second World War, German soldiers took steroids before battle to enhance aggressiveness. This assertion, although often cited, has yet to be documented, in spite of efforts in this regard. Furthermore, the Nazis were opposed to organism-altering drugs in general. [17] There was a concerted campaign against the 'poisons' alcohol and tobacco, and the Nazis were not particularly interested in the popular gland transplant techniques of that period, since their idea of race improvement was genetic. [18]

Bøje, [19] writing in the *Bulletin of the Health Organization of the League of Nations* in 1939, appears to have been the first to suggest that sex hormones, based on their physiologic actions, might enhance physical performance. At the same time, the anabolic effects of anabolic steroids were being confirmed in eunuchs and in normal men and women. [20]

Uncontrolled studies also demonstrated improvements in strength and dynamic work capacity in eugonadal males [21] and otherwise healthy older males complaining of fatigue. [22]

The first recorded case of an 'athlete' using testosterone was a gelding trotter named Holloway. Prior to the implantation of testosterone pellets, this eighteen-year-old horse had 'declined to a marked degree in his staying power and during February of 1941 in several attempts at ice racing, failed to show any of his old speed or willingness'. [23] After the administration of testosterone and several months of training, Holloway won or was placed in a number of races and established a trotting record at age nineteen.

In *The Male Hormone,* de Kruif further raised hopes and expectations for the newly synthesized anabolic steroids. He argued that these hormones had the potential to rejuvenate individuals and improve their productivity, and he assuredly reported that testosterone 'caused the human body to synthesize protein [and] ... to be able to build the very stuff of its own life'. [24] De Kruif went on:

> I'll be faithful and remember to take my twenty to thirty milligrams a day of testosterone. I'm not ashamed that it's no longer made to its old degree by my own aging body. It's chemical crutches. It's borrowed manhood. It's borrowed time. But just the same, it's what makes bulls bulls. [25]

With regard to athletes, de Kruif commented: 'We know how both the St Louis Cardinals and the St Louis Browns have won championships supercharged by vitamins. It would be interesting to watch the productive power of an industry or a professional group (of athletes) that would try a systematic supercharge with testosterone. [26]

Rapid expansion during the 1960s and 1970s

De Kruif's writings were not without effect. When these were combined with the significant positive observations reported from clinical studies in professional journals, it was a relatively easy extrapolation for some in the physical culture of bodybuilding to expect that additional anabolic-androgenic hormones, at that time universally assumed to exert no adverse effects when taken in therapeutic dosages, would allow development of greater-than-'normal' body size and strength. According to several interview reports, experimental use of the new testosterone preparations began among West Coast bodybuilders in the early 1950s. [27] Also suggestive of anabolic steroid use are physique photos of this time showing highly significant changes over relatively short periods in the muscle mass of established elite bodybuilders. Since then, body-building has been and continues to be strongly and consistently linked to steroid use, [28] as has the sport's most well-known participant, Arnold Schwarzenegger. [29] The elite bodybuilding community has maintained its position at the 'cutting edge' of experimentation with performance-enhancing drugs. By the early 1980s and beyond, the use of human growth hormone (hGH) was well-established on that community's drug menu. [30] In 1982, Fred Hatfield in his controversial book, *Anabolic Steroids: What Kind and How Many*, stated that hGH had 'become "the state of the art" strength and size drug in the free world'. [31]

The initiation of systematic use of anabolic steroids in sport has been attributed to reports of their use by successful Soviet weightlifting teams in the early 1950s. Statistical analysis of the performance of the Soviet lifters during this period is consistent with this assertion. [32]

Dr Zeigler and Dianabol

In 1954, at the world weightlifting championships in Vienna, Dr John Ziegler, the US team physician, reportedly was told by his Soviet counterpart that the Soviets were taking testosterone. [33] Ziegler returned to the United States and experimented with testosterone on himself and a few weightlifters in the York Barbell Club. Dr Ziegler was concerned, however, with the androgenic effects of testosterone, and in 1958, when the Ciba Pharmaceutical Company released Dianabol (methandrostenolone), he began experimentation with this new drug. After several of the weightlifters with whom Ziegler was working achieved championship status while using anabolic steroids, news of the efficacy of these drugs apparently spread by word of mouth during the early 1960s to other strength-intensive sports, from field events to football.

Emergence of adverse effects

The short-term health effects of anabolic-androgenic steroids have increasingly been studied, and a number of authors have reviewed the physiological and health effects of these drugs. [34] Although anabolic steroid use has been associated (mainly through case reports) with several adverse and even fatal effects, the incidence of serious effects reported has been extremely low. [35] However, for decades experts have consistently stated that the long-term health effects of anabolic steroid use are unknown. [36] Specifically, long-term health effects related to type of steroid, dose, frequency of use, age at initiation and concurrent drug use have not been elucidated. Assessment of health consequences is confounded by the fact that many individuals use other performance-enhancing and illicit drugs concurrent with steroids, and/or use large doses of anabolic steroids for prolonged periods of time, whereas others use therapeutic doses intermittently. [37]

Although the role of anabolic steroids in the etiology of various diseases in both animals and humans is still uncertain, steroid use in clinical trials and in laboratory studies is associated with numerous acute deleterious changes in risk factors for cardiovascular disease, liver tumours and infertility, and in the physiology of various sundry organs and body systems, suggesting potential for subsequent health problems. [38] The best-documented effects are those on the liver, serum lipids, and the reproductive system. Other areas of concern include the psyche and behaviour, cardiomyopathy, coronary artery disease, cerebrovascular accidents, prostatic changes and the immune function. [39]

Steroid use has been related to cardiovascular risk factors. The most important are changes in lipoprotein fraction, increased triglyceride levels, increased concentrations of several clotting factors, changes in the myocardium such as increased left ventricular mass and dilated cardiomyopathy, [40] and hyperinsulinism and diminished glucose tolerance. [41] Although these effects vary significantly between different types and doses of anabolic steroids, and between individuals and situations, [42] all of the effects (except postulated changes in the myocardium) are fully reversible within several months after cessation of steroid use. [43]

Acute thrombotic risk has been linked to steroid use in case reports of non-fatal myocardial infarction and stroke in several athletes who were using anabolic steroids. [44] Although there is no direct evidence that anabolic steroids are thrombogenic in humans, [45] the clinical circumstances of these reports suggest a possible causal relationship. These reports further suggest that if a causal relationship exists, anabolic steroids could have serious short-term effects.

Liver structure and function are also altered by administration of anabolic steroids: these changes include cholestatic jaundice, peliosis hepatis, hepatocellular hyperplasia, and hepatocellular adenomas. [46] It has not been demonstrated convincingly that anabolic steroids can cause, at least with therapeutic doses, development of hepatocellular carcinomas. Virtually all histological changes in the liver are associated with the use of 17 alpha-alkylated (oral) steroids, [47] and the cause-and-effect relationship between oral anabolic steroids and these conditions is strengthened by the return of normal blood values and excretory function, the regression of tumours, a general recovery and a return towards normal liver function after cessation of steroid use. [48]

The effects of anabolic-androgenic steroids on the male reproductive system include reductions in levels of endogenous testosterone, gonado-trophic hormones and sex hormone-binding globulin, reductions in testicle size, sperm count and sperm motility, and alterations in sperm morphology. [49] When steroid use is stopped, the testes resume sperm production. In women, anabolic steroids are associated with several adverse effects, some of which are not reversible upon discontinuation of steroid use. [50] These adverse effects include menstrual abnormalities, deepening of the voice, shrinkage of the breasts, male-pattern baldness, and an increase in sex drive, acne, body hair and clitoris size. Premature halting of growth in younger users has not been systematically studied, although such effects have been described in case reports for several decades. [51]

A positive pattern of association between endogenous testosterone levels and aggressive behaviour in males has been increasingly established. [52] Although studies using moderate doses of exogenous testosterone for contraceptive and clinical purposes reveal few adverse effects on male sexual and aggressive behaviour, other investigations and case reports of athletes using substantially higher doses suggest the possibility of affective and psychotic syndromes (some of violent proportions), psychological dependence, and withdrawal symptoms. [53] Whereas several recently published reports support a pattern of association between the use of anabolic steroids by athletes and increased levels of irritability, aggression, personality disturbance and psychiatric diag-noses, others do not. [54] Only a few prospective, blinded studies documenting aggression and adverse overt behaviour resulting from steroid use have been reported. [55] As Bjorkqvist and colleagues [56] point out, much of the psychological and behavioural effect of steroid intake may be placebo. Anticipation of the aggressiveness related to steroid use may lead to actual violent acts and become, in effect, an excuse for aggression.

Although prevalence of anabolic steroid dependency is difficult to determine, and there may be as many as 300,000 yearly anabolic steroid users in the United States, [57] it appears that only a very small percentage of users experience psychological dependence requiring clinical treat-ment.

Rationale for initial banning

The most obvious reason we are concerned about anabolic steroid use in sport is that it is cheating – the use of these drugs violates the rules of virtually every sports federation. A more important question, however, is, why have sport federations outlawed the use of these drugs?

Our concern over drug use in sport is generally founded on one or more of the following moral and ethical issues:

- The athlete may suffer physical or psychological harm as the result of drug use;
- The use of drugs by one athlete may coerce another athlete to use drugs to maintain parity;
- The use of drugs in sport is unnatural in that any resulting success is due to external factors;
- The athlete who uses drugs has an unfair advantage over athletes who do not use them.

Sport should be a quest for personal excellence through competition, as well as a source of fun, enjoyment, and camaraderie. Drugs are unnecessary to achieve these ends. If the primary objective of participants in sport, however, is to achieve victory over an opponent, the use of drugs to achieve that end becomes an increasingly rational behaviour.

Legacy for anti-doping campaigns

Efforts to ban the abuse of drugs in sports started in the late 1960s when the International Olympic Committee created its Medical Commission and when state-of-the-art laboratory techniques were introduced to detect stimulants and narcotics at the 1968 Olympic Games. This successful move was immediately blurred by the advent of anabolic steroids and by the elaboration of sophisticated programmes to avoid their detection at major competitions. For a variety of complex political issues, testing during training periods was not conducted until 1989 – after the Ben Johnson scandal of the Seoul games – and many sports organizations are still reluctant to allow out-of-competition controls on a large scale.

The establishment of the World Anti-Doping Agency (WADA) in 1999 marked an important development of global anti-doping policy. It represented an effort to create an independent entity to deal with doping in sport – quite unlike prior efforts where sports federations policed themselves. One of the first actions of the agency was to form a working group to prepare a World Anti-Doping Code that would be the cornerstone for the global anti-doping campaign. The draft code was published in 2003 with the intention of it being operational in time for the Athens Olympic Games in 2004. On 1 October 2000, the United States Anti-Doping Agency (USADA) began operations. USADA is the independent anti-doping agency for Olympic-related sport in the United States. It was created as the result of recommendations made by the US Olympic Committee's Select Task Force on Externalization to uphold the Olympic ideal of fair play, and to represent the interests of Olympic, Pan American Games and Paralympic athletes. USADA was given full authority to execute a comprehensive national anti-doping programme encompassing testing, adjudication, education and research, and to develop programmes, policies and procedures in each of those areas. The level of success of WADA and USADA in achieving their goals is a matter of significant controversy.

Prevalence of stimulant use

Many of the early stimulants were of plant origin. The legendary Berserkers of Norse mythology used bufotein to 'increase their fighting strength twelve fold'. [58] This drug came from fly-agaric (*Amanita muscaria*), a mushroom containing muscarine (a deadly alkaloid). [59] The Samoyeds used the same stimulant to induce a heightened state of combativeness. The African plant *Catha edulis* contains norpseudoephedrine, a psychomotor stimulant that has been used by the people of the region to increase strength and delay the onset of fatigue. [60] From ancient times West Africans used *Cola acuminita* and *Cola nitida* for running competitions. [61] For centuries the Andean Indians of Peru have chewed coca leaves or drunk coca tea to increase endurance and protect against mountain sickness. [62] The Tarahumara Indians of northern Mexico used peyote (which has strychnine effects) in their multi-day runs that were among the requirements of a fertility ritual. [63] The Australian aborigines ate the pituri plant for its stimulant effect. [64] In Styria and Tyrol in Austria, lumberjacks ingested large amounts of arsenic to increase their endurance. [65]

Stimulant use, war and sport

The stimulant effect of coffee (caffeine) has long been recognized. According to Catton in *The Army of the Potomac*, during the Civil War 'the coffee ration was what kept the [Union] army going'. The ration was 'ample for three or four pints of strong black coffee daily. . . . Stragglers would often fall out, build a fire, boil coffee, drink it, and then plod on to overtake their regiments at nightfall.' [66] The use of coffee by foot soldiers also serves as an early example that such ergogenic practices were not universally embraced: 'cavalry and artillery referred to infantry, somewhat contemptuously, as "coffee boilers"'. [67]

Coffee was also 'the drug of choice for any number of literati, scientists, and artists' of that period whose work necessitated a well-functioning brain. [68] Liquors, too, were considered artificial stimulants to be used by soldiers and labourers working in stressful conditions. [69]

In the last third of the nineteenth century, the use of stimulants among athletes was commonplace, and moreover there was no attempt to conceal drug use, with the possible exception of some trainers who guarded the proprietary interest in their own special 'doping recipes'. Swimmers, distance runners, sprinters and cyclists used a wide assortment of drugs to gain an edge over their opponents. [70] As early as 1865, a doping episode involving Amsterdam's canal swimmers was reported. [71] Boxers of the day used strychnine tablets and mixtures of brandy and cocaine. [72]

In 1879, 'six day' bicycle races began, each race proceeding continuously, day and night, for 144 hours. It is not surprising that stimulants and a variety of doping strategies were employed in these gruelling contests of prolonged athletic exertion: 'French racers preferred mixtures on a caffeine bases, the Belgians preferred sugar cubes dipped in ether, and others used alcohol-containing cordials, while the sprinters specialized in the use of nitroglycerine.' [73] The cyclists of the day also used coffee 'spiked' with caffeine; and as the race progressed, they would add increasing doses of cocaine and strychnine. [74] (Note that strychnine when taken at low doses has a stimulant effect, while at higher doses it is poisonous.) As trainers continued their experiments with a variety of powerful drugs and poisons, it is little wonder that someone died. The first fatality attributed to doping was reported in 1886: Arthur Linton, an English cyclist, is said by some to have overdosed on 'tri-methyl' (probably a compound containing either caffeine or ether) during a 600-kilometre (373-mile) race between Bordeaux and Paris. [75] Others have argued that in fact Linton won the race in question and did not die until ten years later, in 1896, of typhoid fever. [76] Whatever the case, given the potency of many of the doping substances being used at that time, it is clear that the health of the athlete was at risk.

Another popular sport during that period in both the United States and England was the professional sport of pedestrianism (or ultramarathoning). These 'go-as-you-please' walking and/or running marathon races usually lasted six days and six nights. The contestant who had covered the most miles at the end of the six days was declared the winner. During some of the more famous ultramarathons, several of the contestants in one race each completed over 500 miles (805 km), and in 1884 George Haezel of England became the first man to cover 600 miles (966 km) in the six-day period. [77] By their very nature, stimulants lent themselves to use in this sport. Trainers employed a variety of concoctions to keep their man going. These included milk-punch champagne and brandy, as well as belladonna, strychnine and 'morphine in hot drops'. [78]

Continuing the practices of their nineteenth-century counterparts, athletes during the first three decades of the twentieth century used a variety of substances (alcohol, cocaine, strychnine, caffeine and nitroglycerine) for their purported 'stimulant' effects. [79] Noticeably absent from this doping menu is any mention of the use of amphetamines, even though they were first synthesized in 1887. [80] In the 1920s and 1930s other derivatives of amphetamines were synthesized. However, it was not until the mid-1930s that amphetamines were identified as a central nervous system stimulant, and in 1937 they became available as a prescription tablet. [81] In the late 1930s, amphetamines were publicized as 'a means of dissipating mental fog' and were thereafter adopted by college students 'to ward off sleep and clear their minds'. [82]

Both Axis and Allied powers used these drugs to combat fatigue and improve endurance. The British Army used amphetamines when men 'were markedly fatigued physically or mentally and circumstances demanded a particular effort'. [83] According to a report in the *Air Surgeon's Bulletin*, 'one pill (*Benzedrine*) may be worth a Flying Fortress when the man who is flying it can no longer stay awake'. [84] Going beyond staving off fatigue, the Japanese were said to have used heavy doses of amphetamines to arouse or 'psych up' their kamikaze pilots in preparation for the suicide missions. [85] Similarly Mandell [86] suggested that amphetamines could be used by soldiers to create a sense of fearlessness.

Impact of stimulants

The use of these 'pep pills' by pre-war college students, combined with the experiences of servicemen who used them to competitive advantage in armed services football, appears to have laid the foundation for the introduction of amphetamines to professional and collegiate sport at the end of the Second World War. [87] The spread of amphetamine use must have proceeded rather quickly, because by 1969 Gilbert concluded:

On good evidence – which includes voluntary admissions by physicians, trainers, coaches, athletes, testimony given in court or before athletic regulatory bodies, and autopsy reports – amphetamines have been used in auto racing, basketball, baseball (at all levels down to children's leagues), boxing, canoeing, cycling, football, golf, mountain climbing, Roller Derby, rodeo, rugby, skating, skiing, soccer, squash, swimming, tennis (both lawn and table), track and field, weightlifting and wrestling. [88]

Deaths of cyclists

Cycling plays a central role in the explosion of stimulant use in sport after the Second World War. Prokop describes cycling competitions of that era as 'special hotbeds of doping'. [89] Of twenty-five urine samples taken from riders in a 1955 race, five were positive for stimulants. In the 1960 Rome Olympic Games, Knud Jensen, a twenty-three-year-old Danish cyclist, collapsed during competition and died. Autopsy results revealed the presence of amphetamines. [90] During the thirteenth leg of the 1967 Tour de France, English cyclist Tom Simpson, twenty-nine, collapsed and died. His autopsy showed high levels of methamphetamine, 'a vial of which had been found in his pocket at the time of his death'. [91] The impact of Simpson's death was extensive, in part because 'this was the first doping death to be televised'. [92] His death substantially added to the mounting pressure on the IOC and member federations to establish doping control programmes, which they did at the end of 1967. [93] One year later another cyclist, Yves Mottin, died from 'excessive amphetamine use' two days after winning a race. [94]

Pushing anti-doping on to the agenda

Even with the gaping loopholes in drug testing, during the past fifteen years we continue to be bombarded with a steady stream of major doping scandals: Ben Johnson, the East Germans, the Communist Chinese, Michelle Smith, the Tour de France, Mark McGuire, the revelations of anabolic steroid and amphetamine use in Major League Baseball (MLB) and now Balco. This latest scandal stands apart in several ways. First, star athletes from multiple sports (track and field, American football and MLB) appear to be involved. Second, and by far more important, the President of the United States in his State of the Union address voiced concern about the impact that doping among elite athletes has on our children.

One thing the Balco case has in common with many major scandals of the past ten years is that drug testing had very little or nothing to do with bringing these episodes of drug abuse and cheating to the public's attention. It was a former East German athlete and her husband who were courageous enough to remove Stasi files from the notorious Leipzig Laboratory after the Berlin Wall came down and documented the heinous doping activities that had taken place. It was the French border police who intercepted the drug-packed car of one of the team trainers and helped expose the culture of doping that is pervasive in pro cycling. It was Australian customs agents who caught Communist Chinese athletes trying to smuggle human growth hormone. It was a disgruntled coach who mailed a syringe containing THG to the USADA, and the subsequent actions of the DEA, FBI and IRS that led to the startling revelations of Balco.

The litany of scandals appears to have impacted on many fans, politicians, journalists, sports officials and even the athletes themselves to the point they have increasingly decried the notion of 'better athletic performance through chemistry'. Indeed, if sport fans were polled and asked 'Are you upset by doping?' or 'Are you against doping?' many, perhaps even a substantial majority, would say 'Yes'. However, a far more relevant question is: 'Are you upset enough about doping to turn off your television set and not watch sports?' Judging by the continuing profitability and popularity of both amateur and professional sports, most would probably answer 'No'. If we do not have the will-power to turn off our television in protest against doping, will we have the stomach to tolerate federal arrests, prosecutions and convictions of our sports icons?

Notes

[1]   C.E. Brown-Sequard, 'The effects produced in man by subcutaneous injections of a liquid obtained from the testicles of animals', *Lancet*, 2 (1889), pp. 105–107, p. 105.
[2]   Ibid., p. 106
[3]   M. Borell, 'Brown-Sequard's Organotherapy and its appearance in America at the end of the 19th century', *Bulletin of the History of Medicine,* 50 (1976), pp. 309–320.
[4]   J. Hoberman and C. Yesalis, 'The history of synthetic testosterone', *Scientific American* (February 1995), pp. 61–5.
[5]   J. Herman, 'Rejuvenation: Brown-Sequard to Brinkley', *New York State Journal of Medicine*, 82 (1982), pp. 1731–9.
[6]   J. Hoberman, *Mortal Engines* (New York, 1992).
[7]   Hoberman and Yesalis, 'Synthetic testosterone', pp. 61–5.
[8]   Ibid., p. 61.

[9]   D. Hamilton, *The monkey gland affair* (London, 1986); Hoberman and Yesalis, 'Synthetic testosterone'.

[10] V. Lespinasse, 'Transplantation of the testicle', *Journal of the American Medical Association*, 61 (21) (1913), pp. 1869–70; L. Stanley, 'An analysis of one thousand testicular substance implantations', *Endocrinology*, 6 (1922), pp. 787–94.

[11] M. Fishbein, *Medical Follies* (New York, 1925).

[12] A. Parkes, Off-beat biologist: the autobiography of A.S. Parkes, Vol. 1 (Cambridge, 1985); A. Parkes, Biologist at large: the autobiography of A.S. Parkes, Vol. 2 (Cambridge, 1988).

[13] A. Butenandt and G. Hanisch, 'Uber Testosteron Umwandlung des Dehydroandrosterons in Androstenediol und Testosteron; ein Weg zur Darstellung des Testosteron aus Cholesterin' *Zeitschrift Physiologische Chemie*, (About testosterone transformation of the dehydroandrosterons and androstenediol and testosterone; a way to the representation of the testosterone from cholesterol. *Journal of Pysiological Chemistry*) 237 (1935), pp. 89–97; C. Kochakian and J. Murlin, 'The effect of male hormone on the protein and energy metabolism of castrate dogs', *Journal of Nutrition*, 10 (1935), pp. 437–59.

[14] C. Francis, *Speed Trap* (New York, 1990).

[15] J. Hoberman, 'The early development of sports medicine in Germany', in J.W. Berryman and R.J. Park, eds., *Sport and exercise science: essays in the history of sports medicine* (Champaign, IL, 1992), p. 207; Hoberman, *Mortal Engines*.

[16] N. Wade, 'Anabolic steroids: doctors denounce them, but athletes aren't listening', *Science*, 176 (1972), pp. 1399–1403.

[17] Hoberman, 'Early development'; Hoberman, '*Mortal Engines*'.

[18] Ibid. Hoberman, *Mortal Engines*.

[19] O. Bøje, 'Doping', Bulletin of the Health Organization of the League of Nations, 8 (1939), pp. 439–69.

[20] A. Kenyon, K. Knowlton, I. Standiford, F. Koch and G. Lotwin, 'A comparative study of the metabolic effects of testosterone propionate in normal men and women and in eunuchoidism', *Endocrinology*, 26 (1940), pp. 26–45; A. Kenyon, I. Sandiford, A. Bryan, K. Knowlton and F. Koch, 'The effect of testosterone propionate on nitrogen, electrolyte, water and energy metabolism in eunuchoidism', *Endocrinology*, 23 (1938), pp. 135–53.

[21] E. Simonson, W. Kearns and N. Enzer, 'Effect of oral administration of methyltestosterone on fatigue in eunuchoids and castrates', *Endocrinology*, 28 (1941), pp. 506–12.

[22] E. Simonson, W. Kearns and N. Enzer, 'Effect of methyltestosterone treatment on muscular performance and the central nervous system of older men', *Journal of Clinical Endocrinology and Metabolism*, 4 (1944), pp. 528–34.

[23] B. Kearns, R. Harkness, V. Hobson and A. Smith, 'Testosterone pellet implantation in the gelding', *Journal of the American Veterinary Medicine Association*, C/780 (1942), pp. 197–201, p. 199.

[24] P. de Kruif, *The Male Hormone* (Garden City, NY, 1945), p. 130.

[25] Ibid., p. 226.

[26] Ibid., p. 223.

[27] J.E. Wright *et al.*, unpublished data (1998).

[28]   D. Duchaine, *Underground steroid handbook* (Santa Monica, CA, 1982); D. Duchaine, *Underground steroid handbook II* (Venice, CA, 1989); W. Fussell, *Muscle* (New York, 1990); A. Klein, 'Pumping irony: crisis and contradiction in bodybuilding', *Sociology of Sport Journal*, 3 (1986), pp. 112–33; A. Klein, 'Of muscles and men', *The Sciences*, 33 (1993), pp. 32–7; W. Nack, 'The muscle murders', *Sports Illustrated*, 18 May 1998; W. Phillips, *Anabolic reference guide*, 5th edn (Golden, CO, 1990); J. Wright, *Anabolic steroids and sports* (Natick, MA, 1978).

[29]   R. Johnston, 'The men and the myth', *Sports Illustrated*, 14 Oct. 1974, pp. 106–20; W. Leigh, *Arnold: the unauthorized biography* (New York, 1990).

[30]   Duchaine, *Handbook*; Duchaine, *Handbook II*; T. Fahey, 'Growth hormone: Muscle-building miracle drug or dark side of the force?', *Muscular Development*, 38 (4) (2001), pp. 174–7.

[31]   F. Hatfield, Anabolic steroids: what kind and how many (n.p., 1982), p. 21.

[32]   J. Fair, 'Olympic weightlifting and the introduction of steroids: A statistical analysis of world championship results, 1948–72', *International Journal of the History of Sport*, 5 (1988), pp. 96–114.

[33]   J. Fair, 'Isometrics or steroids? Exploring new frontiers of strength in the early 1960s', *Journal of Sport History*, 20 (1993), pp. 1–24; B. Starr, *Defying gravity: how to win at weightlifting* (Wichita Falls, TX, 1981); T. Todd, 'Anabolic steroids: the gremlins of sport'. *Journal of Sport History*, 14 (1987), pp. 87–107.

[34]   K.E. Friedl, 'Effect of anabolic steroids on physical health', in C.E. Yesalis, ed., *Anabolic steroids in sport and exercise*, 2nd edn (Champaign, IL, 2000), pp. 175–225; H. Haupt and G. Rovere, 'Anabolic steroids: a review of the literature', *American Journal of Sports Medicine*, 12 (6) (1984), pp. 469–84; D. Lamb, 'Anabolic steroids in athletics: how well do they work and how dangerous are they?', *American Journal of Sports Medicine*, 12 (1) (1984), pp. 31–8; J. Wilson, 'Androgen abuse by athletes', *Endocrine Reviews*, 9 (2) (1988), pp. 181–99; J.E. Wright, 'Steroids and athletics', *Exercise Sports Science Reviews*, 8 (1980), pp. 49–202.

[35]   Friedl, 'Anabolic steroids'.

[36]   C.E. Yesalis, J.E. Wright and M.S. Bahrke, 'Epidemiological and policy issues in the measurement of the long term health effects of anabolic-androgenic steroids', *Sports Medicine*, 8 (1989), pp. 129–38.

[37]   Duchaine, *Handbook II*; S. Gallaway, *The steroid bible*, 3rd edn (Sacramento, CA, 1997).

[38]   American College of Sports Medicine, 'Position stand on the use of anabolic-androgenic steroids in sports', *Sports Medicine Bulletin*, 19 (1984), pp. 13–18; Friedl, 'Anabolic steroids'; F. Hartgens, G. Rietjens, H.A. Keizer, H. Kuipers, and B.H. Woffenbuttel, 'Effects of androgenic-anabolic steroids on apolipoproteins and lipoprotein (a)', *British Journal of Sports Medicine*, 38 (2004), pp. 253–9; H.L. Kruskemper, *Anabolic steroids* (New York, 1980); Wright, 'Steroids and athletics'.

[39]   Friedl, 'Anabolic steroids'.

[40]   A. Urhausen, T. Albers and W. Kindermann, 'Are the cardiac effects of anabolic steroid abuse in strength athletes reversible?', *Heart*, 90 (5) (2004), pp. 496–501.

[41]   Friedl, 'Anabolic steroids'; G. Glazer, 'Atherogenic effects of anabolic steroids on serum lipid levels', *Archives of Internal Medicine*, 151 (1991), pp. 1925–33;

Haupt and Rovere, 'Anabolic steroids', pp. 469–84; R. Rockhold, 'Cardiovascular toxicity of anabolic steroids', *Annual Review Pharmacology Toxicology*, 33 (1993), pp. 497–520; M.L. Sullivan, C.M. Martinez, P. Gennis and E.J. Gallagher, 'The cardiac toxicity of anabolic steroids', *Progress Cardiovascular Disease*, 41 (1) (1998), pp. 1–15; Wright, 'Steroids and athletics'.

[42]   Kruskemper, *Anabolic steroids*.

[43]   Friedl, 'Anabolic steroids'; Haupt and Rovere, 'Anabolic steroids', pp. 469–484; Wright, 'Steroids and athletics'.

[44]   Rockhold, 'Cardiovascular toxicity'.

[45]   J. Ansell, C. Tiarks and V. Fairchild, 'Coagulation abnormalities associated with the use of anabolic steroids'. *American Heart Journal*, 125 (2) (1993), pp. 367–71.

[46]   R.D. Dickerman, R.M. Pertusi, N.Y. Zachariah, D.R. Dufour and W.J. McConathy, 'Anabolic steroid-induced hepatotoxicity: is it overstated?', *Clinical Journal of Sport Medicine*, 9 (1999), pp. 34–3; Friedl, 'Anabolic steroids'; K. Soe, M. Soe and C. Gluud, 'Liver pathology associated with the use of anabolic steroids', *Liver*, 12 (1992), pp. 73–9.

[47]   Friedl, 'Anabolic steroids'; Kruskemper, *Anabolic steroids*; Wilson, 'Androgen abuse by athletes'; Wright, 'Steroids and athletics'.

[48]   Friedl, 'Anabolic steroids'.

[49]   Ibid.; Wright, 'Steroids and athletics'.

[50]   D.L. Elliot and L. Goldberg, 'Women and anabolic steroids', in C.E. Yesalis, ed., *Anabolic steroids in sport and exercise*, 2nd edn (Champaign, IL, 2000), pp. 225–46.

[51]   A. Rogol and C.E. Yesalis, 'Anabolic-androgenic steroids and the adolescent', *Pediatrics Annual*, 21 (3) (1992), pp. 175–88.

[52]   M.S. Bahrke, 'Psychological effects of endogenous testosterone and anabolic-androgenic steroids', in C.E. Yesalis, ed., *Anabolic steroids in sport and exercise*, 2nd edn (Champaign, IL, 2000), pp. 247–78.

[53]   Ibid.

[54]   S. Bhasin, T. Storer, N. Berman, C. Callegari, B. Clevenger, J. Phillips, T.J. Bunnell, R. Tricker, A. Shirazi and R. Casaburi, 'The effects of supraphysiologic doses of testosterone on muscle size and strength in normal men', *New England Journal of Medicine*, 335 (1) (1996), pp. 1–7; W.R. Yates, P.J. Perry, J. MacIndoe, T. Holman and V.L. Ellingrod, 'Psychosexual effects of three doses of testosterone cycling in normal men', *Biological Psychiatry*, 45 (1999), pp. 254–60.

[55]   C.J. Hannan, K.E. Friedl, A. Zold, T.M. Kettler and S.R. Plymate, 'Psychological and serum homovanillic acid changes in men administered androgenic steroids', *Psychoneuroendocrinology*, 16 (1991), pp. 335–42; E.M. Kouri, S.E. Lukas, H.G. Pope and P.S. Oliva, 'Increased aggressiveness responding in male volunteers following the administration of gradually increasing doses of testosterone cypionate', *Drug Alcohol Dependence*, 40 (1) (1995), pp. 73–9; H.G. Pope, E.M. Kouri and J.I. Hudson, 'Effects of supraphysiologic doses of testosterone on mood and aggression in normal men', *Archives of General Psychiatry*, 57 (2000), pp. 133–40; T.-P. Su, M. Pagliaro, P.J. Schmidt, D. Pickar, O. Wolkowitz and D.R. Rubinow, 'Neuropsychiatric effects of anabolic steroids in male

normal volunteers', *Journal of the American Medical Association*, 269 (1993), pp. 2760–4.

[56] K. Bjorkqvist, T. Nygren, A.-C. Bjorklund S.-E. Bjorkqvist, 'Testosterone intake and aggressiveness: real effect or anticipation', *Aggressive Behavior*, 20 (1994), pp. 17–26.

[57] Monitoring the Future Study (Ann Arbor, 2003), online at www.monitoringthefuture.org.

[58] L. Prokop, 'The struggle against doping and its history', *Journal of Sports Medicine and Physical Fitness*, 10 (1) (1970), pp. 45–8.

[59] Bøje, 'Doping'.

[60] J. Ivy, 'Amphetamines', in M. Williams, ed., *Ergogenic aids in sport* (Champaign, IL, 1983).

[61] Bøje, 'Doping'.

[62] E. Jokl, 'Notes on doping', in E. Jokl and P. Jokl, eds., *Exercise and altitude* (Basel, 1968).

[63] Hoberman, *Mortal Engines*.

[64] Bøje, 'Doping'; P.V. Karpovich, 'Ergogenic aids in work and sports', *Research Quarterly*, 12 (suppl.) (1941), pp. 432–50; M. Williams, *Drugs and athletic performance* (Springfield, IL, 1974).

[65] T. Csaky, 'Doping', *Journal of Sports Medicine and Physical Fitness*, 12 (2) (1972), pp. 117–23.

[66] B. Catton, *The Army of the Potomac* (Garden City, NY, 1951), p. 182.

[67] Ibid., p. 182.

[68] Hoberman, *Mortal Engines*, p. 112.

[69] Ibid.

[70] Bøje, 'Doping'; Hoberman, *Mortal Engines*; Prokop, 'The struggle against doping'.

[71] Prokop, 'The struggle against doping'.

[72] Ibid.

[73] Ibid., p. 45.

[74] T. Donohoe and N. Johnson, *Foul play? Drug use in sport* (Oxford, 1986).

[75] Prokop, 'The struggle against doping'.

[76] Donohoe and Johnson, *Foul play?*

[77] J. Lucas, 'Pedestrianism and the struggle for the Sir John Astley belt, 1878–1879', *Research Quarterly*, 39 (3) (1958), pp. 587–94.

[78] T. Osler and E. Dodd, *Ultra-marathoning: the next challenge* (Mountain View, CA, 1979).

[79] Bøje, 'Doping'; Prokop, "The struggle against doping'; Jokl, 'Notes on doping'.

[80] J. Hart and J. Wallace, 'The adverse effects of amphetamines', *Clinical Toxicology*, 8 (2) (1975), pp. 179–90.

[81] O. Ray and C. Ksir, *Drugs, society, and human behavior*, 7th edn (St Louis, MO, 1996).

[82] 'Benzedrine alert', *Air Surgeon's Bulletin*, 1 (2) (1944), pp. 19–21, p. 20.

[83] P. Robson, *Forbidden drugs*, 2nd edn (Oxford, 1999). p. 99.

[84] 'Benzedrine alert', p. 20.

[85] J. Scott, 'It's not how you play the game, but what pill you take', *New York Times Magazine*, 17 Oct. 1971.

[86]   A. Mandell, 'The Sunday syndrome: from kinetics to altered consciousness', *Federation Proceedings*, 40 (1981), pp. 2693–8.

[87]   A. Mandell, 'The Sunday syndrome', *Psychedelic Drugs*, 10 (1978), pp. 379–83.

[88]   B. Gilbert, 'Drugs in sport: part 2. Something extra on the ball', *Sports Illustrated*, 30 June 1969, pp. 30–42, p. 32.

[89]   Prokop, 'The struggle against doping', p. 46.

[90]   Donohoe and Johnson, *Foul Play?*

[91]   Gilbert, 'Drugs in sport.', p. 37.

[92]   Donohoe and Johnson, *Foul Play?*, p. 8

[93]   J. Ferstle, 'Evolution and politics of drug testing', in C.E Yesalis, ed., *Anabolic steroids in sport and exercise*, 2nd edn (Champaign, IL, 2000), pp. 363–413.

[94]   J. Todd and T. Todd, 'Significant events in the history of drug testing and the Olympic movement: 1960–1999', in W. Wilson and E. Derse, eds., *Doping in elite sport* (Champaign, IL, 2001), p. 69.

Knud Enemark Jensen's Death During the 1960 Rome Olympics: A Search for Truth?

Verner Møller

On the opening day of the 1960 Olympic Games in Rome, the twenty-three-year-old Danish racing cyclist Knud Enemark Jensen died. During the team time trials he became sick and fell off his bicycle: an ambulance was called, but he was beyond rescue. That much we know. We also know that it was an extremely hot day with temperatures above 40 degrees Celsius. What is not known for certain is why he died. We do know, however, that every death has a cause. That is, a truth about Jensen's death does exist, and that truth forms the basis of this article. Given some of the conceptual developments within the humanistic study of sport since the 1980s, it is necessary to begin with a discussion of the problem of truth.

The fascination with the impossible thought that the truth was false

It is probable that laymen with an interest in the history of sport or the history of drugs in society will find the attempt to uncover the truth about Knud Enemark Jensen's death both legitimate and relevant. Within the humanistic and social sciences, however, it is a controversial project. Fashionable ideas such as postmodernism, social constructivism, deconstruction and neo-pragmatism have – with their emphasis on concepts such as construction, perspective, relativity, discourse and narrativity – put truth under pressure and nearly driven the humanistic sciences insane. Prestigious publishers have published books containing interesting but, at their core, meaningless statements such as 'we make stars by drawing certain boundaries rather than others. Nothing dictates whether the sky shall be marked off into constellations or other objects. We have to make what we find, be it the Great Dipper, Sirius, food, fuel or a stereo system'. [1]

The field of history has not escaped this trend. Thus, in *The Saturated Self*, the social-constructivist psychologist Kenneth J. Gergen enthusiastically shares with us his discovery of the work of Hayden White:

> Consider the writing of history. We generally think of proper history as furnishing us with an accurate account of the past. It is through the teaching of history that we come to understand our heritage, our accomplishments and our failings, and enrich our wisdom for the future. Yet, proposes the historian Hayden White, if historians are to be intelligible they must inevitably rely on the existing conventions of writing within their culture. These conventions are themselves subject to historical growth and decay, and our understandings of the past are thus rooted in the literary traditions of the day, particularly our tradition of storytelling, or narrative tradition. [2]

The insight that Gergen finds particularly fascinating is that historians are unable to present all the documents, bodily movements and statements that might be relevant. In other words, they are unable to present history as it really was. 'Rather they select and interpret the evidence in a way that will fit the cultural demands for proper narratives.' And this is not all: 'In White's terms, "historical narratives . . . are verbal fictions, the contents of which are as much 'invented' as 'found.'" (Reader beware, the same may be said of this book, and as well of the saying so).' [3] In the way Gergen reads White, what we assume to be historical reality is therefore – to put it radically – a fiction. Gergen's fascination with the fact that everything could be different is all too conspicuous – and odd. If he really meant what he wrote, it ought to have made him hesitate and consider whether it was worth writing the book at all. Of course, he might simply enjoy writing in the same way that some people enjoy doodling when they are talking on the phone. But why then publish the book? If he claims that – like novelists – he wants to tell a story to an audience, why then choose the genre of non-fiction? Why not just write freely from his imagination – as if it were a novel – instead of going to the trouble of referring to a huge range of books (e.g. Hayden White's) to provide support for his arguments? What is the use of footnotes and quotations? There seems to be a remarkable discrepancy here between form and content. This discrepancy gives rise to the suspicion that Gergen does not quite dare to trust his own point of view: that truth does not exist but is invented. If he did, his arguments would be completely in vain, as there is no reason to argue for a point of view that does not value truth.

This is not to say that I believe historical accounts to be perfect reflections of the past as it really was. It is obviously impossible to give a complete rendition of the events of the past. Reading some of the many accounts of the Second World War will provide anyone with ample evidence of this: none of them are identical. The reader would even find significant differences between Danish, Norwegian and English history books. However, one would also discover another essential fact at the same time, namely that Hitler, Himmler, Göring and Goebbels, as well as a range of events such as *Kristallnacht*, the extermination of the Jews and D-Day appear in all of the accounts. They do so because a range of sources and personal testimonies about the events exist: this is a strong indication that we are not dealing with pure fiction.

There is a qualitative difference between novels and history books. Whereas novels can be fiction from one end to the other, historical accounts are based on a real past. The historian tries to give an account of real events and stay as close to the truth as possible, which is not to say that he tries to give an account of everything that took place: the object of his laborious work with sources is to find the essence of past events. The point of departure is that, although history is influenced by coincidences (for example natural disasters), it does not evolve coincidentally but is shaped by people who act according to certain motives. The writing of history thus requires the writer to assume a perspective and carry out an interpretation. It is necessary to carry out a selection based on debatable criteria of relevance. Hence, historians will often focus on events that influenced developments in their own countries and have a tendency to disregard what might be important for areas further away. This, however, *neither* means that the events did not in reality have effects outside the historian's horizon – that the reality is not greater than as presented by the historian – *nor* that the result reached by the historian is pure fiction without any truth value. It does mean that history is presented by the historian as a subject and is hence a subjective account and interpretation of historical facts: and, moreover, that the truth which the historian believes his interpretation to uncover is *a truth about something*. He could also have sought the truth about a second, third or fourth matter within the same – or a completely different – field. These other truths were left out of consideration due to the historian's choice of focus. Despite this, his or her account may very well accord with the truth. Perhaps the agents of history really did act on the basis of the motives ascribed to them in the account. Due to the nature of the subject, this cannot be known for sure, but by investigating various sources, presenting documentation and arguing in a consistent way the historian strives to validate his or her interpretation. It is then left up to the reader to judge.

These are not the same criteria one would use to judge a novel. The essential thing is not whether it is a good story, whether it has a good plot and is well told and well composed. The main criterion is whether the account is *credible* and in accordance with the historical evidence. A badly written story about Auschwitz that accords with the comprehensive documentation of the camp is therefore better history writing than an excellently written denial of the existence of Auschwitz and what happened there. The first story is, in spite of its stylistic imperfections, closer to the truth than the well-written denial. The denial is very aptly called a falsification of history, thereby implying that there is a (true) history to falsify. The fact that this consists of an almost endless number of truths does not support the statement that there is no truth, or that we cannot get close to this truth by finding factual information about past events. Claiming that there is no objective truth – that truth is always a construction – is in reality claiming that there is no qualitative difference between the statement that mass exterminations took place during the Second World War in Auschwitz and the statement that mass exterminations never took place.

This is clearly untenable. Even if Auschwitz, contrary to all evidence, never did happen, this is a truth that falsifies the story we have been told about Auschwitz. Based on the scholarly criteria and methods according to which historians work, however, it is entirely unlikely that the people who deny the reality of Auschwitz will ever be given scholarly recognition:

the existing evidence is too overwhelming for that to happen. It therefore appears to be more appropriate to compare historical scholarship with legal scholarship rather than literature.

I tried to make this point at a conference arranged by Professor John Bale in the Danish city of Aarhus in response to Professor Jeff Hill's lecture, [4] which was strongly inspired by Hayden White. Hill emphasized the fictitious character of historical writing and maintained that, strictly speaking, there is no difference between the writing of history and the writing of novels. There is undoubtedly good reason to point out the potential value of literature as historical material. However, I was very surprised to hear Hill deny that there is a genre difference and deny that the historian – albeit in a literary form and with the use of certain artifices and additions – tries to the best of his ability to give an account of the past that is as close to the truth as possible. 'I don't believe in Truth with a capital T' was the answer, which clearly struck a chord in the audience but which, rightly considered, evades the problem. In order to clarify whether the concept of truth was valid at all, I asked whether it was not a truth that Kant was born in 1724, which made one of the historians present, Murray Philips from the University of Queensland, exclaim spontaneously 'No! That's a fact!' And thus ended the discussion.

From the linguistic turn to pure nonsense

The reason it has become necessary to argue that there *is* a truth (consisting of a number of truths) is that a great part of the humanistic disciplines have been seduced by the 'linguistic turn' in philosophy. For unknown reasons the (re)discovery of the language dependency and discursive creation of science possesses such centrifugal force that it has apparently slung cognition within certain humanistic fields beyond the gravitational pull of reason. Hayden White goes exactly as far as he can – and no further – when he states that:

> recent philosophers of history have typically treated narrative less as a verbal structure than as a kind of explanation by storytelling and have regarded the story told in a given history as a structure of argumentative concepts, the relations among whose parts were logical (specifically syllogistic) rather than linguistic in nature. All this implied that the content of a historical discourse could be extracted from its linguistic form, served up in a condensed paraphrase purged of all figurative and tropological elements, and subjected to tests of logical consistency as an argument and of predicative adequacy as a body of fact. This, however, was to ignore the one 'content' without which a historical discourse could never come into existence at all: language.

During the very period in which this argument model predominated among analysts of historical discourse, philosophers such as
Quine, Searle, Goodman, and Rorty were showing the difficulty of
distinguishing what was said from how it was said even in the
discourse of the physical sciences, let alone in such a nonformalized
discourse as history . . . this implied that the very distinctions between
imaginative and realistic writing and between fictional and factual
discourse, on the basis of which historiographical writing had been
analyzed since the disengagement from rhetoric in the early nineteenth
century had to be reassessed and reconceptualized. [5]

In this connection it is essential to point out that White's invoking of the
role of language in historiography is not aimed at abandoning truth, but
to get even closer to it. It is fair to demand that we reflect on the
consequence of the language dependency of scholarship, just as it is fair to
doubt whether history allows us to know the past as it really was.
However, it does not follow from this that one has to walk the plank of
relativism. White's objective is to contribute to the development of the
science of history, since he believes the traditional writing of history to be
inadequate. Instead he opts for a modernist writing of history, which takes
into consideration the linguistic staging, because 'modernist modes of
representation may offer possibilities of representing the reality of both
the Holocaust and the experience of it that no other version of realism
could do'. [6] He argues for this re-conceptualizing, not for the sake of
renewal, but because he believes that historical research would gain from
this and become even better at what it aims to do: to provide us with
insight into and understanding of, for example, the past political, financial
and national developments that have contributed to shaping the
conditions in which we currently live.

In fact, White is working for a laudable purpose that is similar to the
cognitive development of the natural sciences, in which one attempts to
develop new theories when too many questions have accumulated which
the previous paradigm is unable to answer. Einstein's relativity theory and
Bohr's quantum mechanics are examples of revolutionizing breakthroughs within physics. The difference, however, is that when these
theories saw the light of day, the advocates had to prove that the power of
explanation of the new theories was greater than that of previous ones.
And the reason why these theories hold to this day is that Bohr and
Einstein succeeded in convincing the scientific community that their
theories possessed a greater power of explanation than the physics of
Newton.

Within the natural sciences, new theories have to prove their worth. This is not the case within the humanistic disciplines. These do not have the same tradition of making strict demands on new theories that must be proved to be better than the existing ones in order not to be rejected. Within the humanities it is, for example, possible to put forward revolutionary claims such as that the idea of truth is an illusion or that the difference between men and women is a social construction, and then leave it to opponents to repudiate the claims. This is often cumbersome, and in certain circumstances even impossible, because the advocates of the new theories reject rationality as the basis for conversation. Thus there are still professional academics who read the French sociologist Bruno Latour in earnest and believe in his argument that it is problematic for new studies of the mummy of Ramses II to show that he died from tuberculosis, as this bacillus was first discovered and hence constructed socially by Robert Koch in 1882, which prompts him to write that 'Before Koch the bacillus has no real existence'. [7]

Hence, it was not particularly surprising, but still a shock to many people, when the physicist Alan D. Sokal demonstrated the receptiveness of the humanities to nonsense with the publication of his mock article 'Transgressing the boundaries: towards a transformative hermeneutics of quantum gravity', which, in fact, provided ample hints to the editors that the article was pure humbug. Already in his introduction he wrote what ought to have made even the most naive and vain humanist suspicious:

> There are many natural scientists, and especially physicists, who continue to reject the notion that the disciplines concerned with social and cultural criticism can have anything to contribute, except perhaps peripherally, to their research. Still less are they receptive to the idea that the very foundations of their worldview must be revised or rebuilt in the light of such criticism. Rather, they cling to the dogma imposed by the long post-Enlightenment hegemony over the Western intellectual outlook, which can be summarized briefly as follows: that there exists an external world, whose properties are independent of any individual human being and indeed of humanity as a whole; that these properties are encoded in 'eternal' physical laws; and that human beings can obtain reliable, albeit imperfect and tentative, knowledge of these laws by hewing to the 'objective' procedures and epistemological strictures prescribed by the (so-called) scientific method. [8]

The quotation should speak for itself.

However, the newly developed theories in the humanities are often well thought out in their original form, and are − if they are read in the same vein that they were written − worth studying. Most often one will then discover that they are not nearly as revolutionary as they are made out to be. The problem lies with inadequate reflection, objectivity and insight. It may be those who elaborate and radicalize the new theories, because small distortions can make them appear to be in accordance with a certain belief, policy or ideology. Or it may be that opponents of the new theories are tempted to present them in a way that makes it easier to repudiate them, but for which the original texts, strictly speaking, do not provide grounds.

The linguistic turn has sent much of the humanities into a cognitive muddle. Increased awareness that reality is thought and expressed in concepts has tempted people to draw the faulty conclusion that concepts such as truth and reality are no more than socio-linguistic constructions without foundation outside language. This has caused some to believe that a change of concepts would cause a change of (what we experience as) reality. Thus feminists used to believe that it would contribute to sexual equality if gender-specific terms such as 'chairman' and 'sportsman' were replaced with gender-neutral terms such as 'chair' and 'sportsperson'. These linguistic innovations seemed slightly comical at first. Now that we have become used to them, we are able to see that this was the only effect they had on anyone. In reality these innovations have changed absolutely nothing, because language complies with and takes shape from reality, not the other way around.

It is important to be aware that there are differences between concepts, and that it is neither reasonable to maintain a purely concept-relativist nor a purely concept-realistic point of view. If we take a word such as 'doping', for example, it is easy to see that this is a highly arbitrary concept, which might as well have been called 'performance-enhancing drugs' and might as well have been legal as well as illegal. At the time of Knud Enemark Jensen's death, doping was not illegal; today a veritable crusade has been launched against it. There are reasons for this. Nevertheless, it is impossible to ignore the fact that the problem of doping is a social construction. If, on the other hand, we look at a concept like 'death', it refers to a real condition, namely the lifelessness of a previously living organism; a condition which, irrespective of whether we choose to use a different term for it, remains a reality independent of human decisions. The fact that Jensen died during the Olympics in Rome in 1960 is beyond any doubt: it is a truth that can be changed by neither language nor historical account. Death is no construction, and neither is the cause of death. Even though the problem of doping is a social construction, and the means of doping are as well (in the sense that they have been produced – possibly in a laboratory), doping drugs are also substances with an effect on the organism, and this cannot be changed. This effect is no social construction. For example, a well-trained marathon runner will acquire enhanced endurance by consuming small doses of strychnine, whether he knows this or not. Whether or not he chooses to call the drug something different, the lethal dose is about 5mg/kg; if he consumes 15mg/kg death will be certain. Thus truth does exist, and this is what historians are chasing when they search through archives for material which may throw light on this or that. That the truth is not very easy to find, on the other hand, will be demonstrated by the following.

The Jensen mystery

In many publications about doping, Jensen's death during the 1960 Olympics is mentioned as a significant reason why politicians and sports organizations became aware of doping as a problem which needed to be fought actively. Barrie Houlihan is the author of one of these publications, and he writes the following about the episode in his excellent book *Dying to win*: 'In 1960 the Danish cyclist, Knut Jensen, collapsed and died at the Rome Olympic Games during the 175-kilometre team time trials following his use of amphetamines and nicotine acid. Jensen's two team-mates, who had taken the same mixture, also collapsed but later recovered in hospital.' [9]

This piece is written without references. It is therefore impossible to know where Houlihan got his information. On the other hand, it is possible to spot three factual errors and one unsubstantiated claim: (1) The cyclist who died was not called Knut, but Knud; (2) The discipline was not 175 kilometres but the 100-kilometre team time trials; (3) Jensen did not have two team-mates, but three, namely Niels Baunsøe, Vagn Bangsborg and Jørgen B. Jørgensen, and there is no evidence to support Houlihan's claim that they, too, had taken amphetamine. Even before finishing the first half of the race, Jørgensen could no longer keep up with the others. He felt unwell in the heat and let himself fall behind the team. As the performance of the team was measured by the finishing time of the third cyclist, it was thus vital for Jensen to keep up with the team to the finish, even though he also complained about feeling unwell during the race. A photo in the Danish tabloid *Ekstra Bladet* on 27 August, the day after the tragedy, shows how the two remaining team-mates are holding Jensen's shirt on both sides and are unsuccessfully trying to support him and prevent him from falling down. The text accompanying the photo is: 'The team-mates Baunsøe and Bangsborg try to keep Knud Enemark on his bike as he suffers heatstroke.' Underneath is the famous photo where Jensen falls, hits his head on the ground and sustains a concussion. The text reads: 'They did not succeed in holding him up. Knud Enemark falls onto the road while Niels Baunsøe watches in horror.'

Even though these are part of the circumstances surrounding Jensen's death, Houlihan does not mention them. He also does not mention that thirty-one other cyclists suffered heatstroke during the infamous race, which points to the extreme heat as a crucial factor. Similarly, he remains silent about the presumably fatal factor: that, unlike the other collapsed cyclists, Jensen was not cooled down but was placed by the first-aid team in a tent, where he lay for about two hours in a temperature of approximately 50 degrees Celsius. [10] Houlihan's loose description of the situation is probably due to the fact that he only needs to use the tragedy to document that the use of doping has had fatal consequences, a fact that contributed to the initiation of an anti-doping policy in the 1960s. Considering the context in which Houlihan writes, it is understandable that he relies on knowledge that has generally been accepted by doping researchers, even though one wonders why he does not carefully pass the buck by referring to the work he paraphrases.

Ivan Waddington has apparently taken this precaution. He writes:

> Writing about the more recent period, Mottram (1996: 92) noted that 'there are numerous examples of fatalities arising from the use of amphetamines by cyclists', two of the most famous amphetamine-related deaths being those of the Dane Knut Jenson in the 1960 Olympic Games and of the British rider Tommy Simpson in the 1967 Tour de France. [11]

Apart from the fact that Waddington has given the poor Dane an un-Danish name, there seem to be no real problems here. We can see that he is talking about Knud Enemark Jensen, and it would appear that we can get the full story by consulting David R. Mottram. However, consulting Mottram's text [12] proves rather disappointing because although Mottram does write what Waddington quotes him as saying, he does not mention a word about Jensen and Simpson. Thus, Waddington does not provide any support for his knowledge about Jensen's death, but similarly draws on the well-known 'fact' that it was a consequence of amphetamine use.

It is remarkable that experienced researchers such as Houlihan and Waddington do not make the effort to cover their backs with references in the Jensen case. This is, after all, a serious allegation to circulate without evidence. But since Jensen died, and the rumours that his death was caused by amphetamine use began, it seems that these rumours have acquired the status of public knowledge. However, this does not mean that they are true, if the truth, which we do not know yet, was in reality different. Waddington might as well have quoted from or referred to Chapter 2 of Mottram's book and thereby passed the blame on to 'former director of ethics and anti-doping at UK Sport', Michele Verroken, who gives the impression of possessing evidence that Jensen's death was doping-related. She states with great confidence: 'At the 1960 Rome Olympics, the cyclist Knud Jensen died on the opening day of the Games as he competed in the 100 km team time trial. Two team mates were also taken to hospital. The post-mortem revealed traces of amphetamine and nicotinyl nitrate in Jensen's blood.' [13] The only thing missing here is documentation. Verroken writes as if she has personally seen the post-mortem report, which she probably has not. She, too, seems to be writing on the basis of rumours, because it is not easy to gain access to this report. So in the quest for the truth about Jensen's death, a reference to Verroken would have been a *dead end* after all.

The reason why the truth about Jensen's death seemingly does not interest doping researchers may actually be that, although doping was not illegal in Jensen's time, he has since become a symbol of unethical behaviour. Therefore there is no mercy regarding his posthumous reputation. Robert Voy writes:

> Perhaps the landmark amphetamine-related tragedy in Olympic history occurred when Danish cyclist Knud Enemark Jensen collapsed and died during the 175.38-km road race at the Summer Olympiad in Rome. It was reported at the time that, leading up to his death, Jensen was taking, supposedly on doctor's orders, a combination of nicotynal alcohol and amphetamine, sarcastically nicknamed by his competitors the 'Knud Jensen diet'. Several of the other athletes competing in Jensen's race collapsed like Jensen had at the finish; however, Jensen was the only fatality. An autopsy revealed that Jensen probably died from dehydration caused by the amphetamine in his system, though his skull had also been fractured. [14]

Once again, no evidence is provided for the claim that Jensen had used amphetamine, (and once again we find factual errors in the account). However, the story has gained a new dimension, as it is implied that Jensen was known by his rivals for using a certain 'doping diet'. This is certainly a good story. Nevertheless it seems scientifically irresponsible to present this kind of claim without substantiating it. Only if Voy actually claimed to have been present and heard about the 'Knud Jensen diet', as well as having had this confirmed by several people independently, would it have been defensible to tell the story in this way. The way it is presented by Voy, the story falls into the category of gossip, which has no place in scientific literature. The fact that the sensational story about the Knud Jensen diet has not appeared in the doping literature after Voy's reference to it indicates a generally high standard of scientific ethics. Still, one is tempted to ask whether the circulation of the story about Jensen's death from doping does not indicate the opposite, in so far as the researchers do not seem to support their claims properly. This may be too hasty a conclusion, as certain pieces of circumstantial evidence speak for this claim, even though one may object that this evidence has never been evaluated properly in the international sport and doping literature.

Circumstantial evidence

Under the headline 'Olympic Trainer Admits Giving Drug to Danish Cyclist Who Died', the *New York Times* on 29 August 1960 wrote the following:

> The trainer of Denmark's Olympic cycling team revealed tonight that the Danish bicycle rider who died after a race in the Olympics last Friday had been given a drug. The rider was Knut Enemark Jensen, 22 years old [he was in fact 23]. He collapsed during the 100-kilometer (62.5-mile) team road race in Rome and died later in that day. The trainer Oluf Jorgensen, told the Danish Government organ Aktuelt that he had given the drug roniacol to Jensen and other members of the Danish cycling team. Preben Z. Jensen, the leader of the Danish Olympic cycling team, confirmed Jorgensen's statement in a report to the Danish Road Biking Union. Preben Jensen told the union that the trainer had given a stimulant to the team's four members prior to the race. He said Jorgensen admitted Friday night, only a few hours after Enemark Jensen's death, that pills had been given to the cyclists. No reason was given why the report had been withheld until now. Jorgensen said the purpose of the drug was to intensify blood circulation. He said he had obtained the prescription from his doctor.

It thus seems indisputable that Jensen consumed a medical preparation before the race, presumably expecting it to enhance his performance. However, Roniacol is a drug that causes vascular dilation but has no real performance-enhancing effect. While it does make the blood flow more easily to the muscles, it also causes the blood pressure to fall and the blood supply to other non-working muscles and organs not to be shut off as effectively as normal when the body is exposed to great performance demands. This means that the blood supply to the working muscles is not optimal, meaning that Roniacol actually has a performance-inhibiting effect. This would have resulted in a drop in blood pressure, which was probably made worse due to dehydration. When blood pressure falls, it causes dizziness and general indisposition. Given these facts, the journalist Lars Bøgeskov's account of the circumstances sounds plausible:

> There are very few hills, but not much shade either. It is a fast race. Just after the four Danes start the second round, Jørgen B. Jørgensen is suddenly gone – he just falls behind all of a sudden. A little while later, he is taken to the central hospital in Rome. On their way up the only small incline towards the turning point, both Knud Enemark and Vagn Bangsborg complain about stiffness in their legs. Only Niels Baunsøe still has any real strength left in his legs. 'Follow me' Baunsøe says, and then he pedals like mad towards the turning point. And Niels Baunsøe rides really fast. At the sharp corner of the turning point a spectator shouts that the three Danish riders are now only ten seconds from a bronze medal. Again, Baunsøe goes in front in the light headwind on the sun-baked plain. 'Homeward bound', says Knud Enemark, ready to endure the final pain in the hope of winning an Olympic medal. But eight kilometres from the finish, Knud Enemark shouts 'I am dizzy'. And when the riders have only five kilometres left, Enemark is only semi-conscious. He lags behind, and his bicycle falters. Niels Baunsøe keeps him up on his bicycle by holding his shirt; Vagn Bangsborg sprays water on his face. His bicycle reels, but then Enemark regains consciousness. 'Are you OK?' Baunsøe asks. 'Yes' replies Enemark; Baunsøe lets go of his shirt, but the next moment Enemark passes out and falls heavily onto the scorching asphalt. Team manager Preben Z. Jensen, who was driving the 100-kilometre team car, turned the car around immediately and fetched an ambulance, which the riders had passed 400 metres earlier. Meanwhile, other teams passed the prostrate Knud Enemark from behind. Knud Enemark was put on a stretcher and inside the ambulance, which took him to the finish area. Here, the unconscious Knud Enemark was placed in a military hospital tent. Niels Baunsøe and Vagn Bangsborg passed the finish, but Bangsborg also felt dizzy. He was sick and was taken to the Olympic village. Baunsøe rode his bicycle. In the military tent the heat was even more oppressive than on the route, and here the 23-year-old Knud Enemark died – the exact time was 1530. [15]

People had high expectations of the Danish team in this race for good reason. Two months earlier, Jensen had won a Nordic Championship and earlier in the year the team had drawn with the Germans, who were considered favourites together with the Russians and Italians. The conditions were the same for all teams, but if the Danish team had been given Roniacol by their coach ahead of the Olympic race, it is understandable that they all felt dizzy, unwell and performed below normal levels in the extreme conditions. The real enigma is Niels Baunsøe, who was the only person to ride well, and who was even well enough after the hardships to cycle back to the Olympic village.

There are two possible explanations. One is that he was the only person in the team who refused to take the Roniacol tablet. The other is that, in addition to Roniacol, he also took amphetamine. The latter seems more plausible. Firstly, amphetamine has a performance-enhancing effect (and Baunsøe did cycle so fast that the others had difficulty in keeping up). Secondly, it enhances the effect of noradrenalin which is, in popular terms, the 'flight-and-fight' hormone of the body that causes vascular contraction. In other words, amphetamine would neutralize the negative effect of Roniacol. In spite of this, no allegations have ever been made against Baunsøe and this is understandable. First of all, doping was not illegal at the time; secondly, the attention was focused on Jensen; and finally, this reasoning was not immediately obvious, as the emerging campaign against doping was based on a growing scepticism towards modernity and the medical progress made by modernity. [16] Nevertheless, it actually seems more likely that the use of amphetamine helped or even saved Baunsøe than it is that it killed Jensen.

Considering Jensen's poor performance, it does not seem likely that his death should later be ascribed to the use of amphetamine. Jørgensen's admission that he had given the riders a medical preparation probably contributed to the view that Jensen's death was doping-related. The public are probably ignorant as to what kind of preparation Roniacol really is, and may therefore have believed that is was probably the name of a potent performance-enhancing drug (like amphetamine). However, it takes much more than just the rumour that Jensen might have taken amphetamine for this to become historical fact. The Danish journalist and Olympic expert John Idorn gives us a clue as to what this *more* is. In his book about the history of the Olympics he writes:

> In the Danish cycling camp it was admitted that the drug in question was Roniacol, said to be harmless, and an 'official' report from November 1961 maintained that the cause of death was sunstroke. The post-mortem showed something different, however. The IOC account, written by Prof. Dr Ludwig Prokop, claims that it was a case of doping with methamphetamine and pyridic carbinol. [17]

Idorn thus refers to Prokop's account, and Prokop seems confident about the matter. According to Bøgeskov, who investigated the case thoroughly in 1998, the IOC account from 1972 is impossible to get hold of, but it is supposed to be 'a historical account about doping cases up until the present' which 'quotes the post-mortem report from the Italian doctors back in 1960, according to which the doctors found amphetamine and the drug pyridic carbinol in Knud Enemark's blood'. [18] I strongly suspect that the report Bøgeskov was unable to get hold of is identical to Prokop's article in Helmut Acker's anthology *Rekorde aus der Retorte* from 1972. Here Prokop briefly describes doping cases through the ages and states authoritatively that Jensen 'broke down and died during the Olympics in Rome as a result of an overdose of amphetamine and Roni[a]col provided by his coach'. [19] The article is, however, written without documentation. Those who claim that Jensen was cycling on amphetamine have only the words of Prokop for support. And his claim that, apart from handing out Roniacol to the riders, the coach supposedly handed out amphetamine as well seems to be just as much of a haphazard guess as the above claim that Baunsøe did better than his team-mates due to the use of amphetamine. It is worth remembering that, after the tragedy, the coach himself volunteered the information that he had distributed Roniacol within the team. And as doping had not been made illegal yet, it would not have incurred any legal sanctions to tell the whole truth. Although there is hardly any reason to doubt Prokop's credibility (he is, after all, one of the pioneers of the campaign against doping), it seems likely that he accidentally 'invents' the provision of amphetamine by the coach based on the Italian post-mortem report.

In the course of his thorough research, Bøgeskov interviewed John Idorn, who refers directly to Prokop's account of the case. In the interview Idorn says:

> I was at the press centre [in 1972], when Ludwig Prokop delivered his account. He gave a speech on various doping cases and mentioned the Enemark case as being central. .... I had the account in my hands; I do not have it anymore, but I have no doubt that Enemark was under the influence of amphetamine and pyridic carbinol – it isn't something I made up in my book. Everybody involved in the race knew that it was a case of doping. [20]

Idorn's statement indicates that he may have fallen victim to an illusion. In 1972 he hears Prokop state that Knud Enemark Jensen had taken performance-enhancing drugs and is even told the names of the drugs in question. He links this with rumours heard at the scene of the event in 1960, where everybody involved in the race believed that it was a case of doping without any other evidence than the admission by the coach that he had handed out the infamous drug Roniacol to the riders. In combination, the rumours and Prokop's account eliminate any shadow of a doubt in Idorn's mind, which is why he simply quotes in his book from 1996 what he heard from Prokop twenty-four years earlier.

The fact that Prokop's account (which is impossible to get hold of) has become the primary source of the doping shadow looming over Jensen's grave is even more regrettable due to the fact that Bøgeskov interviewed the author of the account in 2001 and gained an admission that Prokop never saw any documentation to prove that Jensen had been doping:

> 'I was there when Knud Enemark died, and from the beginning I suspected that doping might be the cause. I sought information straight away but I couldn't gain access to the post-mortem report. A couple of months later in Monte Carlo I met the Italian professor who carried out the post-mortem on Knud Enemark, and he told me that, among other things, he had found amphetamine in the Danish cyclist. However, I have to admit that I have never seen documentation to prove that his death was caused by doping. Perhaps it was wrong of me to draw it out in the report,' says Ludwig Prokop, who does not believe, however, that Enemark died in vain. 'Remember that Knud Enemark's death initiated the fight against doping', says Ludwig Prokop. [21]

Bøgeskov's interview leaves no doubt that Prokop's commitment to the early work against doping led him to make unsubstantiated claims, because it happened in the service of a good cause. Confronted with the question several years later, he reveals a doubt as to whether the statement by the Italian professor was sufficient reason to maintain as a fact that Jensen had been doped by amphetamine. In those days, the methods used for tracing drugs were not as sophisticated as today. It therefore seems a very reasonable demand to see documentation, stating what kind of data the professor bases his statement on, before declaring with medical authority to the public that Jensen was doped by amphetamine. And the case becomes even more precarious for Prokop, as the Italians produced a medico-legal report in 1961 clearing Jensen of suspicion.

This report caused the then president of the Danish Olympic Committee, Leo Frederiksen, to write the following letter in 1962 to the editor of the *Bulletin du Comité International Olympique*, which had published an article providing new fuel for the suspicions against Jensen:

> Dear Sir,
> I refer to the article *Waging War Against Dope* on page 46 of the International Olympic Bulletin, No. 77, which includes, *inter alia*, the following lines: 'We do not wish to cite the case of the unfortunate Danish cyclist during the last Games in Rome, the medical and legal sport [report] on whose death was communicated only to the family, so that we shall never know the real cause of this death.' I would like to

comment on this paragraph as follows: The official report from the Italian authorities has not been made available to the Olympic Committee of Denmark, but the report was handed to the Danish police authorities, who submitted it to the Danish public health authorities. 'In due course, our Committee received from the Copenhagen Police a letter of the following wording: "The Italian authorities" report on the death of the cyclist Knud Enemark Jensen and the results of the subsequent post mortem and pharmacological and toxicological examinations have been submitted to the Danish Public Health Board.' On returning the report, the Board declares that no grounds have been found for comment of any importance on the case. In consequence, the Copenhagen Police want to establish as final the conclusion of said report, viz., that the death of Knud Enemark Jensen was caused solely by heatstroke. No charge whatsoever will be brought against anybody in connection with this case. I would much appreciate it if you would include this comment in your next issue of the International Olympic Committee Bulletin.
Yours faithfully
For the Olympic Committee of Denmark
Leo Frederiksen
President. [22]

The letter was published and followed by the editor's thanks for the comment 'which put an end to this regrettable accident which happened during the Rome Games'.

So what is the truth?

Today we know that the editor was wrong. Frederiksen's comment did not put an end to the story. The rumour lives on. Presumably due to the highly esteemed Austrian doctor Prokop's circumstantial account, it has been written into the scientific literature as fact. But the only accessible official document about the case acquits Jensen of doping. This raises doubts whether there is any way to substantiate the repeated claim by the doping researchers: that Jensen died as a result of doping with, among other drugs, amphetamine. As the case stands, it seems scientifically dishonest for Tom Donohoe and Neil Johnson to maintain that 'While the official verdict cited sunstroke as the cause of death, the autopsy revealed that Jensen had taken the stimulant amphetamine and also nicotinyl tartrate to increase the blood supply to his muscles'. [23] As nothing indicates that they have ever seen this post-mortem report, what they communicate as fact is only what they have read or heard through the grapevine. This is not to say that it is necessarily wrong. Lars Bøgeskov concluded his research into the case in 2001 by phoning one of the doctors, Dr Alvaro Marchiori, who carried out the post-mortem. With reservations about his weak memory now forty years after carrying out the examination, he says: 'But of course I remember the examination of the cyclist who died during the 100-kilometre race. Because it was the first time we had a doping case at our institution. And I remember that we found traces of several things – amphetamine among others.' [24]

Bøgeskov thus receives the same message from Marchiori as Prokop received from the professor who carried out the post-mortem a few months later. So what are we to believe? It is odd that the doctors who carried out the post-mortem claim to have found traces of amphetamine, whereas the official report, which was published on the basis of the post-mortem and sent to the Danish authorities, does not mention this finding at all. It complicates the matter further that the only currently accessible document is an unfinished nine-page translation, which can be found at the National Archive in Copenhagen. The Italian authorities will not allow access to the full medico-legal analysis report. It is beyond understanding what motives the Italian authorities may have had for publishing a report which acquits Jensen, if they, in reality, did find amphetamine in his blood. On the other hand, it is also beyond understanding that the doctors who carried out the post-mortem would claim to have found traces of amphetamine if this was not the case. In my view, the best explanation for this is that there were doubts about the finding. The doctors could not prove that they had found amphetamine. We will only know whether this is the truth when the Italian authorities release the post-mortem report and the medico-legal analysis in its entirety.

This is not to say that we know nothing, and that there is no historical truth about the event. Even though our knowledge is communicated to us in a narrative form and using literary means, it is beyond any doubt– it is true – that during the Olympics in 1960 a 100-kilometre team time trial race was run with Danish participation in temperatures of over forty degrees Celsius. We also know for certain that Knud Enemark Jensen was a rider on the Danish team, that he had been given a drug, Roniacol, which causes vascular dilation, became unwell, collapsed and died a few hours after the race in a hot military tent. Furthermore, we know that there were rumours to the effect that he had been doped, that those who carried out the post-mortem claimed to have found traces of amphetamine, but also that the report which was forwarded to the Danish authorities did not mention this finding, for which reason the case was shelved. Against the background of these and other truths (call them facts if you wish) presented here, it is possible to offer a plausible explanation of the cause of death. It seems unlikely that Jensen cycled with amphetamine in his blood. And if he did, this still is not grounds for maintaining that he died as a result of amphetamine doping. On the contrary, there is good reason to believe that if, indeed, he had taken amphetamine, he did not die because of but rather *in spite* of this, inasmuch as amphetamine would have countered the fatal effect of the Roniacol tablet. It is therefore more likely that his death was caused by a combination of factors. The extreme heat combined with the consumption of Roniacol, which would have contributed to an already significant level of dehydration, is presumably an essential part of the explanation. From the Danish Sports Association's biography of Danish Olympic athletes, it appears that the Swedes had measured a loss of fluid in their cyclists of six litres. Furthermore, it says that in that era the Danish cyclists and coaches did not believe 'that it was worth carrying fluids on the bicycle (they were too heavy)'. [25] Insufficient intake of fluids thus seems to have been a critical factor. Jensen's team spirit and his ambition to win an Olympic medal are also factors to be included. If he had not raced in order to win, but simply for the joy of participating, he would probably have stopped when he started to feel ill. Finally, placing Jensen in a hot military tent with insufficient cooling or treatment with fluids seems to have contributed to the tragedy. We are not likely to get any closer to the truth unless new material about the case appears. Nevertheless, we have now substantiated that there is a truth about Jensen's death, and for this reason it does matter what is claimed about the cause of death; it would not matter unless it were the purpose of (historical) science to search for the truth. Thus, there is good reason to support the opinion rejected in mockery by Sokal that 'human beings can obtain reliable, albeit imperfect and tentative knowledge' also about history'.

Notes

[1]   Nelson Goodman, *On mind and other matters* (Cambridge, MA, 1984), p. 36.
[2]   Kenneth J. Gergen, *The saturated self. Dilemmas of identity in contemporary life* (New York, 1991), p. 108.
[3]   Ibid., p. 109.
[4]   Jeff Hill: "Sport as Ideology: History, Literature and Culture". Lecture held at the conference "Educational and Sociological Issues in Sports and Physical Education" Aarhus University 8–10 December 2004.
[5]   Hayden White, 'Literary theory and historical writing', in *Figural realism: studies in the mimesis effect* (Baltimore, MD, 2001), p. 5.
[6]   Hayden White, 'Historical emplotment and the problem of truth in historical representation', in ibid., p. 41.

[7]   Here quoted from David Favrholdt, *Filosofisk Codex. Om begrundelsen af den menneskelige erkendelse* (Copenhagen, 1999), p. 230. Philosopical codex. On the basis for human understanding.

[8]   Alan D. Sokal, 'Transgressing the boundaries: towards a transformative hermeneutics of quantum gravity', in *Social Text*, 46/47 (1996), p. 217.

[9]   Barrie Houlihan, *Dying to win – Doping in sport and the development of anti-doping policy* (Strasbourg, 1999), p. 36.

[10] Lars Bøgeskov, 'Doping-mysteriet uden løsning', *Politiken*, 9 April 2001, sportsmagasinet, p. 12. All excerpts from the original article translated by Mette Bollerup Doyle. The doping mystery without solution.

[11] Ivan Waddington, *Sport, health and drugs* (London, 2002), p. 154.

[12] David Mottram eds. *Drugs in Sport* (London 1996).

[13] Michele Verroken, 'Drug use and abuse in sport', in David R. Mottram, *Drugs in sport* (London, 1996), p. 19.

[14] Robert Voy, *Drugs, sport, and politics* (Champaign, IL, 1991), pp. 6ff.

[15] Lars Bøgeskov, 'Dopingsagen der ændrede verden', *Politiken*, 20 Sept. 1998, section 1, p. 14. All excerpts from the original article translated by Mette Bollerup Doyle. The doping case that changed the world.

[16] For a further discussion of this, see Verner Møller, 'The anti-doping campaign – farewell to the ideals of modernity', in John Hoberman and Verner Møller, eds., *Doping and public policy* (Odense, 2004).

[17] John Idorn, *OL-Historie Strejftog gennem myter, legender og danske medaljer* (Copenhagen, 1996), p. 92. Excerpt translated from the original by Mette Bollerup Doyle. Incursion through myths, legends, and Danish medals.

[18] Lars Bøgeskov, 'Dopingsagen der ændrede verden', *Politiken,* 20 Sept. 1998, 1. section, p. 14. The doping case that changed the world.

[19] Ludwig Prokop, 'Zur Geschichte des Dopings', in Helmut Acker, ed., *Rekorde aus der Retorte* (Stuttgart, 1972), p. 25.

[20] Lars Bøgeskov, 'Dopingsagen der ændrede verden', *Politiken*, 20 Sept. 1998, section 1, p. 14. The doping case that changed the world.

[21] Lars Bøgeskov, 'Intet bevis i historisk dopingsag', *Politiken*, 9 April 2001, sportsmagasinet, p. 1. Excerpt translated from the original by Mette Bollerup Doyle. No evidence in historical doping case.

[22] Leo Frederiksen, 'Correspondence', *Bulletin du Comité International Olympique*, 78 (May 1962), p. 47.

[23] Tom Donohoe and Neil Johnson, *Foul play – drug abuse in sports* (Oxford, 1986), p. 6.

[24] Lars Bøgeskov, 'Doping-mysteriet uden løsning', *Politiken*, 9 April 2001, sportsmagasinet. p. 12. The doping mystery without solution.

[25] Danmarks Idrætsforbund, *De Olympiske biografi af danske OL-deltagere 1896– 1996* (Copenhagen, 1996), p. 313. Excerpt translated from the original by Mette Bollerup Doyle. (author: The National Olympic Committee and Sports Confederation of Denmark) title: The Olympic – a biography of Danish participants in The Olympic Games 1896–1996.

Changing Patterns of Drug Use in British Sport from the 1960s

Ivan Waddington

Although there is a large and growing body of literature on the use of performance-enhancing drugs in sport, there have been few attempts to estimate systematically the level of drug use in sport, or to examine changes in patterns of drug use over time. Perhaps this is not surprising for, as Mottram has noted, '[m]eaningful data on the prevalence of use of performance-enhancing drugs in sport are difficult to obtain'. [1] However, it is the case that, because of the data that have become available since the collapse of the Communist regime in East Germany, we now know much more about the prevalence and organization of doping in that relatively closed society than we know about the recent history of drug use in Western democracies. [2] The objective of this paper is systematically to examine the evidence relating to the prevalence and the changing patterns of drug use in British sport in the period from the 1960s to the present.

However, before we examine these issues, it is important to remind ourselves of a point of fundamental importance: modern elite sport is a global phenomenon. One consequence of the globalization of sport is that it is not possible adequately to understand any aspect of elite sport, including the illicit use of drugs, within a single country simply by looking at processes which might be considered 'internal' to that country.

A clear example is provided by the early development and use of anabolic steroids in sport in the Soviet Union and the United States in the 1950s, a development that can only be properly understood if we locate it within the context of the cold war rivalry between those countries at that time. For both superpowers, sporting competition was an extension of the political, economic and military competition associated with cold war rivalry and each saw sporting success as a means of demonstrating the claimed superiority of its own political and economic system; in this context, the military arms race between the superpowers was complemented by the so-called 'big arms' race involving the use of steroids in sports such as weightlifting. [3] We will return to the importance of the globalization of sport later.

Some historical questions about modern drug use in sport

The relationship between drugs and sport has a long history in Britain, as in many other countries. Houlihan has suggested that the death of the English cyclist Arthur Linton in the 1886 Bordeaux to Paris race may be the first recorded death of an athlete from an overdose of drugs, [4] while one of the highest-profile drugs-related deaths in sport was that of the English cyclist Tommy Simpson, who collapsed and died during the 1967 Tour de France.

The death of Simpson came during a period of, and gave further impetus to, growing concern about the use of drugs in sport. This concern gave rise to the first anti-doping regulations in the 1960s. In Britain, the

British Cycling Federation carried out drug tests at the 1965 Milk Race and by 1967 it had introduced a set of anti-doping regulations for cycling. At the international level, the International Olympic Committee (IOC) introduced the first Olympic drug tests at the winter games in Grenoble in 1968. [5]

The fact that anti-doping regulations were only introduced in the 1960s serves as a useful reminder of an important but neglected fact about drug use in sport, namely that our current attitudes towards the use of drugs are very recent in origin. In this regard, it is useful to remind ourselves of two key points about the history of drug use: (1) the use of performance-enhancing substances within the sporting context is not new but is a long-standing phenomenon that can be traced back through sports such as cycling in the late nineteenth century to the knights in mediaeval jousts and even as far back as the games of ancient Greece and Rome; [6] and (2) it is only very recently – specifically since the 1960s, when anti-doping regulations were introduced – that the use of drugs has come to be seen as a problem.

It is therefore important to note that performance-enhancing drugs have been used by people involved in sport and sport-like competitions for some 2,000 years, but it is only very recently – specifically since the 1960s – that this practice has been regarded as unacceptable. In other words, for all but the last four decades, those involved in sports, both in Britain and elsewhere, have used performance-enhancing drugs without infringing any rules and without the practice giving rise to condemnation or punishment. A recognition of this fundamental point throws up a series of important questions. How can we explain the development of this specifically modern approach to drug use in sport? In this context we need to ask not just 'Why are performance-enhancing drugs banned?' but, no less importantly, 'Why was their use *not* banned until relatively recently?' How did this process come about? What is it about the structure of specifically modern sport, and of the wider society of which sport is a part, that has been associated with the development of anti-doping policies in sport? It is not appropriate to examine these problems in detail here, for the primary focus is on other issues; these are however important questions to which I have sought to provide the beginnings of an explanation elsewhere. [7] But having raised these issues, let us turn to the central concern of this paper, namely the development of drug use in British sport.

Doping in British sport: some methodological problems

There seems to be general agreement that the modern era of drug use in sport in Britain, as elsewhere, can be traced to the post-war period and, more particularly, to the period from the 1960s. As Houlihan has noted, the 'first sign that the use of drugs to enhance sporting performance was systematic and regular rather than exceptional emerged in the 1960s'. [8] Verroken has similarly pointed to the growing use of amphetamines by athletes in the 1940s and 1950s and has suggested that the use of drugs in sport had become widespread by the 1960s. [9] Donohoe and Johnson have also pointed to the significance of the development of amphetamine-like stimulants in the 1930s, and they suggest that in recent times 'a massive acceleration in the incidence of doping in sport has occurred'. [10] There is, then, substantial agreement that the use of performance-enhancing drugs in sport was established by the 1960s. But is it possible, in relation to British sport, to describe more accurately this 'massive acceleration' in the use of drugs in recent times?

As Yesalis *et al.* have pointed out, there are numerous difficulties involved in trying to arrive at a precise estimate of the extent of illicit drug use in sport. [11] They note that there are four major sources of information about the prevalence of drug use among athletes: investigative journalism, including the writings and testimonials of athletes and others involved in sport; government investigations; surveys; and results from drug testing. However, all four sources suffer from significant methodological problems. Yesalis *et al.* suggest, for example, that those who have used drugs and who serve as informants 'may project their own behaviour onto others in an attempt to rationalize their drug use – as they may say, "Everybody does it"' and that, as a consequence, an overestimate of the level of drug use may result. [12] However, they argue – almost certainly correctly – that most of the methodological difficulties are more likely to lead to an underestimate of the level of drug use. In particular, they argue that

> the responses of athletes to the questions of journalists, drug use surveys, or even government investigations may be influenced by the athlete's desire to respond to questions in a socially desirable manner, memory lapse, the illegal nature of the substances being surveyed, and a general distrust of those doing the questioning.

They also note that drug testing 'is hamstrung by significant limitations in technology' and conclude that 'All these limitations would likely result in a significant under-reporting bias'. [13]

There are, then, real difficulties in trying to arrive at a precise estimate of the changing prevalence of drug use in British sport. This does not however mean that we should simply abandon the attempt to estimate past or current patterns of prevalence. There are two key points in this regard. Firstly, problems involved in estimating levels of drug use by athletes are by no means unique; indeed, social scientists not infrequently have to deal with very similar problems. For example, it is difficult to obtain accurate information about a whole range of social activities, particularly those which are illegal or which normally incur other sanctions. To cite two examples which are not unrelated to the subject of this paper, it is difficult to obtain accurate data on the extent of illegal drug use within the wider society while, within the sporting context, it is extremely difficult to obtain reliable data on the extent of child abuse and sex abuse within sport. [14] Nobody, however, suggests that we should not seek to estimate, as accurately as we can, the size of such problems; indeed, those responsible for anti-drugs policies and child protection policies would be failing in their duties if they abandoned any attempt to estimate the size of these problems. The same is true of those who have the responsibility for developing and implementing anti-doping policy in sport. The key issue in this regard can be simply put: if we do not know the size of the problem and we do not seek to monitor whether the problem is increasing or decreasing, then how can we know whether current policies are working? In this regard, it might be argued that a critical weakness of anti-doping policies in Britain (and within the IOC) has been the failure even to try to monitor properly – and also the failure, for public relations purposes, to admit publicly – the prevalence of doping within sport. It is therefore imperative that, while recognizing the difficulties involved, we seek to estimate, as accurately as we can, the prevalence of drug use in sport.

The second point is that while each of the sources of information on drug use in sport raises particular methodological difficulties, the fact that we are not dependent on a single source but that we have several different sources of information gives us a triangulation of sources which helps to increase the validity of our conclusions. As Goode has noted in relation to the problems of estimating the extent of drug use more generally in American society:

> As a general rule, the greater the number of *independent* sources of information that reach the same conclusion, the more confidence we can have in that conclusion. That is what we mean by triangulation: getting a factual fix on reality by using several separate and disparate sources of information. To the extent that several independent data sources say the same thing, we can say that their conclusions are more likely to be true or valid. [15]

What, then, are the key sources of information on doping within British sport? Firstly, there is a good deal of evidence from investigative journalism, including the writing of athletes and ex-athletes and others involved in elite sport within Britain. Secondly, the Amateur Athletic Association (AAA) appointed in 1987 a committee of inquiry to investigate allegations of drug use in British athletics. The inquiry reported in 1988, but it is important to note that this was not a government inquiry and that it did not have the wide-ranging powers of the Black Inquiry, established in 1988 by an Australian Senate standing committee to investigate doping in Australian sport, or the Dubin Commission of Inquiry, established in Canada following the positive drug test on Ben Johnson at the 1988 Olympic Games. Unlike these inquiries, the Coni Inquiry in England was not acting in a quasi-judicial capacity and was unable to give to witnesses any guarantee that their evidence would be treated confidentially in the event of any subsequent legal proceedings arising from their evidence. These limitations almost certainly had a serious impact on the number (and probably also the type) of witnesses who were prepared to give evidence and, probably largely because of this, the committee's report was by no means as penetrating as those of Senator Black or Commissioner Dubin. Notwithstanding these limitations, however, the report did provide some useful data.

Thirdly, there have been several surveys of athletes and others involved in sport-like situations (e.g. bodybuilders in gyms) which have been designed to elicit information about athletes' use of drugs and their attitudes towards drug use and anti-doping policies. These studies have been variously carried out by academics, by those working with drug users in the community and by the Sports Council, while major surveys have also been carried out by newspapers as part of journalistic investigations into drug use in sport.

Fourthly, there are data from the drug testing programme carried out in Britain by the anti-doping directorate of UK Sport. These are often cited by sports administrators as evidence of low levels of drug use in sport. However, as will be explained later, data from positive test results are of so little value as to be almost worthless as an indication of the prevalence of drug use in sport. Some of the problems with data from the drug testing programme are examined in detail towards the end of this paper.

Finally, while it is important to reiterate the difficulties of estimating the prevalence of drug use in sport, it is equally important not to use such difficulties as an excuse for abandoning the effort. We have to work with the data sources that are available, whatever their limitations, and the best guard against the cavalier use of those data is constantly to remind ourselves of the methodological problems involved. With this cautionary note, let us examine the data relating to drug use in British sport.

Drug use in British sport

In December 1987, *The Times* newspaper published a three-part investigation into doping in British sport. It concluded there was 'no evidence to suggest that the majority of British athletes, the club competitors, take drugs' but that, despite the claims of the British Amateur Athletic Board to the contrary, 'there is little doubt that many British internationals do take them'; this, *The Times* claimed, was confirmed by 'athletes with whom we spoke, by coaches who advise them, and by doctors who both monitor and supply them'.

The Times characterized the history of drug taking among British athletes during the previous fifteen years as involving three processes: 'the spread from the throwing events to all the track and field disciplines; the spread from international down towards club level and the involvement of youngsters; and official connivance to cheat the testing system'. [16] The allegations of connivance as they related to British athletics officials will be examined later; for the moment, let us focus on the developing pattern of drug use among British athletes in the late 1970s and 1980s.

The Times noted that when Barry Williams, a British international hammer thrower, admitted in 1976 that he had used anabolic steroids, it was widely assumed that their use was restricted to athletes in the heavy throwing events – the shot, discus and hammer. However, it went on to say that 'the spread into the other power events, the sprints, hurdles and jumps, had already begun. In the 1980s, with increasingly sophisticated products, the athlete using drugs is as likely to be a long jumper as a hammer-thrower and even the once sacrosanct middle- and long-distance events are not immune'.

Among the athletes with whom *The Times* spoke was Dave Abrahams, a former United Kingdom indoor record-holder in the high jump. Abrahams described the journey home following the 1982 Commonwealth Games in Brisbane, Australia: 'On the plane back, most of the English team were talking about drugs. I'd say 80 per cent of them were, or had been on them.' John Docherty, a former Scottish international 400-metre hurdler who at the time lived in the south of England, said that drug taking was already spreading down from the elite level to Southern League athletics, which *The Times* described as 'the equivalent of non-League football'. [17]

Following *The Times* investigation, the Amateur Athletic Association established a committee of enquiry chaired by Peter Coni, a barrister and prominent figure in rowing. The committee was asked to investigate 'allegations of drug abuse within British athletics' and, in its report, the Coni Inquiry confirmed that there was indeed widespread use of drugs in at least some sports within Britain. Coni noted:

> It is a matter of common knowledge that the use of drugs to aid sports performance surfaced in sports other than athletics in the late 1940s and early 1950s, notably with the use of anabolic steroids in weightlifting. We are in no doubt that by the later 1950s, the use of at least anabolic steroids had spread into athletics. . . . By the mid-1960s, there were few countries in which a number of the top athletes in a range of events were not experimenting with drugs; and Great Britain was no exception. [18]

The report continued:

> The evidence we have heard leaves us in no doubt . . . that by the later 1960s, anabolic steroids were being used by an appreciable number of the more successful power event athletes in this country. We have heard nothing to suggest that the banning of the use of certain drugs by the IAAF in 1974 caused any substantial reduction in this use. . . . The institution of a testing programme at certain levels of competition in 1977 led to a temporary check in the progress and extent of drug use, but not to any major reversal of the practice . . . as it became clear both that the claims that had been made as to the possibility of detection had been grossly overstated, and that the testing systems initially introduced were far less rigid than they ought to have been, the fear of detection receded and the use of drugs continued and even increased. [19]

It is clear that, by this time, there was already developing in at least some sports within Britain a culture that was shared by some athletes and coaches and which involved not only an acceptance of doping but also a significant degree of organization to obtain drugs and avoid detection. Coni described overseas training camps involving British athletes in which athletes 'sat down with their coach to work through the coming competitive season, dividing up between them the events at which testing might occur so that each would have "come off" drugs for only the minimum period to evade the risk of detection if called for testing'. Clearly there was already a substantial demand for, and use of, performance-enhancing drugs by British athletes; a particularly striking revelation by Coni related to a training camp in Portugal in the early 1980s at which the local chemists' shops 'ran out of anabolic steroids because of the purchases by British athletes'. Coni was also provided with evidence of American athletes who, after competing in Europe, stopped over in Britain 'to sell off at a profit anabolic steroids they had been able readily to buy on the continent before returning home'; [20] such an arrangement not only points to the development of an international network of relationships through which athletes obtained drugs, but the fact that it was worthwhile for the Americans to stop off in Britain also suggests that the trade in drugs must by that time already have been substantial.

The Coni Report also accepted another key claim made in *The Times* articles: that there were doctors in Britain who were involved in 'monitoring athletes on a regular basis in circumstances which can only be construed as checking the effect upon those athletes of the drugs they have been taking to aid their performances'. [21] Coni concluded:

> We have evidence of a few doctors prepared to prescribe banned drugs to athletes. . . . Medical support arises more often, though, on the basis of the doctor who says that, whilst he would never advocate the taking of drugs for the sake of athletic achievement, it is his responsibility if an athlete has made that decision for himself to monitor the athlete's health to ensure so far as the doctor can that he does so without physical harm. Since availability of banned drugs presents few problems, the end result from the standpoint of drug use by athletes – that medical advice is available for those who care to look for it – is of course the same, whether the doctor is prescribing, or simply monitoring the effects. We are also told that test centres are readily to hand at which a British athlete who has been using banned drugs in training can check in advance of competition that his urine sample will no longer disclose the presence of the banned drug. We are told that such centres are available in London, in Birmingham and in Edinburgh, and no doubt there are others. [22]

If we consider both the evidence of *The Times* and of the Coni Inquiry it is clear that, by the 1980s, there was already developing within British sport a 'doping network', consisting of networks of relationships between athletes, coaches, doctors and – as we shall see later – some sports administrators, who were involved in supplying, using, monitoring and concealing (or at least 'turning a blind eye' to) the use of drugs. Of course British sport was not, and is not, unique in this respect. In the same year that the Coni Report was published in Britain, Ben Johnson tested positive at the Seoul Olympics and, following Johnson's disqualification, the Dubin Commission of Inquiry was appointed in Canada to examine 'the use of banned practices intended to increase athletic performance'.

The commission, which had much greater legal powers than did the Coni Inquiry in Britain and which also received a great deal more evidence, produced a biting and incisive analysis of the social organization of these 'doping networks' in Canadian sprinting, weightlifting and other sports. More recently, the 'doping network' in professional cycling, involving not just the cyclists themselves, but also team managers, masseurs, doctors and others, was laid bare during the doping scandal in the 1998 Tour de France. [23]

In many respects, the findings of the Coni Inquiry are broadly consistent with the allegations made by *The Times*. However, there was one important difference. This related to the fact that, although Coni confirmed that the use of drugs had been widespread in some sports, it differed from *The Times* in claiming that the period from 1976 to 1982 was the 'high point' of drug use by British athletes and that 'since perhaps 1983 the level of drug abuse in British athletics has reduced'. [24]

The report stated: 'we do not think we are being over-optimistic in concluding that British athletics is at present enjoying a noticeable recession in the level of drug use'. [25] It claimed that this conclusion was based on 'an overwhelming burden of evidence' which it had received, though significantly none of this evidence was cited in the report. The report did, however, offer what it called two 'very plain' reasons for this claimed reduction in drug use. The first of these related to the out-of-competition testing which had been introduced by the British Amateur Athletics Board in 1986 and which, Coni claimed, had been a deterrent to the use of drugs by significantly increasing the possibility of detection. This argument is entirely unconvincing for, whatever the advantages of out-of-competition testing compared with testing in competition, it is difficult to see how a testing system which was not introduced until 1986 could have produced a reduction in drug use from 1983!

The second 'explanation' for the assumed decrease in the use of drugs after 1983 is hardly more convincing. The report argued that 'there is an increasing disapproval amongst the athletes themselves of the way that drug use in athletics has spread and, still more importantly, of the forms that it is now taking'. [26] The reference to 'the forms that it is now taking' related to concerns about the side effects associated with the use of some drugs. Again, however, the evidence on which this claim is based is extremely tenuous. Firstly, although the committee interviewed a total of twenty people involved with athletics, just four of these were athletes, which is hardly a secure basis for such a sweeping generalization about the views of British athletes. Secondly, it is extremely unlikely that athletes who were using drugs, and who might therefore have taken a contrary viewpoint, would have been prepared voluntarily to provide evidence to a committee which had no power to subpoena witnesses and no power to protect them against further legal action resulting from any evidence which they might have provided to the committee; indeed athletes who were competing at the time and who admitted to drug use would have been inviting disciplinary action against themselves.

Thirdly, and perhaps most importantly, the committee provided no direct evidence to support its claim that athletes were increasingly opposed to the use of drugs; rather it appears to have *assumed* that athletes' attitudes towards drugs would have been decisively shaped by evidence of the side effects associated with some drugs. As the report put it,

> we are in no doubt that even the most cynical and determined achiever in athletics, prepared to consider going to any lengths to attain world and world record status, is obliged to accept that there are now good reasons to fear serious adverse side effects from at least some of the forms of drug abuse that are currently in use in athletics internationally. [27]

In assuming that the claimed side effects of some drugs would be a decisive factor in deterring most athletes from using drugs, the Coni Inquiry was revealing – not, as we shall see, for the only time in the report – its naivety and, in particular, how little it understood about the motivation and commitment to winning of many elite athletes; perhaps significantly, the report made no reference to the evidence provided to a US Senate committee in 1973 by Harold Connolly, the 1956 Olympic hammer-throw champion, in which he said that the majority of athletes 'would do anything, and take anything, short of killing themselves' to improve athletic performance. [28] Nor did they refer to Mirkin's study [29] of over a hundred competitive runners, more than half of whom indicated that they would take a 'magic pill' that guaranteed them an Olympic gold medal, even if it would kill them within a year. Nor did they refer to the admission by Gideon Ariel, an American discus thrower, that if he had had to choose during his days as an Olympic thrower between an extra five inches in distance or an extra five years of life, he would have chosen the distance. [30]

There is, in fact, no evidence to support the claim that there had been a significant reduction in drug use by British athletes from the early 1980s; indeed, public statements from other experienced British athletes ran directly counter to this claim. For example, in 1986, Tessa Sanderson, Britain's gold-medal winner in the javelin in the 1984 Olympics, wrote that 'a year or two ago, a well-known former international thrower said he believed 60 per cent of the British team had at some time used drugs, specifically steroids ... from my observations I guess he would not be too far out'. [31] And shortly after the Coni Inquiry was constituted, Daley Thompson, who won the gold medal in the decathlon in both the 1980 and 1984 Olympics, estimated that among Britain's elite athletes (that is, the top ten per cent), 80 per cent were using drugs. [32]

There seems little doubt that Coni was mistaken in believing that there had been a significant reduction in the level of drug use by British athletes in the 1980s. The reasons for this erroneous conclusion are not difficult to see. As we noted earlier, the inquiry was not acting in a quasi-judicial capacity; it had no power to subpoena witnesses and no power to guarantee that their evidence would be treated confidentially in the event of any subsequent legal proceedings arising from their evidence. No doubt as a result of these considerations, very few people directly involved in sport were prepared to be interviewed by the inquiry team, which was able to interview only six coaches, ten officials and just four athletes (by comparison, the Dubin Commission in Canada heard evidence from 119 witnesses). The committee acknowledged this weakness in its evidence base in its comment that 'our refusal to accept evidence on a basis of total confidentiality has meant that few of the athletes who are currently competing have wished to come forward'. [33] This unwillingness of current athletes to give evidence about doping – unless they are compelled to – is well established; as Yesalis *et al.* have noted, testimonies on drug use 'are generally given only by former athletes, because current athletes fear possible retribution from coaches, team-mates, or sport federation officials'. [34] It may well be this that accounts for the fact that the committee's evidence relating to drug use in the earlier period of the 1970s and early 1980s is not only more revealing but also rather more secure than its evidence relating to the more recent period nearer the time of the inquiry.

In addition, it is important to emphasize that the Coni Inquiry was not a genuinely independent inquiry in the manner of the Black Inquiry in Australia or the Dubin Commission in Canada; it was an enquiry established by a body – the Amateur Athletic Association – which was itself centrally involved in administering those sports which were the focus of the allegations made by *The Times*. Moreover, two of the three members of the inquiry team were also centrally involved in sports administration. The chairman was not only a barrister but also a prominent figure in rowing and had been chairman of the organizing committee of the 1986 World Rowing Championships, while a second member of the inquiry team had been a leading track and field official and a vice-president of the AAA and was at the time the treasurer of the Midland Counties AAA.

These points are important because, in many respects, the Coni Inquiry responded to *The Times* allegations of doping in the way in which sports federations normally respond to such allegations. As Yesalis *et al.* have noted, sports federation officials, when faced with such allegations, 'have often tended to deny that a major doping problem exists … or have at least played down its magnitude', and they add that 'When pushed, sport officials have stated "we've had problems in the past, but now things are different"'. [35] The Coni Report fits exactly into this pattern.

Notwithstanding these problems, the Coni Report and *The Times* investigation, taken together, do provide useful data about the use of drugs in British sport up to the late 1980s. What evidence is there relating to the use of drugs in more recent years?

As noted earlier, there has been no systematic attempt by any national sporting body to monitor the extent of doping in British sport. For an understanding of doping in the 1990s, we are therefore dependent once again on occasional studies and reports by investigative journalists. However, these investigations in the 1990s did not use similar methods, nor ask the same questions, as earlier ones and therefore the data are not directly comparable. It is important to bear these methodological problems in mind when considering the data below.

In 1995, the Sports Council carried out a survey of the experiences and views of British elite athletes concerning doping control in the United Kingdom. Of the 448 British Olympic athletes who took part in the survey, 48 per cent felt that drug use was a problem in international competition in their sport, and in track and field the figure was as high as 86 per cent. It is also clear that these elite British athletes did not feel that the problem was being effectively tackled by the existing system of doping controls; 23 per cent of athletes felt drug use had increased over the previous twelve months, while only 6 per cent felt that it had decreased. [36] It is important to emphasize that these data do not relate to their own use of drugs or to the use of drugs by their fellow British athletes, but to their perception of the extent of drug use in their own sport in international competition. Such perceptions are nevertheless of some value.

In the first place, they are consistent with the views of other influential 'insiders' such as Anthony Millar, research director at the Institute of Sports Medicine in Sydney, Australia, who in 1996 wrote of an 'epidemic of drug usage' in international sport and suggested that the use of drugs was 'widespread and growing'. [37] (Miller also argued that drug use was growing among recreational athletes, thus echoing similar views expressed in 1988 by Professor Arnold Beckett of the drugs-testing centre at King's College, London, and in 1989 by Sir Arthur Gold, the chairman of the British Olympic Committee.) [38]

Secondly, although these data do not provide information about the extent of drug use by British athletes, they do provide important information about British athletes' perceptions of the changing character of international competition. We noted at the beginning of this paper that it is not possible to understand drug use within a particular country without taking into account the international context and, in this regard, it is important to note that one of the constraints on athletes to use drugs is the knowledge (or belief) that their competitors are using drugs. Thus although this study did not provide any direct evidence about the extent of drug use by British athletes, it does suggest that, in so far as drug use was becoming still more common in international competition, then the constraints on all international athletes, including British athletes, similarly to use drugs, would also have been increasing; at the very least, one could say that an increase in the use of drugs in international competition would not provide conditions conducive to a reduction in their use among elite athletes in Britain (or, indeed, in any other major sporting nation).

Three years after the Sports Council survey, the *Independent* newspaper, in December 1998, published a week-long investigation into drug use in sport. The *Independent* sent out questionnaires to over 1,300 British elite sportsmen and sportswomen, of whom over 300 replied. The questionnaire, which was anonymous, included questions about the use of drugs by the respondent and by other British athletes in the respondent's sport. The results reflect the views of elite competitors in nine sports: athletics and swimming (leading lottery-funded competitors from both sports), cricket (first-class county players), football (Premier and Nationwide Leagues), horse racing (leading jockeys), rugby league (Super League players), rugby union (Premiership One teams), tennis (all Britons in top world 100), and weightlifting (international level). In cycling and rowing, the governing bodies declined the invitation to take part and in boxing and snooker the response rates fell below ten per cent and the results were not included.

The summary results were as follows. Across all sports, 54 per cent believed that up to 30 per cent of competitors in their sport were using performance-enhancing drugs; 5 per cent believed that between 30 and 60 per cent were doing so and 4 per cent believed that over 60 per cent of competitors were using drugs. Not surprisingly, there were substantial variations between sports. Not a single respondent from weightlifting (including powerlifting) or rugby league believed their sport was 'clean' and only 3 per cent of athletes did so. Among elite swimmers, 65 per cent believed that the use of performance-enhancing drugs was 'widespread' in their sport. In some sports, many competitors admitted using drugs. In weightlifting and powerlifting, for example, 20 per cent of respondents admitted using anabolic agents, 10 per cent admitted using testosterone, 10 per cent admitted using narcotic analgesics, 10 per cent admitted using stimulants such as ephedrine or amphetamines, 10 per cent admitted using diuretics, while 40 per cent admitted caffeine loading. In rugby league, 46 per cent of respondents indicated that they had been offered drugs by other players or professional dealers and, in relation to their own drug use, 31 per cent admitted using caffeine loaders, 15 per cent admitted using testosterone, 15 per cent admitted using stimulants, 8 per cent admitted using narcotic analgesics and 8 per cent admitted using diuretics. In horse racing, 35 per cent of jockeys admitted using diuretics, 30 per cent admitted caffeine loading, 10 per cent admitted using narcotic analgesics and 5 per cent admitted using stimulants. [39]

Although considerable numbers of respondents did admit using performance-enhancing drugs it is fairly safe to assume that these data understate – possibly substantially – the real level of drug use in British sport for, even in an anonymous survey, some of those using performance-enhancing drugs would have been reluctant to have admitted to their use. To take just one example, there is reason to believe that in the two forms of rugby the level of drug use may well be considerably higher than that admitted by players.

As we noted above, a substantial percentage of rugby league players admitted that they had used performance-enhancing drugs and the *Independent* claimed, with some justification, that the results of its survey indicated that there was 'widespread' use of drugs in rugby. The paper also quoted the former Welsh international J.P.R. Williams as saying that drug use was also 'fairly rife' in rugby union. [40] However it is striking that, although many players admitted using drugs, only 4 per cent of rugby union players and no rugby league players admitted using anabolic steroids. This should not, however, be taken as an indication that steroid use is rare in the two forms of rugby, for there are grounds for suspecting that the use of anabolic steroids in rugby may be much more common that the results of the *Independent* survey suggested.

Firstly, it might be noted that anabolic steroids are, in terms of performance enhancement, the obvious drugs of choice for rugby players because of their effectiveness in building bulk and power. This does not of course mean that they will necessarily be used by rugby players. However, it is difficult to see why players who do use performance-enhancing drugs – as many rugby players admitted to doing in the *Independent* survey – would eschew the use of precisely those drugs (that is, anabolic steroids) that offer the most obvious advantages in terms of performance enhancement. But, secondly, there is also direct evidence to suggest that the use of steroids is common in both rugby union and rugby league.

Three years before the *Independent* investigation, a BBC radio documentary claimed that the use of anabolic steroids was widespread among rugby union players in Wales and their counterparts in English rugby league. The programme claimed that at least 150 players in rugby union and league were taking anabolic steroids, while the director of the Drugs and Sport Information Service in Liverpool said that his organization had dealt with 30 to 40 players from the two rugby codes, some of whom were internationals. [41] One year after the *Independent* investigation, the *Observer* drew attention once again to the extent of doping in rugby union and claimed that the use of steroids was 'commonplace'. It claimed that the use of steroids began to become increasingly widespread from the early 1990s and cited a former international player as saying that rugby was 'awash with drugs' and that the use of steroids had been associated with 'incredible changes in players' size, shape and bulk in recent years'. [42]

How can we account for the conflicting results of, on the one hand, the *Independent* survey and, on the other, the claims of other investigative journalists working for the BBC and the *Observer*? Given the absence of more reliable data, it is not possible to provide a definitive answer to this problem, though it is probable that the *Independent* survey substantially underestimated the use of anabolic steroids in rugby. In this regard, we might note that there are several reasons why sportspeople who might be prepared to admit to the use of some drugs might be particularly reluctant to admit to the use of steroids. Anabolic steroids are widely seen as both the most effective but also the most dangerous performance-enhancing drugs in use in those sports requiring power and strength. There is also in public opinion a commonly held association between steroid use and uncontrollable outbursts of anger (so-called 'roid rage') with associated connotations of violent, dangerous, anti-social and even criminal behaviour and, because of this, those who use steroids are often stigmatized, or even 'demonized'. [43] Perhaps for a combination of these reasons, the use of anabolic steroids in sport has normally attracted the most severe sanctions and it may be the severity of these sanctions, together with the associated negative public stereotyping of steroid users, which accounts for what may be the reluctance on the part of rugby players to admit to the use of steroids.

It has also become increasingly clear that the use of steroids is not confined to elite sport. Perry *et al.* noted that anabolic steroid use 'is commonly perceived to be the domain of the higher echelons of competitive athletes', but they point out that 'a great deal of anabolic steroid use occurs in ... gymnasia ... among non-competitive recreational athletes'. [44] It is interesting to note that data relating to drug use among recreational and non-competitive athletes are more plentiful than is information about doping among elite athletes; these data also make it clear that the use of performance-enhancing drugs is widespread and increasing at the level of recreational and non-competitive sport.

In 1992, a study among gym users in West Glamorgan found that 38.8 per cent admitted having used steroids. The authors concluded: 'To anyone who attends gymnasia on a regular basis, it is not too difficult to see that the prevalence of anabolic steroid abuse has increased in the past two decades, but especially in the last five to ten years'. [45] Four years later, a study of 1,105 users of 43 gymnasia in the north-west of England found that in 'hardcore' gyms (gyms having predominantly heavy weight training equipment, competitive bodybuilders and relatively few female members), over 29 per cent of gym users were currently using anabolic steroids and over half had at some time used them; even among users of 'fitness' gyms (characterized by light free weights, a large number of female members and an emphasis on cardiovascular training) 15 per cent admitted to having used steroids. [46] Writing in 1996, Lenehan *et al.* noted that in the north-west of England, anabolic steroids (AS) 'have been easily available since the mid-1980s. Liverpool has seen a remarkable increase in the number of AS users accessing needle exchange services over the last five years'. [47] In the following year, Bellis reported that whereas 87 users of anabolic steroids were recorded as having used the needle exchange scheme on Merseyside in 1991, by 1995 the number had increased to 546. [48] In 1993, Charles Walker, head of the sports section of the Council of Europe, estimated that in a city the size of London there will be at least 30,000 and probably as many as 60,000 regular users of anabolic steroids. [49]

What conclusions, then, can be drawn about the prevalence of drug use in British sport? Although the data are too fragmented and characterized by too many methodological problems to allow us to estimate very precisely the extent of drug use, it is nevertheless possible to point to some general trends with a fair degree of confidence. In particular it is clear that there has been a substantial increase in the illicit use of performance-enhancing drugs by British athletes since the early 1960s; that their use has spread from relatively few sports to many sports; that the prevalence of drug use varies from one sport to another but that in some sports drug use has increased to the point that it is now widespread; and that the use of performance-enhancing drugs has diffused down from elite sport and is now widespread in recreational and non-competitive sport.

However, if the above analysis is correct, it raises a major question: why has the widespread use of drugs in at least some sports not been reflected in large numbers of positive tests among British athletes? This raises some key questions about the value of data derived from drug testing programmes.

Data from drug testing in Britain

As Coomber has noted, bodies such as the IOC sometimes point to the relatively small numbers of athletes testing positive for banned drugs as evidence that international sport is relatively drug free. [50] Similarly, sports organizations in Britain have frequently claimed that the small number of athletes testing positive is an indication that British sport is relatively drug-free. For example a spokesman for the British Athletic Federation claimed in 1995 that test results showed that 'over 99 per cent of British athletes are not using performance-enhancing drugs'. [51] Two years later, the then director of the United Kingdom Sports Council's ethics and anti-doping directorate, in commenting on the fact that only 2 per cent of the 4,000 samples analysed in the previous year were positive, said: 'It is a great testament to the integrity of our competitors that 98 per cent tested negative'. However, such claims are spurious, as *The Guardian* argued in a pointed editorial in 1998. It wrote:

> Any reader of yesterday's annual report from the UK Sports Council could be forgiven for believing that Britain enjoys a Rolls-Royce drug prevention programme. ... It describes in detail the work of its anti-drugs directorate. ... It refers to its computerized records ... its systematic reports to the governing bodies of the various sports, and its internationally accredited laboratory setting new performance-standards for analysis, secure reporting, and the provision of expert evidence. Is it any surprise, with such a superb system, that there were only seventy-nine cases last year in which prohibited substances were found or athletes refused to provide a sample? Anyone who believes this is the extent of Britain's problems with drugs in sport ... is living in as unreal a world as elite Japanese Sumo wrestlers. To have produced such a complacent report in a year in which the sports world has once again been wracked by drugs scandal ... suggests the worst aspects of amateurism still permeate British sports administration. [52]

Despite the claims of organizations such as the IOC and, within Britain, the Sports Council (now UK Sport), there is among informed analysts a growing recognition that positive test results are an extremely poor – indeed, almost worthless – indication of the extent of drug use in sport, for it is widely acknowledged that those who provide positive tests simply represent the tip of a large iceberg. The most spectacular indication of the inadequacy of using positive test results as an indication of the extent of doping was provided by the 1998 Tour de France, during which the actions of the French police and customs clearly established that drug use among professional cyclists was widespread, systematic and organized. However, despite routine drug tests at the end of each stage of the Tour, *not a single rider was excluded from the Tour as a result of failing a doping control carried out by the Tour organizers*; all the riders who tested positive did so as a result of tests which were conducted following the police action, rather than as a result of tests which were carried out as part of the Tour itself. [53]

The inadequacy of using positive tests as an indication of doping prevalence has been noted by many writers. Within the American context, Yesalis *et al.* have noted that, during the last ten years, 'less than 3 per cent of Olympic and National Football League athletes who were tested were shown to be positive for banned substances. These results appear to be at great odds with most of the conclusions of investigations conducted by journalists and the government organizations.' [54] In Canada, the Dubin Commission concluded that 'many, many more athletes than those actually testing positive have taken advantage of banned substances and practices' and that 'positive test results represent only a small proportion of actual drug users'. [55] And as we have seen, the Coni Inquiry accepted that there was widespread use of drugs by British athletes in some events but, despite this fact, British athletes have never tested positive in large numbers.

If the use of drugs by British athletes is as widespread as much of the evidence suggests, then why do so few athletes provide positive test results? There are many reasons for this. As Yesalis *et al.* have noted, there are some performance-enhancing substances for which reliable tests are not yet available; [56] it has been relatively easy to avoid testing positive in competition testing (where most testing has taken place) for, as Sir Arthur Gold observed, the only people who get caught in testing at major competitions are 'the careless or the ill-advised'; [57] and, when faced with unannounced, out-of-competition testing, there are a number of strategies to successfully circumvent the testing process. [58] In addition, a good many informed observers, including reputable sports journalists,

[59] senior sports physicians who have held major positions of responsibility [60] and elite level athletes [61] have all argued that senior sports administrators often collude with drug-using athletes to beat the testing system, while it is also clear that drug-using athletes are often able to beat the system by virtue of their access to expert advice from team doctors or other sports physicians. [62] British sport has not been free of such allegations.

In addition to investigating allegations of drug use by British athletes, the Coni Inquiry was also asked to 'investigate allegations made by *The Times* newspaper against certain officials in athletics and against the sport in general'. [63] *The Times* alleged that British officials had colluded with athletes and with officials of foreign teams to beat the doping control system. Among these allegations were claims that a senior official of the British Amateur Athletic Board (BAAB) had acceded to a demand by East German officials that their athletes would not be tested at a meeting between East Germany and Britain in London in 1982 and that a similar deal had been struck with a United States team in 1983. [64]

The Coni Inquiry examined these specific allegations within the context of the general development of drug testing in Britain. Coni accepted that 'it is painfully evident now that the detailed regulations for testing and the way that they were put into effect by both BAAB and AAA were at best naive'. [65] However, other statements by Coni make it clear that what was involved was not merely naivety but deliberate collusion by British officials to beat the testing system. For example Coni noted that

> once the choice of event and position for testing has been made, that information must be kept secret from the athletes competing until the competition is taking place and the athlete will have no opportunity to avoid finishing in the position that will lead to testing. We had evidence, not only from athletes but from a dope control steward, that in the early years, this secrecy from time to time was broken. There are many stories of dope control stewards telling athletes in advance of competition that their event was providing a test that day; and in cases where current form made the probable finishing order obvious, telling a specific athlete that he or she had been chosen for testing. . . . We have also heard of draws for testing which were far from random, including the practice of omitting a specific event from the draw to protect a leading British athlete from the risk of testing. [66]

With regard to *The Times's* allegations, Coni concluded that the claim that there had been an agreement not to test members of the American team was untrue, but it did accept that the secretary of the BAAB had agreed to a demand from the East Germans that, in the match between Great Britain and the GDR, East German athletes would not be tested. However, in a paragraph which many would regard as remarkable for its naivety – there were at the time many allegations of systematic doping by East Germany, allegations that were shown to be true following the collapse of the Communist regime in East Germany – Coni took the view that this was not evidence of collusion between British and East German officials to undermine the testing system, but that it was due to administrative difficulties. Coni wrote: 'It is easy for the cynic to assume that the GDR stance was taken because they were afraid of positive results if some of their athletes were to be tested' but, he suggested, it would be entirely wrong to assume that this was so. The refusal of the GDR representatives to agree to testing was, Coni said, something which 'we do not find either surprising or in the least sinister'. [67] However, shortly before the Coni Inquiry was established, the then Minister for Sport, Colin Moynihan, who was conducting his own inquiry into drug taking in sport, told *The Times* that some British governing bodies had 'made deals' to ensure that certain competitors would not be tested for drugs at important events. He said this had happened 'regularly'. Asked whether he had any concrete evidence of malpractice, Moynihan said: 'We took a considerable amount of evidence in confidence. There is no doubt at all that the answer is "yes".' [68]

Several years later, the *Sunday Times* revealed that Dr Jimmy Ledingham, who was a doctor to the British Olympic men's team between 1979 and 1987, had provided steroids to British athletes, monitored the effect of the drugs on the athletes and provided advice about how to avoid testing positive. It also claimed that Frank Dick, Britain's national director of coaching from 1979 until 1994, had 'turned a blind eye' to athletes who told him they were using steroids; according to the *Sunday Times*, Dick took a pragmatic view that 'positive drug tests on British athletes had to be avoided'. [69] Despite the seriousness of these allegations, the British Athletic Federation (BAF, which had been formed in 1988 as the new umbrella organization for British track and field) declined to hold an inquiry. The BAF's spokesman refused to comment on the allegations and said that the BAF was 'disappointed so much space is given to allegations that are not relevant to what is happening today', with the clear implication that it did not want to know about wrongdoing in the past. [70]

Conclusion

Although it is not possible to arrive at a precise estimate of the extent of drug use in British sport, the data do suggest that since the 1960s there has been a substantial increase in the use of performance-enhancing drugs by

British athletes. It is clear that, in athletics, the use of drugs has spread from the heavy throwing events to many other track and field events, and that it has spread from athletics and weightlifting – the sports in which drugs were most frequently used in the 1960s – to many other sports. It is also clear that the use of performance-enhancing drugs has spread down from the elite to much lower levels, and that the use of anabolic steroids is widespread among non-competitive recreational athletes in other sport-related contexts. In all these respects, the development of the pattern of drug use in sport in Britain appears to have been broadly similar to that in most other Western liberal democracies and to the development of the pattern of drug use in international sport more generally. [71]

It is also clear that, on occasions, the administration of British sport has been characterized by what Hoberman has called 'sportive nationalism', [72] which has involved at least some officials and doctors in collaborating with athletes to beat the drug-testing system. Moreover it might be argued that, even today, structural problems remain within the administration of British sport which limit the effectiveness of anti-doping policies. In this regard, many governing bodies within British sport – and indeed, to some degree, the British government itself – would appear to have a continuing conflict of interest. This was one of the conclusions of a report on doping in sport, published by the British Medical Association in 2002. That report noted that successive British governments have in recent years adopted a high-performance sports strategy aimed at achieving international sporting success and it added that for much of that time, 'it has not appeared that drug-free sport was central to the government's high-performance sports strategy'. The report concluded:

> The overriding impression of anti-doping efforts in the UK has been that government enthusiasm has been intermittent and that many organizations have a conflict of interest. The major governing bodies are in the position of seeking to maximize international success while at the same time rigorously enforcing an anti-doping policy which is certainly perceived by some as a major threat to the achievement of that success. It is certainly questionable whether governing bodies can be both gamekeeper and poacher with equal enthusiasm'. [73]

Notes

[1]   David R. Mottram, ed., *Drugs in sport*, 3rd edn (London, 2003), p. 357.

[2]   Giselher Spitzer, *Doping in der DDR* (Cologne, 2000); Giselher Spitzer, 'Sport and the systematic infliction of pain: a case study of mandatory doping in East Germany' in Sigmund Loland, Berit Skirstad and Ivan Waddington, eds., *Pain and injury in sport: ethical and social analysis* (London, 2006), pp. 109–26.

[3]   James Riordan, *Sport in Soviet society* (Cambridge, 1977); Robert Voy, *Drugs, sport and politics* (Champaign, IL 1991); Ivan Waddington, *Sport, health and drugs* (London, 2000).

[4]   Barrie Houlihan, *Dying to win: doping in sport and the development of anti-doping policy* (Strasbourg, 1999). However, it has been suggested that Linton did not die during or close to competition but that he died many years later from typhoid; see Tom Donohoe and Neil Johnson, *Foul play: drug abuse in sports* (Oxford, 1986).

[5]   Houlihan, *Dying to win*, pp. 202–3.

[6]   Michele Verroken, 'Drug use and abuse in sport', in Mottram, *Drugs in sport*, pp. 29–62; Donohoe and Johnson, *Foul play*, pp. 2–3; Houlihan, *Dying to win*, p. 33.

[7]   Waddington, *Sport, health and drugs*, pp. 96–113.

[8]   Houlihan, *Dying to win*, pp. 201–2.

[9]   Verroken, 'Drug use', p. 30.

[10]   Donohoe and Johnson, *Foul play*, pp. 2–4.

[11]   Charles E. Yesalis, III, Andrea N. Kopstein and Michael S Bahrke (2001), 'Difficulties in estimating the prevalence of drug use among athletes', in Wayne Wilson and Edward Derse, eds., *Doping in elite sport: the politics of drugs in the Olympic movement* (Champaign, IL, 2001), pp. 43–62.

[12]   Ibid., p. 45.

[13]   Ibid. p. 56.

[14]   Celia Brackenridge, *Spoilsports: Understanding and preventing sexual exploitation in sport* (London, 2001).

[15]   Erich Goode, *Between politics and reason: the drug legalization debate* (New York, 1997) p. 14 (emphasis in original).

[16]   *The Times* (London), 16 Dec. 1987.

[17]   Ibid., 16 Dec. 1987.

[18]   Peter Coni, Gilbert Kelland and Dan Davies, *AAA drug abuse enquiry report* (Amateur Athletics Association, 1988), paragraph B 5.

[19]   Ibid., paragraph B 15.

[20]   Ibid., paragraph B 16.

[21]   Ibid., paragraph B 20.

[22]   Ibid., paragraph B 21

[23]   Waddington, *Sport, health and drugs*, pp. 153–69.

[24]   Coni *et al.*, *AAA drug abuse enquiry*, paragraph B 19.

[25]   Ibid., paragraph B 27.

[26]   Ibid., paragraph B 19.

[27]   Ibid., paragraph B 19.

[28]   Jay J. Coakley, *Sport in society: issues and controversies*, 6th edn (Boston, MA, 1998), pp. 167–8.

[29]   Gabe Merkin, 'High risk gamble to obtaining winning edge' San Diego Union, 13 July 1982, Secton C, p. 1.

[30]   Terry Todd, 'Anabolic steroids: the gremlins of sport', *Journal of Sport History*, 14 (1987), pp. 87–107.

[31]   Tessa Sanderson with Leon Hickman, *Tessa: my life in athletics* (London, 1986) p. 159.

[32]   Coni *et al.*, *Drug abuse enquiry*, paragraph B 25.

[33]   Ibid., paragraph A 4
[34]   Yesalis *et al.*, 'Difficulties in estimating', p. 45.
[35]   Ibid.
[36]   Sports Council, *Doping control in the UK: a survey of the experiences and views of elite competitors*, 1995 (London, 1996), pp. 33–4.
[37]   Anthony P. Millar, 'Drugs in sport', *Journal of Performance Enhancing Drugs*, 1 (1996), pp. 106–12.
[38]   *Sunday Times*, 2 Oct. 1988; Sir Arthur Gold, interview in *Athletics Today*, 3 (52) (28 Dec. 1989), pp. 10–11.
[39]   *The Independent*, 9 Dec. 1998.
[40]   Ibid., 10 Dec. 1998.
[41]   *The Guardian*, 4 Sept. 1995.
[42]   *The Observer*, 24 Oct. 1999.
[43]   Lee F. Monaghan, *Bodybuilding, drugs and risk* (London, 2001).
[44]   H.M. Perry, D. Wright and B.N.C. Littlepage, 'Dying to be big: a review of anabolic steroid use', *British Journal of Sports Medicine*, 26 (1992), pp. 259–61.
[45]   Ibid., pp. 259–60.
[46]   Pat Lenehan, Mark Bellis and Jim McVeigh, 'A study of anabolic steroid use in the north west of England', *Journal of Performance Enhancing Drugs*, 1 (1996), pp. 57–70.
[47]   Ibid. pp. 58–9.
[48]   Mark Bellis, 'Prevalence and patterns of anabolic steroid use', paper presented at Third Annual Conference of the Drugs and Sport Information Service, Liverpool, 2 July 1996.
[49]   Charles Walker, *Conference Proceedings: the 4th Permanent World Conference on Anti-doping in Sport*, 5–8 Sept. 1993 (London, 1994).
[50]   Ross Coomber, 'Drugs in sport: rhetoric or pragmatism', *International Journal of Drug Policy*, 4 (1993), pp. 169–78.
[51]   *The Guardian*, 30 Oct. 1995.
[52]   Ibid., 10 Oct. 1998
[53]   Waddington, *Sport, health and drugs*, p. 166.
[54]   Yesalis *et al.* 'Difficulties in estimating', p. 47.
[55]   The Right Hon. Charles L. Dubin, *Commission of inquiry into the use of drugs and banned practices intended to increase athletic performance* (Ottawa, 1990), pp. 349–50.
[56]   Yesalis *et al.* 'Difficulties in estimating', pp. 47–8.
[57]   Sir Arthur Gold, interview in *Athletics Today,* p. 10.
[58]   Yesalis *et al.*, 'Difficulties in estimating', pp. 47–8.
[59]   For example, Pat Butcher and Peter Nichols, *The Times*, 15–17 Dec. 1987.
[60]   Voy, Drugs, *sport and politics*.
[61]   Paul Kimmage, *Rough ride: behind the wheel with a pro cyclist* (London, 1998); Werner Reiterer, *Positive* (Sydney, 2000).
[62]   Waddington, *Sport, health and drugs*, pp. 135–52.
[63]   Coni *et al.*, *Drug abuse enquiry*, paragraph A 1.
[64]   *The Times*, 15 and 17 Dec. 1987.
[65]   Coni et al., Drug abuse enquiry, paragraph D 2.
[66]   Ibid., paragraphs D 4 – D 5.
[67]   Ibid., paragraph E 9.

[68] *The Times*, 17 Dec. 1987.

[69] *Sunday Times*, 29 Oct. 1995.

[70] *The Guardian*, 30 Oct. 1995.

[71] Waddington, *Sport, health and drugs*, pp. 170–5.

[72] John Hoberman, Sportive nationalism and doping, in *Proceedings from the Workshop: Research on Doping and Sport*, Norwegian University of Sport and Physical Education, Oslo, 2001, pp. 7–9.

[73] British Medical Association, *Drugs in sport: the pressure to perform* (London, 2002), p. 110.

The Legacy of Festina: Patterns of Drug Use in European Cycling Since 1998

Ask Vest Christiansen

The 1998 Tour de France scandal made it clear to everyone that doping was being systematically used within the sport of cycling. [1] The investigations by the French police revealed that an entire cycling culture – riders, coaches, doctors and officials – had secretly lived with and practised doping as part of their particular lifestyle.

Since then, a major effort has been made to clean up the sport. Cycling's governing bodies and a number of public institutions have been involved and have contributed to the intensified campaign against the use of drugs in the sport. A key event in this campaign was the establishment of the World Anti-Doping Agency (WADA) in 1999 and the signing of the

Common Code in March 2003, a document which aims to develop a unified and systematic response to the use of doping in sport in general.

The 1998 Tour de France served as a powerful catalyst in the struggle against doping, and it is significant that cycling has produced many of the most recent prominent cases, as examples from the 2004 season as well as the beginning of the 2005 season show. Thus in January 2004 it was revealed that riders from the French team Cofidis had organized a major doping network. In February of that year the doctor working for the French Cycling Association, Armand Mègret, stated that at least 30 per cent of the French riders were still using EPO. In March, the sacked Spanish Kelme rider, Jesus Manzano, told his story to the press about the systematic use of doping by the Kelme team. In June, the reigning individual world time-trial champion, David Millar, was charged with the use of EPO. In August, the Phonak rider Oscar Camenzind was accused of taking the same substance. In September, his two team-mates Tyler Hamilton and Santiago Perez tested positive for blood doping. In October the Belgian rider Johan Museeuw, a specialist in the classic races, was banned for four years for using EPO and other performance-enhancing drugs. The 2005 season opened with serious accusations against the Italian Acqua & Sapone squad; the sprinter Danilo Hondo tested positive for a stimulant; in August seven - time Tour de France Winner Lance Armstrong was accussed by French paper L'Equipe of having used EPO when he won in 1999, and in September four - time Vuelta a España winner Roberto Heras tested positive for EPO.

In the light of these events, it is not difficult to understand why cycling is perceived by many people as particularly affected by doping. This perception is not only due to the media's focus on the problem, but is also confirmed by WADA's statistics for 2003 which show cycling to be one of the Olympic sports [2] with the highest number of positive doping tests. Cycling was responsible for 3.93 per cent of the positive tests in 2003, which was more than in boxing (3.68 per cent), almost twice as many as in weightlifting (2.06 per cent), nearly three times as many as in athletics (1.46 per cent) and more than four times as many as in soccer (0.93 per cent). [3]

Along with the many prominent doping cases, these statistics raise a central question: have the attitudes towards, and the use of, performance-enhancing drugs among professional cyclists changed at all since 1998? This is the question I will seek to answer in this article. The choice of 1998 as a defining year is due to the fact that the 1998 doping scandal involving the French Festina team kick-started a renewed campaign against doping. My point of departure is the Danish version of this situation, and my analysis is based on material from qualitative research interviews with thirty-four Danish riders, interviewed by myself and my colleague, Kristian Rasmussen, in 2002 and 2003. [4] Danish riders compete all over the European continent, are employed by multinational teams and often live in central and southern Europe. Hence their views and experiences are to a large extent formed by what they encounter at an international level. Which means that even though the Danish experiences are central to this article, they also serve to address issues affecting the broader European situation.

The focus of this essay is thus on contemporary history. However, in order to understand the current situation it is necessary to take a general look at training methods and drug use in cycling from 1950 until the present, since these practices are relevant to the situation in which riders find themselves today.

Preparation for races, 1950 to 2004

In the following description of the development of training methods and drug use, I will distinguish between three historical phases: the 'classical' period from 1950 to 1984, a period of change and reform from 1984 to 1989 and the post-reform contemporary period from 1990 to 2004. This is the division used by Benjamin Brewer in his recent article about the commercialization of cycling. [5]

The 'classical period': 1950–84

The training methods and riders' preparations for races were relatively unsophisticated during the classical period. There were few major breakthroughs in the development of training techniques that were explicitly based on scientific ideas during the years from 1950 to the mid-1970s. The general consensus was that riders should spend most of their winter and spring training on long endurance rides in order to build up a 'base' for competitions during the racing season.

However, there has always been a progressive attitude within cycling towards the medical and technological products made available by modernity. [6] And with the availability of amphetamine in the 1950s, riders gained access to a potent stimulant drug which became widely used within the sport during the 1960s. However, as is the case with performance-enhancing drugs today, this did not mean that all riders had equal access to stimulants. In the spring of 1967 the English former world champion Tom Simpson spent £800 on what he expected to be one year's supply of amphetamines. This was a significant amount of money at the time, and a support rider earning between £4 and £16 a week would never have been able to sustain such an expensive habit. [7]

Professional cycling was among the first sports to introduce compulsory drug tests. A few years earlier, sporadic and imprecise tests had been carried out, but after the World Championships in 1966 the tests became more regular, precise and carried legal authority in terms of sanctions and exclusions. [8] Several prominent riders were strongly opposed to these tests. Among them was the five-times Tour de France winner Jacques Anquetil, who spoke out against the tests on several occasions. He argued that these tests constituted an infringement of the integrity of the riders, and he defended their right as adult, autonomous individuals to manage their own lives and health: 'We find these tests degrading' he said when the controls were introduced in 1966. 'Why should cyclists have to be suspected and controlled while any other free man can do what he likes and take what he likes?' [9]

After the ban on doping came into force in the late 1960s, the use of drugs was hidden from public scrutiny. But consumption was not significantly reduced. Riders, trainers and masseurs were behind the distribution of the drugs, and the dosages were determined according to other riders' experiences, through 'trial and error' and according to 'traditional advice'. In this way the use of drugs reflected the social organization of training and preparation which was common at the time: unsophisticated and bound by tradition. [10]

In certain respects amphetamines and other stimulants are easy to manage. They are taken on the day of the race; the effect on the nervous system is immediate (reduced fatigue and a feeling of enhanced strength and self-confidence) and wears off relatively quickly. Hence, the use of these drugs does not require close medical supervision. From the 1970s, however, the use of a different type of drug – anabolic steroids – became widespread within the sport, and initially they too were used in an unregulated way. [11] But unlike the stimulants, these drugs have a real and longer-lasting physiological effect, and it was therefore most productive to take them on a more regulated basis – during training periods – in order to enhance recovery and rebuild muscles. [12]

The reform period: 1984–89

In 1984 the Italian champion Francesco Moser set a new world record for the one-hour time trial. At the time the holder of the record was the Belgian Eddy Merckx, and Moser was the first rider ever to cover more than 50 kilometres in an hour. Both Moser's specially built aerodynamic bicycle and the scientifically structured training regime he followed in preparation for the record attempt caused widespread astonishment within the sport. Watching a senior professional rider who had adopted new training methods attack the mythical world hour record on a bizarre-looking bicycle was a clear indication that the classical period was coming to an end. [13] Moser's training programme was based on the newly invented portable heart-rate monitor, and he worked in close cooperation with the physiologist Professor Francesco Conconi. [14] During the 1980s Conconi and his protégé Dr Michele Ferrari (and later also Dr Luigi Cecchini) became the most prominent doctors within cycling circles. They acquired a high status within the sport which they have maintained to this day, and it was primarily due to their work that riders made great progress during the 1980s. Training became more scientifically based, and the tradition-bound focus on marathon distances was replaced by interval training and more careful and precise periodization.

Changes in the use of drugs were still in a developmental phase and were not as important as the implementation of new training methods. The use of amphetamine was apparently still common, [15] but more significant changes occurred along with the development of steroid hormones. [16] In January 1985 it was revealed that the great success experienced by the American cycling team at the Olympics in Los Angeles six months earlier had involved extensive use of blood doping. [17] However, as Brewer points out, even though the blood doping scandal was controversial at the time, it proved to be a portent of the paradigmatic change in drug use which occurred about six years later, rather than a revolution in the use of doping within the sport in the mid-1980s. [18]

The contemporary period: 1989–2004

The season for professional riders has become longer. Normally they now have only two months without any racing, but even during these months they cover around 2,000 kilometres of basic training and attend training camps. Close scientific monitoring of the riders has become the norm, and in addition to the normal bicycle computer and heart-rate monitor, many riders today also train with the so-called SRM system (*Schoberer Rad Messtechnik* – Schoberer Bike Measurement Technique), which measures the effect of pedalling and stores these measurements in a computer. Thus, every step on the pedal can, in principle, be made the object of analysis and be adjusted for optimization. During the post-reform period the scientifically supervised training that arrived in the wake of Moser's hour record became fully institutionalized.

Modern doping drugs represent a fundamentally different approach to performance enhancement. The most common doping drug of the 1990s in cycling has been EPO, a hormone found naturally in the body which stimulates the bone marrow to produce more oxygen-carrying red blood cells. In addition to this, anabolic steroids are still used primarily for faster recuperation (rather than the bulking up of muscles), and growth hormone has also become very popular for the same purpose. [19] Unlike steroids, growth hormone is still impossible to detect in a drug test. Steroids and growth hormone are often taken in preparation for important races in order to optimize training and to enable the rider to train even harder. With the technique used until 2005 EPO could only be detected in the urine for about two to three days (see below); hence this has also primarily been used during the riders' build-up phase rather than during races. The effectiveness of the so-called EPO urine test, introduced in 2000 has, however, led to a resurgence of blood doping within the sport. [20]

All these modern drugs and techniques require close medical supervision, calibration and monitoring, which is normally beyond the competence of the average rider. In this way they represent a radical change both in relation to their physiological effect on the athlete and in relation to the social organization of doping. As the sports sociologist Ivan Waddington has pointed out, however, the increased presence of medical expertise within the sport is not just a consequence of the need to monitor drug use. The experts have also played a major role in connection with the introduction of drugs into the sport:

> [T]he growing involvement of practitioners of sports medicine in high-performance sport, especially from the 1950s, has increasingly involved them in the search for championship-winning or record-breaking performances, and this has led them in the direction not only of developing improved diet or mechanical and psychological techniques but, on occasions, it has also led them ... to play an active part in the development and use of performance-enhancing drugs. [21]

This seems to be the case in cycling. The doctor employed by the Festina team in 1998 was a central figure associated with the distribution of drugs and with monitoring the doping programme of the team; in addition, doctors such as Conconi and Ferrari have, over the past few years, assisted with the systematic doping of riders. [22] In the case of these doctors, Waddington's claim is even more relevant: during the 1990s, Conconi's research laboratory had been receiving funding from the International Olympic Committee and the International Cycling Union for the development of a reliable test to detect the use of EPO. At the same time, he had been coaching a number of top riders and managing their drug use. [23] Moreover, it is worth noting that the periodization and careful planning that is characteristic of the management of modern performance-enhancing drugs reflect the development of scientific training programmes, several of which were developed and refined by Conconi and Ferrari themselves during the 1980s and 1990s.

Periodization of training is one of the great steps forward in the development of practical training physiology over the past few decades. [24] This method has been made even more sophisticated through the use of accurate measuring equipment such as the SRM system mentioned earlier. But the increased volume of data generated by this sophisticated equipment also ensures the necessity of medical professionals for the management, analysis and revision of training programmes. The riders e-mail their training data to their trainers/doctors, with whom they are in contact on a weekly or, during their peak periods, daily basis. Developed by the practitioners of sports medicine themselves, the new sophisticated training principles hence contribute to consolidating the hegemonic position of these doctors in relation to training and preparation.

We have seen that the way in which riders prepare for their races has developed significantly during the last fifty years. Training and drug use have become much more complex, and the sport makes increasing use of medical and technological expertise. With the Tour de France doping scandal of 1998, the public became aware of the widespread, and not always legal, use of medicines within the sport. But the media and the public were not the only ones to find these revelations shocking. Within the sport the drug scandal came as a great shock, making it clear to riders and teams that, from that moment on, the sport had acquired a new set of rules.

Three scenarios for the use of doping

Since 1998 the official attitude has been that there must be no more scandals. [25] It has therefore been necessary to intensify the testing of riders to try to eliminate drugs from the sport. Looking only at the Tour de France, there have been no major cases in the seven years from 1998 to 2005. (Whether the case concerning Armstrong's 1999 urine samples can be considered a major case is debatable).

This might indicate that efforts in the campaign against doping have been successful. The first scenario for the new rules of the game might therefore be that, as a consequence of the increased testing and enhanced testing methods, the majority of riders now race without the use of illegal performance-enhancing drugs. This corresponds with the statements from the majority of the Danish riders we interviewed, to which I will return later.

However, the fact that in 1999, 2003, 2004 and 2005 the riders achieved higher average speeds than ever before, along with the many doping cases outside the Tour de France, points toward alternative scenarios. An alternative view of the current rules of the game might thus be based on the revelations concerning the professional teams Phonak, Cofidis and Kelme. In the Kelme team (and to a lesser extent in the Cofidis and Phonak teams), the use of drugs has apparently been organized in the same way as it was in the Festina team during the 1990s. If we are to believe the sacked Kelme rider Jesus Manzano, the riders in the Spanish team have been more or less forced to take EPO and growth hormone, and they had to endure badly administered blood transfusions in connection with blood doping before the 2003 Tour de France. [26] In my interview material, however, there is nothing to suggest that such methods are used in the teams that employ Danish riders.

The third possible scenario for the new and implicit rules of cycling is a reduced role played by the teams in connection with drug use. Because of the significant risks associated with bad publicity, the teams no longer want to be involved in organized doping. Decisions about the use of drugs are therefore left to individual riders, who also have to organize their own doping regimes. But the organized use of drugs must be kept strictly separate from the joint activities of the team. 'You are not allowed to transport any medicine whatsoever when travelling with the team,' the rider Frederik explains:

> We have a very clear set of rules. I am not allowed to transport anything. In my toilet bag I am only allowed to have normal painkillers and cream for my bum for when I have pressure sores and that's it. It says in my contract that I am not allowed to carry any medicine myself, and the team is allowed to search suitcases as a control measure.

The team doctors do not carry illegal medicines either, as he explains: 'Many of the teams enforce a very strict line. Nobody drives around any more in a car like the one Festina used to have. It just doesn't happen, because the team would be closed down and fifty people would lose their jobs.'

With no illegal drugs circulating inside the teams, they can publicly deny any knowledge of drug use and thereby protect themselves against financially damaging scandals. For those riders who choose to make use of doping, it probably means that they encounter the drugs at a later point in their careers than would otherwise have been the case. This is due to the fact that access to the illegal drugs requires establishing a network which is not connected to the rider's team.

External doping networks

The analysis above suggests that drug use within contemporary cycling is primarily organized through networks outside the teams. If this is correct, the networks do not have the institutional character typical of the Festina team of the 1990s. To a certain extent, this differs from the picture presented by Waddington:

> Perhaps the first point to be made is that this case study [the 1998 Tour de France] brings out in a particularly clear way the figuration of relationships among those involved in what might be called the doping network. It should be noted that, in some respects the situation in cycling may be rather special . . . and, as a consequence, it may also be the case that in cycling these networks are more organized and more systematized – in a word they are more highly institutionalized – than in most other sports. Nevertheless, when placed alongside other detailed and reliable case studies, such as those provided by the Dubin Commission of Canada's 1988 Olympic weightlifting and sprint teams, it is clear that at the elite level it is simply unrealistic to see the individual drug-using athlete as working alone, without the assistance and support of others. [27]

The implications of a 'drug bust' for a team's sponsorship suggest that the strongly institutionalized networks associated with the teams have been dissolved, the Kelme team perhaps being a curious exception. Instead, the riders need to establish their own doping networks external to the teams. Waddington is therefore right in saying that doping requires the cooperation of others. There is a need for contact with people who can help with storage and delivery, for example, but especially with expertise and relevant knowledge. Without people who know which drugs to take, when to take them, and how they work, access to drugs is useless. As one of the elite riders, Christian, emphasizes:

> It is of no benefit to have lots of stuff thrown at you straight away. For example, I have spoken to riders who didn't know what to do. They might have all the drugs in the world in front of them, but they didn't know what to do with them.

The networks that can offer medical assistance are not in place when a rider begins his professional career. They have to be established gradually through friends and colleagues who help the rider gain contact with 'the right people'. The doping networks external to the teams are largely built on trust, which requires time to establish. As one of the interviewees put it:

> It depends to a large degree on confidence and friendships. You don't just go to Bologna and ring Dr Ferrari's door bell, who will then receive you with his arms open, and then you pay €5,000 and go home with a full suitcase. It doesn't work like that at all, because it requires a confidence which takes many years to build up. It is – how can I explain it? – it is a gradual introduction to the professional environment.

Frederik is one of the Danish riders who, at a critical point in his career, gained access to such a doping network outside his team. He took the initiative due to problems caused by over-training, which almost resulted in anaemia – 'and it's certainly not healthy when your haematocrit count is thirty-six, and you are supposed to be doing sports. That puts you right at the other end of the scale,' he says. [28] A close friend, who vouched for him, introduced him to people who would be able to help. At first they provided vitamins and minerals, but later he also gained access to more potent drugs. At the core of the network were only five or six people, including a masseur and a doctor, and a couple of other riders. This small group of people constituting the network did not find each other on the basis of previously existing professional relations but through friends and friends of friends. As Frederik gradually became a part of this community, he came to owe his loyalty to the others because they had trusted him. Presented with the hypothetical possibility that he might one day be caught in a test, he emphasizes that he would never reveal the activities of the others in such a situation. In general, riders are very careful and speak as little as possible about doping. Even though the activities within the network have led to what Frederik describes as warm and lasting friendships, he is also aware that these strong ties are strictly necessary, 'because what is done is in reality a criminal offence'. For this very reason, they have to be certain that they can trust each other.

Even though such a network may look like a criminal mafia from the outside (and in some cases it is a criminal arrangement according to the doping laws of some countries), it is primarily seen by the riders as a necessary arrangement which enables them to pursue their ambitions. For them the criminal aspect of the network is a practical rather than an ethical problem. As Frederik explains, though, these risks are taken for the sake of sporting success: 'What I think should be emphasized is that it isn't done for money. Because that's not possible. It's simply too tough for that. Nobody injects this or that drug into their body to make money. The driving force is ambition and passion.'

It is, however, understandable that the structure of a network such as Frederik's, with its demand for loyalty, internal obligations and help for 'friends of friends', feeds the image of a mafia-like brotherhood based on the law of silence, *omertà*. The problem with this image is that it does not just see the silence as a necessary precaution so that riders can use these small limited networks. It also suggests that the sport is one big conspiracy. The interviews with the Danish riders show that this perception is wrong.

Doping within Danish cycling

Apart from the will to enhance performance in an illegal manner, two basic conditions need to be fulfilled in order for an athlete to make use of doping. Firstly, there has to be a drug that works for the sport in question; and secondly, as has been shown previously, the athlete needs contacts and relations with people who can help him gain access to, and possibly counsel him in the use of, the drug. Even though EPO can enhance performance, this does not automatically mean that even those riders who would like to use it always do so. As noted previously, the modern potent hormone-based drugs require guidance and help from people with medical knowledge. It is not enough to simply distinguish between different sports in order to understand the pattern of drug use. One also has to look at how drugs are used within each sport. This is not only because athletes might have differing opinions on what is right and reasonable, but also because, depending on conditions such as age and performance level, they do not have the same opportunities to establish relationships with experts. It is necessary to distinguish between the most talented young riders, the riders belonging to the national elite, and the riders belonging to the international elite.

The young talents

There is no reason to believe that doping is currently a problem among talented young Danish cyclists. None of those interviewed had experience with illegal drugs or methods. The young riders generally expressed great uncertainty and had little knowledge of what one might use and which drugs actually have a performance-enhancing effect. Of course, they have heard about EPO and, to a limited extent, they know how the drug works. But they remain largely ignorant of the three other potent drugs (amphetamine, anabolic steroids and growth hormone). Similarly, none of the young riders has been offered drugs by team-mates, trainers or others, and they have only a very vague idea of where they should go if they are interested in procuring such drugs. Mikkel, who rides for the under-23 national team, exemplifies this position:

> One may suspect that some people are trying to do something. But I have to admit that I have never come across anyone who has offered me anything. So I find it hard to believe that it is so widespread, because I think I have been quite close to the top of Danish cycling, and I have never ever been offered anything or seen anybody do anything. So it seems a bit strange to me that it should be so widespread.
> *But let's imagine that you wanted something, would you know where to go then?*
> No, I actually wouldn't. Apart from the fact that you can go to your local gym and get something there if you want bigger muscles. But that's not of much use to me.

Anabolic steroids, which Mikkel expects to be able to find at his local gym, have been used (and are still used) by some riders. But his statement that bigger muscles are of no use to him demonstrates the kind of ignorance about these drugs which is characteristic of the young riders in general. This, and the denial of any personal experiences with doping, strengthens the impression that this is a group of riders who train and race without the assistance of illegal drugs.

The national elite

The use of doping among riders in the national elite also seems very limited. The positive tests over the last few years have primarily involved less potent stimulants such as caffeine and ephedrine. The riders in this group have brought the attitudes against doping they developed as young riders into the senior league, so they have only limited knowledge of the effect of drugs and where to get them. Part of the explanation for this is that, unlike the big professional teams, the teams for which the national elite race do not have their own doctors. That means they have no immediate access to knowledge about the effects of medical drugs, which is reflected in their view of the drugs as alien and exotic. This makes some riders, such as Søren, talk about them with a certain awe:

> I have no knowledge of doping inside of cycling. Maybe some people use something, but I know nothing about what drugs to take to get better. I've heard about EPO, of course, but if you don't know how to use it, you're no better off. Or you'll probably drop dead.

However, the lack of knowledge and fear of the drugs' effects are not the only significant aspects of these riders' attitude toward doping. Many of them are students, working part-time or are voluntarily unemployed. On the one hand, this provides them with the best opportunities to spend the necessary time on training, but on the other it means that their financial means are limited. It would thus appear that there are only a few riders in the national elite, if any at all, who have the financial means, knowledge and network to start using a drug such as EPO.

The international elite

The attitude among the very best Danish riders is that doping is a problem they do not want. Thus, the majority of the interviewees in this group claim never to have used illegal performance-enhancing drugs. But even those riders who have doped believe that it would be better if everybody raced 'clean'. The fact that they have not adhered to this ideal themselves is either due to being in situations where they were so exhausted physically that they felt they had to take drastic action in order to recuperate, or their ambitions have forced them to play by the same rules as their rivals. There is thus no reason to suggest that the current situation of the best Danish riders resembles what was happening in international cycling during the 1990s, when doping seems to have been widespread. [29] When asked whether he has ever used doping drugs, Martin, who has raced as a support rider on several professional teams, answered:

> No. I know many people claim that it is impossible to race professionally without doping. But I was racing all the time, and I therefore felt that there was a great risk of being caught in tests if I had taken anything. And you can easily race without doping. I know so many riders who do. But I'm also sure that many riders have, in fact, used something.

The risk of being caught was due to the fact that Martin was a support rider. The support riders are in a situation where they are 'racing all the time', as Martin says, and they rarely decide themselves which races they will be competing in. Even though they have scheduled breaks, they might still be used as replacements for sick or injured riders in races they are not supposed to be competing in. The top riders have more freedom to plan their season in order to give them the necessary breaks before the most important races. Those top riders who use doping are therefore able to make sure that they do not race at times when they know they would test positive. Support riders such as Martin do not have this option. Hence, the risk of being caught doping is much greater for support riders than it is for the stars. This is due to the fact that a rider can only test positive for EPO while being on a course of EPO treatment and for two to three days afterwards. [30] Most of the tests within cycling are carried out around the time of races, unlike other sports where two-thirds take place outside of competitions, since this is more effective. Cycling is an exception, as nine out of ten tests are carried out in connection with competitions.[31] But what about the unannounced tests that *do* take place around Europe? How do the riders avoid getting caught in these? The French paper *Le Monde* posed this question to the Cofidis rider Philippe Gaumont after it was revealed that he was a main figure in a major doping network:

> [The tests] are not unannounced! They're carried out at the sites where we train as a group or at the races: so it's easy to get ready for them so you can be sure that you don't test positive. All the riders know that when they take doping drugs, they have to do it on the basis of exactly when they will arrive at the sites where we train or at the races to calculate when they have to stop. [32]

Thus it seems possible to avoid getting caught even in the unannounced out-of-competition controls. To the top riders, the risk of being caught in connection with an EPO treatment seems to be much less than it is for the support riders.

Some professional riders have chosen not to dope on account of the risk of being caught, and also because it violates their ethical standards. When asked whether he has ever felt tempted to dope in order to enhance his performances, Stig answers: 'No, never. You need to make up your own mind about that and decide what you want. It is, after all, only cycling. You need to stick with what you think and say that it's bloody unnecessary. That's all there is to it.' By saying that 'it is, after all, only cycling', Stig shows that, even though he is a committed professional leading a disciplined life that involves intensive training, cycling is not essential to his life. His ambition is not to win any of the great races but to maintain his position in the bottom half of the hierarchy of his team. However, Bo's attitude demonstrates that not everybody takes this view:

> I have wanted to be a professional rider since I was a boy, and now I have been given the chance. And if this means that I have to use medicine, this will not stop me from chasing my dream. I have not spent all these years cycling only to stop now that I have reached a point where I can fulfil my dream.

Cycling is more than a hobby for Bo, it is where he might fulfil his potential and his talent. The sport is essential to making his life meaningful, so it is far too important for him to give up just because he might have to use drugs.

To reach the very top in sport, it is paramount to have an ambitious and uncompromising will to victory, as Bo does, and perhaps even to view sport as the most important thing in life. On the other hand such an ambitious attitude means that doping becomes a factor that is comparable to diet, training, equipment and other matters that are important for optimal performances. You may not necessarily choose to practise doping, but you have to consider it carefully.

We need to critically challenge the idea that professional racing cyclists all belong to the same subculture in the sense that they share certain norms and values relating to the use of doping. They do not. What separate them are the various combinations of talent and attitude regarding how far they are willing to go in order to fulfil their ambitions. The interview material suggests that most professional Danish riders share the view that doping can and should be avoided. However, a small group of riders do not share this view. These are riders who compete at the highest international level. In the course of their careers they will revise their opinions regarding which resources they should use. In addition to their realistic view of the conditions in the international elite, their burning ambition and disciplined way of life make them choose to play by the same rules as the ones they believe their competitors play by. This means that at precisely defined times during their season, they choose to supplement their strict diets and intensive training with potent performance-enhancing drugs.

Conclusion

The many doping cases in cycling in 2004 and 2005 renewed the discussion about attitudes towards doping among riders. Within the sport there has always been an 'entrepreneurial' attitude towards medical and technological developments. As a logical consequence of the dynamic development of modern societies, riders have, since the beginning of the sport, adopted the performance-enhancing technologies made available by modernity. However, since the mid-1980s the traditional approach to training and doping has changed. Scientific and medical supervision of riders has become increasingly common. The increased focus on the sport after the doping scandal in 1998, however, made the organized use of drugs within the teams impossible. Due to the crucial relationships with sponsors, it became necessary for team managers to deny any knowledge of doping. The riders' use of doping now had to take place through networks outside the teams. It is likely that this change means that riders encounter doping at a later stage in their careers than would otherwise have been the case. This is due to the fact that it takes time to establish the necessary trust and confidence upon which the outside doping networks are built. Thus there is good reason to reject the notion that professional Danish riders belong to one and the same subculture. The talented young Danish riders aspiring to become professionals distance themselves from doping and approach the sport with the belief that it is possible to be successful through legal means. The same can be said of riders who compete in the national elite and the majority of professional riders employed by teams around Europe. However, for a small group of riders the perspective changes in the course of their careers. The ambition and will to succeed on the international scene prompt them to establish contact with networks which are able to help them gain access to legal as well as illegal drugs. Furthermore, the dismantling of internal doping networks in favour of networks external to the teams implies that the role of the team doctor(s) has become more ambivalent. To the extent that they continue to provide riders with illegal drugs, they do not necessarily restrict their help to riders from one team. Even though many teams today emphasize the importance of cooperation and teamwork, this change in the doctors' work role points to the historically variable ways in which the various team members contribute to the functioning of an integrated unit.

Notes

[1]   The article is based on material from the author's doctoral thesis (written in Danish): A.V. Christiansen, 'Rene resultater: En kulturanalyse af cykelsporten – socialization, fascination, træning, kost og doping' ['Clean results: A cultural analysis of cycle sport – socialization, fascination, diet and doping'] (PhD. thesis, University of Southern Denmark, 2005).

[2]   These are sports that are on the Olympic programme. This means that sports such as rugby, baseball, American football and professional boxing not are included in this statistic.

[3]   Cycling had 486 positives out of 12,352 tests, boxing had 70 positives out of 1,904 tests, weightlifting had 110 positives out of 5,347 tests, athletics had 276 positives out of 18,876 tests, and football had 187 positives out of 20,104 tests. See WADA statistics 2003: Overview of results reported by the 31 IOC/WADA-accredited Laboratories, Table C, online at www.wada-ama.org/, accessed 8 November 2004.

[4]   We interviewed three groups of riders: a group of young talents, a group of professional and semi-professional riders and a group of former top riders: thirty-four riders in all. These are the interviews from which the views and quotations presented in this article are taken. Of course I know the identities of the interviewed riders, but all riders were guaranteed anonymity so that they could speak freely. Therefore, the riders quoted in the article appear under assumed names. A discussion of the problems involved in interviewing public figures about taboo subjects such as doping is included in my thesis: see Christiansen, 'Rene resultater', ch. 3.

[5]   Benjamin Brewer, 'Commercialization in professional cycling 1950–2001: institutional transformations and the rationalization of "doping"', *Sociology of Sport Journal*, 19 (2002), pp. 276–301.

[6]   See for example John Hoberman, *Mortal engines: the science of performance and the dehumanization of sport* (New York and Toronto, 1992); Les Woodland, *The crooked path to victory: drugs and cheating in professional bicycle racing* (San Francisco, CA, 2003).

[7]   William Fotheringham, *Put me back on my bike: in search of Tom Simpson* (London, 2002), pp. 143–4.

[8]   Tom Donohoe and Neil Johnson, *Foul play: drug abuse in sports* (Oxford, 1986), p. 6.

[9]   Fotheringham, *Put me back on my bike*, pp. 169–70.

[10]   Brewer, 'Commercialization in professional cycling', p. 285.

[11]   Les Woodland, *Dope: the use of drugs in sport* (London, 1980), p. 58.

[12]   Willy Voet, *Breaking the chain: drugs and cycling, the true story* (London, 2001), pp. 36, 40.

[13]   Brewer, 'Commercialization in professional cycling', p. 287.

[14]   Conconi's own account of how the hour record was beaten can be found in F. Conconi, *Moser's hour records: a human and scientific adventure* (Brattleboro, VT, 1989).

[15]   Paul Kimmage, *Rough ride: behind the wheel with a pro cyclist* (London, 2001), pp. 97–8.

[16]   Voet, *Breaking the chain*, pp. 49–50.

[17]   Robert Voy, *Drugs, sport and politics* (Champaign, IL, 1991), pp. 70–3.

[18]   Brewer, 'Commercialization in professional cycling', p. 287.

[19]   Voet, *Breaking the chain*, pp. 49–50.

[20]   In the spring of 2001, the Danish rider Bo Hamburger became the first rider to test positive after taking the EPO urine test. But now there is also a test against the technique of blood doping. Thus, the American Tyler Hamilton from the

Phonak team was the first rider to test positive for blood doping in September 2004.

[21] Ivan Waddington, *Drugs, health and sport: a critical sociological perspective* (London, 2000), p. 141.

[22] Allessandro Donati, 'The silent drama of the diffusion of doping among amateurs and professionals', in John Hoberman and Verner Møller, eds., *Doping and public policy* (Odense, 2005), p. 51. In March 2004 a judge in Ferrera pronounced Conconi guilty of having aided and abetted in the EPO doping of many athletes (John Hoberman, 'Doping and public policy', in Hoberman and Møller, *Doping and public policy*, p. 11). Similarly, on 1 Oct. 2004, Michele Ferrari received a twelve-month suspended sentence for 'sporting fraud' in connection with a major drug case. However, he was acquitted of distributing doping products which could endanger health ('Ferrari found guilty of sporting fraud', *Velonews*, 1 Oct. 2004).

[23] Donati, 'The silent drama', p. 53.

[24] Christof Weiss, (ed.), *Handbuch Radsport: Geschichte und Entwicklung, Freizeitradsport und Radrennsport, Technik und Training, Ernährung und Medizin, Ausrüstung und Material* (Munich, 1996), and R.J. Gregor and F. Conconi, eds., *Road cycling* (Oxford, 2000).

[25] Dominique Marchetti, 'The changing organization of the Tour de France and its media coverage: an interview with JeanMarie Leblanc', in Hugh Dauncey and Geoff Hare, eds., *The Tour de France 1903–2003. A century of sporting structures, meanings and values*, special issue of *International Journal of the History of Sport*, 20 (2003), pp. 54–6.

[26] 'Spaniard says blood was doped', *The Guardian*, 25 March 2004; 'EPO still widely used, claims Manzano', *The Guardian*, 26 March 2004.

[27] Waddington, *Drugs, health and sport*, p. 159.

[28] Normal haematocrit levels (the percentage of oxygen carrying red blood cells in the bloodstream) for untrained men are approximately 42–45. With intensive endurance training this level will typically fall, rather than increase. However, a value of 36 indicates anaemia.

[29] Voet, *Breaking the chain.*

[30] R. Kazlauskas, C. Howe and G. Trout, 'Strategies for rhEPO detection in sport', *Clinical Journal of Sport Medicine*, 12 (2002), table 1, p. 233. These data are valid for the EPO urine test as it worked until the end of 2004. From the beginning of 2005 WADA has substituted the so-called 80 per cent limit with a qualitative judgement: 'suspicious' or 'very suspicious'. This is done in order to give the national federations the possibility of making decisions about sanctions in the light of the total analytical result, and not only from the question of whether the test result was above or below the 80 per cent limit.

[31] Christiansen, 'Rene resultater', p. 277. These are figures from Anti-Doping Denmark. I have not been able to find international data that compare cycling with other sports regarding the frequency of out-of-competition versus in-competition controls, but Gaumont's statement below indicates that the European figures do not differ a lot from the Danish.

[32] 'Selon Philippe Gaumont, les coureurs se jouent des contrôles', *Le Monde*, 15 March 2004.

The Quest for the Imaginary Evil: A Critique of Anti-Doping

Kristian Rasmussen

Most people associate the 1998 Tour de France with the Festina scandal. As is well known, the Belgian *soigneur* Willy Voet was caught on the border between France and Belgium with a car full of doping substance, a discovery that led to the exclusion of the Festina team from the race. Some of the world's best cyclists, such as Richard Virenque, Alex Zülle and Laurent Dufaux, were then treated as criminals and subjected to solitary confinement and interrogation. It later emerged that the provision and monitoring of drugs within the Festina team involved an extremely well-organized network of managers and doctors. At the same time it seemed remarkable that the 'catch' was made by an ordinary customs control rather than cycling's anti-doping authorities. The sheer quantity of drugs found in Voet's car – all meant for the Festina riders – raised questions over the efficacy of doping tests and procedures during the Tour de France.

The Festina scandal prompted a quick and powerful response. Within a year politicians and representatives from sports organizations all over the world met in Lausanne, Switzerland, for the 'Conference on Doping in Sport'. It was at this meeting that the World Anti-Doping Agency (WADA) was established. In the spring of 2003, the fight against doping was crystallized even further when representatives from governments and international sports organizations met in Copenhagen to agree on the Code, a common set of rules for the global fight against doping, also called the Constitution of Sport. Around 1,200 people from 101 countries took part in the conference. The scale of this meeting – more than double the participants of the 1999 conference – reflected a new and global willingness to fight the so-called 'evil' of doping. The Festina scandal had proved to be a watershed resulting in greater collaboration between sports authorities and politicians.

It is important, however, to understand how this globalized project was implemented within national borders and how it affected national sports. This paper will consider the situation in Denmark.

Politics and the desire to control

The events of the later 1990s had a profound impact on Danish sports policy. Politicians increasingly saw it as their duty to intervene to 'protect' what were assumed to be the 'core values' of sport. In February 1999, the then Minister of Culture, Elsebeth Gerner Nielsen, formed a White Paper Commission with the aim of 'creating a unified insight into the background, extent and consequences of the use of doping within sport in Denmark'. [2] Based on the recommendations of the White Paper, the Danish government increased cooperation between the various national sports organizations, which led to the formation of Anti Doping Danmark (ADD) in 2000 – initially for a trial period of three years. The White Paper recommended increased control measures, which could be seen as a natural reaction to the fallout from the Festina scandal. Specifically, the following extract indicates the priorities to be implemented by ADD:

> A set of rules becomes ineffective if the control function is not optimal.
> In Denmark this control function has a good structure with a doping

committee which has an organized practice of testing and analysing the results. The limitations are found in the number of controls carried out, the choice of time for these controls and the choice of sports subjected to controls. The committee estimates that a reinforcement of all three areas may be necessary in order to achieve credibility and a full preventative effect for doping control. [3]

The emphasis here is important. According to the White Paper, doping control would only achieve full preventative effect if all three areas were increased, by both catching more doping culprits than previously (or catching all the ones there are) and pre-empting wrongdoing by increasing the chances of being caught. This seems logical because the alternative would be absurd – that the number of tests would be increased only for the sake of control and that, in reality, there was no problem to justify these controls. With the implementation of the ADD programme, one would expect more athletes to be caught using doping, not least because the Festina scandal was assumed to be the tip of the iceberg – the thin end of a very thick wedge.

An external evaluation of Anti Doping Danmark, published at the end of its trial period (2003), concluded that it had been a successful venture and suggested making it a permanent body. Legislation was introduced stating that ADD's aim was to achieve 'a continual extension of a target-orientated, effective control policy and an offensive strategic information and communication policy'. [4] The report went on to state that Denmark was 'one of the countries furthest ahead with anti-doping efforts'.[5] In order for Denmark to maintain this position, the report recommended that the current budgetary framework for ADD, which was just under 11 million Danish kroner in 2003, should be extended in the coming years. [6] This would allow a significant increase in doping tests over the next three to five years, rising from around 2,000 tests in 2003 to an annual figure of between 2,500 and 3,000. Of 11 million kroner in the 2003 budget, 7.8 million was spent on controls, 2 million on information and communication activities and 1 million on research activities. Thus, the priority was clearly testing and control.

So what is the current situation in the fight against doping? Has the increased effort in the area of control been fruitful or has it been in vain?

Control activities before and after the Festina scandal – continuity or discontinuity?

ADD's Annual Report in 2001 reflected on the apparent gains made in anti-doping policy and practice:

Doping work in Denmark was characterized by continually increasing and ever more target-orientated control activities together with fresh initiatives in the field of information. It must be noted that as many as sixteen cases of doping were revealed during the year. Considering the increased number of tests, this is not a larger number of positive cases than previously, but the total number for Denmark is high. The primary reason for the large number of revelations is that control is carefully measured today. [7]

In 2001 ADD carried out 1,229 tests, an increase of 11 per cent over the previous year. The sixteen doping cases constituted, 'a significant increase in relation to year 2000 (seven doping cases) but still only 1.3 per cent of those tested. In comparison, there were in 1.98 per cent positive tests in 1999 among those tested at a global level.' [8] Ostensibly, it seemed that the sharp rise in positive tests was a consequence of the increased number of tests. However, the following year saw a fall in the number of doping cases, even though one would expect more cases due to a further increase in the number of tests. ADD wrote in the annual report for 2002:

This year ADD has carried out its highest number of tests to date, 1,669 tests in total. At the same time, thirteen athletes were found to have positive urine samples. This is both a relative and absolute fall, which is very positive and to be expected after the anti-doping efforts of the last years. On the other hand, one might have feared more positive tests, as the existing doping control is run very professionally and efficiently and fulfils the highest standards for doping control as agreed in the ISO 9002 certification. [9]

The number of doping cases fell from 1.3 per cent of all tests in 2001 to 0.9 per cent in 2002. This decrease is remarkable as the number of doping tests had increased by 45 per cent between 1999 and 2002. There were five cases in 1999, seven cases in 2000 and sixteen cases in 2001. Thus it would seem that 2002 proved a turning point which the then chairman of ADD, Professor Bengt Saltin, ascribed to the fact that the anti-doping strategies of both information and control were now starting to bear fruit. The pattern continued in 2003, during which the number of controls was increased to 1,936 doping tests (of which 1,778 were carried out on Danish athletes, while the rest were carried out in connection with international events in Denmark, that is, primarily as tests for WADA). The number of doping cases (within the Danish Sports Association's Special Association) fell to eleven while the number of tests had increased by 69 per cent from the 1999 levels. In his preface to the annual report for 2003, Saltin judged the work of ADD so far as follows:

A review of the results so far shows that we are on the right track in focusing on strict control of the elite, not only in connection with competitions but also increasingly during training, where the use of doping is most common in some sports. Control is the core of anti-doping work, but information is also required. For the first time, we have seen a fall in the number of positive doping tests within the area of organized sport where performance is paramount. We would like to suggest that part of the explanation of this development is due to the extensive information activities carried out by ADD. [10]

Developments in 2003 thus confirmed the impression that the reductions of 2002 were no coincidence. They seemed to show that the fight against doping had both led to better times for sport and restored its credibility. ADD's secretariat director, Finn Mikkelsen, assured us that there were very real reasons to be hopeful in the following statement to a Danish newspaper: 'During the latter years, new drugs have emerged against which we have found test methods relatively quickly. Now we just need an effective test for EPO and growth hormone, and then we will have largely won the fight against doping. [11] The headline of the article, 'IOC: We can win the fight against doping', offered an optimistic sense of change. Thus it seemed to be a well-founded judgement for Saltin to conclude in his review of the efforts against doping that strict control of elite athletes had improved the fight against drug use. The wounds caused by the Festina scandal seemed to be healing well – the response had apparently been a success.

However, if we take a more critical look at the White Paper investigations, which were a significant factor in the formation of ADD and the increased fight against doping, a picture emerges of a Danish situation after the Festina scandal that did not necessarily give cause for concern. On the basis of more than 7,000 replies from questionnaires sent out to various sports communities in 1999, the White Paper concluded the following about doping: 'In all the investigations by the White Paper committee, very few of the athletes stated that they were currently using doping.' [12] Whereas the Festina scandal suggested that elite sport was affected by an almost universal problem of which we had only seen the tip of the iceberg, subsequent investigations contradicted this view. Very few athletes within the elite sports community in Denmark in 1999 admitted to using doping, although perhaps such denials ought to have been expected.

The conclusion of the White Paper is supported by a comparison of the number of doping cases before and after the Festina scandal. A review of the period 1993–8 shows that the number of actual doping tests was between 930 and 1,039. In 1993, five were positive; there were nine in 1994, ten in 1995, seven in 1996, twelve in 1997 and ten in 1998. When comparing the two periods 1993–8 and 1999–2003, it is impossible to say that the increase of control activities by 69 per cent during the period 1999–2003 led to more positive tests. In fact, the two periods are at approximately the same level: 1993–8 had relatively more doping cases, because less testing was carried out. Whereas one would expect a rising number of doping cases as a result of an increased number of doping tests, the reality is that the two periods are very similar. It seems that the intensification of control activities has simply revealed the true extent of the problem: only around 1 per cent of athletes used or are currently using doping in the years before and after 1998.

The myth of the doped elite

However, it is no surprise to find that only a very small minority of Danish athletes use doping. In the article 'The Myth of the Doped Elite' (*Myten om den dopede elite*) published in the Danish paper *Politiken* in 2002, Professor Bengt Saltin wrote:

> Myths appear easily and are – even with the strongest counter-evidence – difficult to eliminate. It is a very widespread misunder-standing that more or less all athletes use doping. The fact is that it only concerns perhaps one per cent of the very best of the absolute elite, and within many sports the number is zero. This is not just the case for Denmark, but for the whole world. The evidence is clear! The 'softer' data come from questionnaire investigations and interviews. There is, of course, a large grey area, but even these numbers, which show only a few per cent, are very far from 100 per cent, or the claim that 'everybody' uses doping. More concrete numbers from very extensive control activities within certain large sports say the same thing. [13]

Saltin's article paints a picture of the situation as viewed by him in 2002 when matters seemed to have improved since the 1990s. For example, he mentions that the haematocrit value, which is normally at 40–45 per cent, was on average about 48 per cent for the best athletes during the last part of the 1990s 'with a few individual cases close to 50 per cent or more. At the start of the Tour de France 2001 the average value was below 45 per cent, and only a few cyclists had a value above this'. [14] This and other examples led Saltin to the following conclusion:

A few sports continue to be affected by the use of doping among the very best athletes. But this use is restricted to a small minority, whereas the large majority – 99 per cent or close to this – do not use doping. This is a fact, but probably not enough to convince the sports critics or eliminate the myth that all athletes use doping. I am not going to discuss in any further detail here why so many people prefer to believe that all athletes use drugs, or why they publicize this misconception in writing and in the media, when they really ought to help dispel this myth. [15]

If Saltin is right, one wonders why this myth has appeared at all. It is reasonable to assume that the activities headed by Saltin himself through ADD have, in fact, contributed to the formation of the myth. It is thus impossible to ignore the fact that both the political decision to form ADD and the extensive efforts initiated by ADD in terms of control and information have contributed to an over-exaggerated perception of the problem.

It was clear from the White Paper on doping that only a small minority of elite sportsmen used illegal drugs. Nevertheless, an anti-doping campaign of hitherto unseen dimensions began. This involved a significant increase of control activities, Internet-based teaching materials, an annual anti-doping prize donated by the Minister of Culture and the organization of the Conference on Doping in Sport in 2003, the biggest event of its kind in Denmark. These are only a selection of the Danish initiatives that followed in the wake of the Festina scandal, and which indicate a high level of activity disproportionate to the 'real problem'. Similarly the formation of ADD was itself symbolic of the fact that politicians and sports organizations exaggerated the problem. ADD has aimed to promote information and enlightenment but paradoxically has helped perpetuate myth rather than fact. Or, put differently, 'enlightenment' is based on myth – there is no doped elite. The role of the media has been vital to this process. Their quest for sensational news has meant that factual aspects of doping have been overtaken by the myth of the doped elite. In other words, reality has become over-exaggerated. It is precisely this point that the French sociologist Pierre Bourdieu makes in his thought-provoking essay *Sur le télévision*. [16] He argues that the presentation of reality in the media is to a large extent characterized by the fact that only the 'sensational' is 'news'. It is not 'sensational' to report that only a small minority of the elite uses doping – just as the ADD report of 2002 is far from 'newsworthy' when it states: 'Most doping users are still non-elite athletes. Since 1995, 80 athletes have tested positive, and of these 30 per cent represent the national elite. More than 95 per cent of those tested during the same period belong to this group. [17]

Other forms of evidence support Saltin's portrayal of doping practice. In 2001 there were sixteen doping cases: four each in both weightlifting and powerlifting, three in working men's sports clubs and one each in athletics, cycling, motor sport, ice hockey and handball. [18] In 2002 the distribution of doping cases was as follows: weightlifting (five), American football (three), cycling and motor sports (two each), DAI (Danish Working Men's Sports Association) and powerlifting (one each). [19] There is some historical consistency in these results: between 1980 and 1998, the highest number of positive tests were in power lifting and weightlifting with thirty-one and twenty-two cases. Thereafter, there is quite a gap to the third sport, cycling, with ten cases during this period, while only four cases of illegal drug use were found in athletics. One of the biggest Danish sports, handball, experienced its first ever doping case in 2001.

The above raises the following question: if doping is as infrequent and as restricted to specific sports, why accuse all sports of being corrupted by drugs? On 7 September 2001 ADD hosted the conference 'Why is Doping Illegal?' Speaking to the delegates, the sociologist Bjarne Ibsen argued that anti-doping policy overlooks a key important aspect of the issue:

> We know that doping within sport is not a general problem. It is a problem within certain sports environments. From the studies carried out in Denmark we know that it is primarily found in certain fitness and bodybuilding environments and in elite cycling. But this general description of those sports is also unfair. According to what we know, it is only in specific training environments – certain fitness centres, training environments or sports clubs – that the use of various doping substances takes place. [20]

However, in spite of this knowledge, the current doping policy with its focus on strict control of the elite together with press handling of the doping issue both suggest that the problem is more widespread and general. It seems that the reality, namely that the problem is of a specific nature, is unable to supplant the view that the elite in general uses doping.

One possible explanation for the discrepancy between doping policy and reality is that the fight against doping is, in fact, fuelled by doped elite athletes, real or imaginary. The myth cannot survive simply on recreational athletes; it needs more high-profile victims. Similarly, it is difficult to imagine that the fight against doping would have assumed the same proportions if recreational athletes had constituted the main threat.

From this perspective, the myth has been created by the anti-doping campaign itself and an increasingly aggressive anti-doping policy, which sends signals of a general problem. Thus it is both a dangerous and laudable project when Professor Bengt Saltin makes efforts to kill off the myth: dangerous because he risks undermining the very foundation for ADD, laudable because he speaks from a position of reason and enlightenment.

The White Paper on doping established what was already known: very few athletes in elite sport use doping. Nevertheless, anti-doping activities of hitherto unseen dimensions were initiated in Denmark. It is, however, easy to imagine the media storm which would have arisen if the White Paper had concluded that there was no reason for further action. The period after 1998 seemed ripe for emotional reactions rather than a reasoned response based on the insights gained. This conclusion is supported by the sociologist Ivan Waddington who, in his book *Sport, health and drugs,* uses the words 'moral panic' as a description of the emotional reactions to the issue of doping. [21]

Following on this one may include the sociologist Ulrich Beck's thoughts on the risk society as an interpretative key enabling us to understand why something that appears to be no major problem grows into an issue of enormous proportions. The event that seriously marked the advent of the risk community was the nuclear disaster in Chernobyl in 1986. While industrial society offered a possibility of eliminating the fear of the unknown and anxiety-provoking events through real or symbolic limits, the nuclear disaster in Chernobyl marked an epoch-making break, pointing towards the fact that everybody is potentially included in the nuclear age threat of dissolving traditional borders.

The problematic aspect of the risk society is that we increasingly see danger everywhere, even where none exists. Danger often takes the form of an encounter with an invisible enemy-how can we know that our food does not contain pesticides and our drinking water is not contaminated? The idea of danger lurking everywhere makes us suspicious. Under the headline 'A speculative age', Beck writes:

> The threats of civilization mean that behind the visible world a new 'kingdom of shadows' appears, which can be compared to the gods and demons of the ancient world; a 'kingdom of shadows' threatening human life on earth. . . . Everything must be seen in a double perspective, and can only be properly understood and evaluated based on this double vision. The visible worlds must be problematized, relativized and evaluated, based on another reality which is con-

structed mentally but nevertheless founded on fact. And the criteria of judgement are found in this other reality, not in the visible world. [22]

One of the consequences of the risk society is that 'new communities and alternative communities, whose world views, norms and certainties are grouped around the centre of the invisible threats' appear – so-called danger communities, where the danger in question may be more or less real. With regard to the doping issue there appears to be a disproportion between the threatening image conjured up and the world of reality. One might therefore call the fight against doping a quest for an imaginary evil: the evil does exist but not to the extent suggested by the quest. With this background, I will take a closer look at one of the greatest doping scandals of our time according to WADA.

The THG scandal

On 16 October 2003 Terry Madden, the leader of the American doping agency, USADA, publicly declared that a number of American athletes had tested positive for a hitherto unknown drug called tetrahydrogestrinone (THG), which is a synthetically produced steroid. On 18 October 2003 the Danish tabloid *Ekstra Bladet* wrote under the headline 'American Doping Shock':

> You run a week's risk. But you gain several months' worth of advantages. That was the reality for American sports stars willing to use doping right until last night (Danish time), when the American anti-doping agency detonated perhaps the biggest bomb for many years. According to USADA, numerous athletes have used the synthetically produced anabolic steroid tetrahydrogestrinone, called THG. It is a drug that has a strong muscle-building effect like other steroids, and it is a drug constructed to be impossible to detect in a doping test. According to USADA's statement in the case, the drug has circulated in a Bermuda triangle between coaches, doctors and willing athletes, and it was only when an athletics coach anonymously revealed this and handed over a syringe with THG to the authorities that they became aware of the drug. . . . 'What we have discovered seems to be determined doping of the worst kind. We are dealing with a conspiracy of chemists, coaches and certain athletes who used what they thought were invisible designer steroids with the purpose of cheating their competitors and the American and global public, who pay to watch the sports events,' says Terry Madden, the leader of USADA. [23]

A total of 350 athletes had already tested positive for THG at the American athletics championships, and 100 other American athletes were also on the list of positive tests. It was expected that the number of doped athletes would rise significantly when the whole world began to test previously frozen urine samples for the presence of THG. For once, doping control had succeeded in being ahead of the situation by developing a test for a new drug without the athletes' knowledge. The almost Sherlock Holmes-like character of the case and the expected great consequences are described in the Danish paper *Berlingske Tidende* under the headline 'The Shadow of the Syringe':

> The whole case surrounding THG started in June, when an anonymous American athletics coach sent a syringe with remnants of the drug to a laboratory in Los Angeles. Here experts succeeded in identifying the drug and cracking its code, which has hitherto made it impossible to trace in doping controls. If the current cases are proved and more appear, it may mean that the Athens Olympics will be held without the participation of some of the most popular and famous athletes in the world. [24]

Among the more prominent names soon added to the list of fallen doping athletes was the European 100-metres champion, the British sprinter Dwain Chambers. He was named and shamed as a THG user on 22 October 2003 when his doping test from a competition on 1 August showed traces of THG. Chambers reacted, as has been seen so often in connection with positive doping tests, by declaring his innocence. His solicitor Graham Shears made this public statement: 'Before we have a satisfactory description of the composition and effect of THG, nobody should condemn Dwain Chambers.' [25] It is interesting that Chambers did not deny having taken the drug; he only appealed for a fair trial. His coach, Ukrainian-born Remi Korchemny, similarly expressed a wish for fairness: 'THG is not an illegal drug. Have you seen the molecular structure? This is a big case in the media, but neither Dwain Chambers nor I have done anything wrong.' [26] It was no use: Chambers received a two-year doping sentence.

The success of doping control not only demonstrated that it had been ahead of the athletes: it also demonstrated that the fight against doping could succeed in uncovering more extensive use. Until then the police had been behind the major discoveries of doping cases such as the Festina scandal, Operation Blitz during the Giro d'Italia in 2001 and the Cofidis revelations at the end of 2003. But the general secretary of WADA, the former New Zealand solicitor David Howman, left no doubt that the THG controversy had considerable implications: 'It is just as serious as the drug use which took place during the seventies in East Germany and the scandals this brought about.' [27] The impact of the case was such that the news agency Ritzau continued to refer to it a year later:

> East Germany, China and the sport of cycling have for many years been considered the strongholds of doping. But the doping arrow now points towards the USA. Accounts of the systematic use of illegal and performance-enhancing drugs have accompanied sport for the last thirty years. . . . But now the epicentre of doping has moved to the USA. [28]

The seriousness of the situation was further emphasized when George Bush took the opportunity in his annual speech to the nation to call for a fight against steroids:

> 'Success through steroids is a dangerous signal to send to the youth of America,' said Bush, and he encouraged all parties in the world of sport to fight against illegal drugs. The words were epoch-making, because for the Republican president to call for a fight against steroids was to acknowledge that the problem existed. [29]

But was there a problem at all? This question was raised by the Danish doping researchers Bengt Saltin and Rasmus Damsgaard from Anti Doping Danmark, when they expressed doubts about whether THG should even be considered an illegal drug, as no scientific studies apparently exist to prove that it is performance-enhancing. The following is a selection of some of the viewpoints presented by the two Danish researchers:

> Dr Rasmus Damsgaard has previously questioned the effect of THG, and he is now supported by the Chairman of Anti Doping Danmark, the Swedish Professor Bengt Saltin, another international heavyweight in the field of doping. 'There are no convincing studies to prove that the drug has an anabolic effect, and as long as it is not performance-enhancing, it cannot be considered doping,' maintains Saltin, who does not understand why WADA have taken such drastic action in the THG case. 'If it has not been clearly established that THG is doping, it is wrong to name and shame a range of athletes as doping users on that basis,' Saltin argues. [30]

> There are many steroid hormones with no effect. The precondition for a breach of the rules is a documented performance-enhancing effect, but it would appear that the international doping agency (WADA), together with the International Olympic Committee (IOC), have stepped into this case in order to make clear to the international public that they are ahead. WADA and the IOC are determined to clean up the sport of athletics in the USA. My only hope is that WADA have

good substantiation for their case,' says the Chairman of Anti Doping Danmark, Professor Bengt Saltin. [31]

The question is whether WADA, together with USADA, the American national anti-doping agency, have unravelled the biggest doping scandal in the history of sport, or whether they have started a 'cry wolf' story of fatal dimensions. In Anti-Doping Danmark, Dr Rasmus Damsgaard has previously called for a bit of deliberation and stated that he lacked evidence to prove that the new drug has any performance-enhancing effect at all. It should, therefore, not be illegal. He fears that the athletes 'have been taken hostage' in a political case, as many ineffective substances sold as miracle drugs have a molecular structure similar to anabolic steroids but nevertheless do not have any anabolic effect. [32]

'I find it deeply problematic for WADA's credibility that they chase doping culprits without having final proof that the drug is perfor- mance-enhancing. We could easily investigate THG ourselves. But for me it has become a matter of principle that WADA, as the world agency, ought to carry out the test,' says Bengt Saltin, chairman of ADD. Saltin was previously engaged in a dialogue with WADA's medical director, Olivier Rabin, about the possibilities of testing whether THG is indeed a doping substance. However, WADA gives 'strange' replies whenever Saltin asks whether a test is on the way. 'The problem is that they hardly say anything at all. As it is a steroid-like preparation, there are obviously indications that it is performance- enhancing, but I simply don't understand why WADA does not investigate this,' says Saltin. . . . 'The biggest problem is that WADA, as a relatively new organization, which needs to unite the world against doping, risks losing credibility through this. It is possible to test THG in three months, so there must be a hidden agenda,' says Saltin. [33]

The scepticism of the Danish doping researchers finally struck a chord with both the Danish Sports Association (DIF) and the Minister of Culture, Brian Mikkelsen. The latter in particular was able to use his influence through being a member of WADA's executive committee – an influence which has become even greater since his election as vice- president of WADA. The Chairman of DIF, Kai Holm, said about the THG case:

> Of course we will follow WADA's policy and recommendations. But we cannot bring any actions against people, if there is any doubt that THG is a doping drug. Hence, DIF will approach WADA in order to have its account about problems with THG. We will then evaluate this account together with Anti Doping Danmark, so that there is no uncertainty about which attitude to assume towards THG in Denmark. There must be no doubt that we will do everything to chase up THG cases if

there is a proper legal foundation for them. However, doubts about this have been raised by our own medical experts among others, and we will therefore have to ask WADA. [34]

Brian Mikkelsen echoes the same demand for explanation and scientific integrity. Under the headline 'Minister demands documentation', he has been quoted as follows:

> THG has now been added to WADA's list of doping. This is a purely medical decision, which I am in no position to criticize, as I am not a medical expert. However, at the forthcoming meeting of WADA's executive committee, I will ask for an explanation of the process, as drugs should only be put on the doping list when there is sufficient documentation. ... I will ask for documentation for the performance-enhancing effect of THG, and if this does not exist, I will suggest that an investigation into the effects of the drug is initiated as soon as possible. However, I expect that a thorough medical analysis of THG does exist as WADA has put it on the doping list and I have no reason to believe that they have acted without reason in this matter. [35]

Later that month, Brian Mikkelsen travelled to a meeting of WADA in Montreal, carrying with him a demand for a scientific explanation of the THG issue. Before the meeting the newspaper *Politiken* confronted WADA's chairman, Dick Pound, with the Danish scepticism, to which he replied: 'I am sorry to hear this, but the rest of the world considers it a steroid, it has been treated as such, and it will be included in the list of illegal drugs.' [36] Pound did not entirely reject the possibility that the case could be investigated further, but the Danish sceptics had to accept that opinions can be difficult to change. On his return from the WADA meeting, Brian Mikkelsen brought this answer with him – here quoted from the tabloid paper *Berlingske Tidende* under the headline 'Saltin put in his place':

> Minister of Culture Brian Mikkelsen, Conservative, does not want to hear any more quibbles about the new designer steroid THG. The drug is included in the international doping list, and hence Anti Doping Danmark must test for it, even though the performance-enhancing effect of the new drug has not been investigated and documented. 'I expect Anti Doping Danmark to do this. The case is closed until a verdict has been reached in the big THG case currently running in the USA,' says Brian Mikkelsen. ... 'It is true that Anti Doping Danmark had told me about their scepticism towards THG. I presented this loyally at the meeting of the international anti-doping agency WADA in Montreal a week ago. But at one of the closed meetings of the executive committee Terry Madden, chairman of USA's anti-doping agency, revealed information which convinced me that THG is a

performance-enhancing, artificially produced steroid. I also accept that due to the current court case in USA against the company Balco, which has produced THG, Madden was unable to present the American documentation. The American court system is different from ours and it has very specific rules surrounding legal justice for the accused. But I am convinced that THG is performance-enhancing. The American statements about the performance-enhancing effects of THG will definitely hold up. [37]

According to Brian Mikkelsen there is no doubt that WADA does have the documentation to prove that THG is performance-enhancing. This is also apparent from the minutes of the congress in Montreal, in which Terry Madden confirmed that THG was a performance-enhancing substance, that Professor Catlin would ensure that evidence would be properly received and that the sanction hearings would probably be completed by the end of January 2004. [38]

More than a year after 2004, the case against Balco is still open: hence WADA has not presented any documentation for the performance-enhancing effects of THG. However, Bengt Saltin doubts that the Americans have any real documentation to prove that THG is performance-enhancing:

> The argument does not stand up. Documentation could easily have been presented to the medical committee of WADA, of which I am a member. For practical reasons we have split the subject areas between us. I am not the expert on steroids, but this case is so big that I would have heard about it from our steroid expert, Christiane Ayotte. She is even based in Montreal, where the WADA congress took place, but according to our electronic correspondence she shares the Danish scepticism about the performance-enhancing effects of THG. [39]

One wonders why it is possible to present an explanation of the performance-enhancing effects of THG to Brian Mikkelsen, whereas it is seemingly impossible to allow the same information to be shared with WADA's medical committee. If this is a question of legal justice, one would assume that the medical committee is bound by the same professional secrecy as Brian Mikkelsen. Similarly, WADA's position might be strengthened if reference could be made to the supporting medical evidence that cannot at present be made public.

As for the two sceptics, they had to give in to a more powerful authority. The Minister of Culture ordered Anti Doping Danmark to test for THG in future. Saltin's comment on the result of the case was 'It is pure politics' – a judgement with which Rasmus Damsgaard agreed. 'Athletes have been taken hostage in this case, and I almost believe it to be an infringement of human rights. The athletes have been branded as doping users with no scientific evidence to support this whatsoever. It is unprofessional, irresponsible and unscientific'. [40]

That is how the case should have ended. The only thing lacking to this day is the documentation to prove that THG really is performance-enhancing. But it is only a matter of time before it will appear once the court case against Balco is completed. And even though the case has been prolonged, many things now seem to indicate that the sceptical doping researchers have made a significant error. Thus, in January 2005 the *San Francisco Chronicle* wrote:

> Victor Conte is the founder of the Burlingame-based Bay Area Laboratory cooperative. He is awaiting trial in the US District Court of San Francisco on steroid-conspiracy charges for allegedly providing banned drugs to more than thirty stars of Major League Baseball, NFL football and Olympic track and field. . . . In an appearance last month on the ABC program *20/20*, Conte confessed that he had distributed drugs to a long list of elite athletes, including track and field superstar Marion Jones, world record sprinter Tim Montgomery and former NFL linebacker Bill Romanowski. Jones has denied ever taking performance-enhancing drugs and sued Conte for defamation after his televised allegation. [41]

In other words, WADA's general secretary, David Howman, seems to be closer to the truth than the two doping researchers in his comparison of the THG scandal with ' the drug use which took place during the seventies in East Germany and the scandals this brought about'. One might ask how Saltin and Damsgaard have been able to ignore the revelations of the Balco case. What serves as an excuse for the two is, of course, that they raised the criticism at a time when the case was in its very early stages. If one asks them today, however, they still have the same view of the matter. Not even Victor Conte's public confession is able to change this, which leaves the impression that the two doping researchers refuse to acknowledge what is visible to anyone. However, the matter is not quite so simple, as will become evident.

Firstly, the argument that Balco founder Victor Conte is said to have distributed doping to a range of athletes is not the same as saying that THG *is* doping. Secondly, one might notice the remarkable fact that WADA decided to change the words in the Code for 2004 as a result of the discovery of THG:

> The discovery of the 'designer steroid' Tetrahydrogestrinone (THG), has made clear that the definition of 'analogue' as defined under

sections S4 and S5 of the former List is inappropriately restrictive. In fact, in its former version, the List required an analogue to have both a similar chemical structure and similar pharmacological effects. However, contrary to good medical and pharmaceutical practice, these 'designer steroids' are administered to athletes despite the lack of any studies on their pharmacological effects. Therefore, in order to be able to cover new 'designer steroids' in future and to prosecute such cases quickly, it is important that substances that have a similar chemical structure or similar pharmacological effects be prohibited. In consequence, the references to 'analogues' and 'mimetics' in sections S4 and S5 have been deleted and replaced by the same wording that is used in sections S1 and S8 namely: '... and other substances with similar chemical structure or similar pharmacological effect(s)'. [42]

At a glance, this seems to be an insignificant change in the words of the code. However, on closer inspection it opens the door to a range of important consequences. In order for a drug to be added to the doping list it must fulfil at least two out of three conditions according to the WADA code:

1. It must be performance-enhancing;
2. It must be injurious to health;
3. It must be against the spirit of the sport.

The problem with THG is that, so far, it is only possible to claim that it is against the spirit of the sport. This problem will, of course, be solved when the court case against Balco has finished, and the documentation for the performance-enhancing effects of THG is presented to the public.

The arguments used by WADA to justify the revised wording of the code are based on the claim that the THG case showed the existing wording to be too restrictive and hence prevented quick action. This might be a valid point, because if the banning of THG was dependent on the conclusion of the Balco case it would not yet be included in the doping list. If the principle of legal justice is inviolable and THG is deemed by scientific research to be a performance-enhancing drug, then it is essential to change the wording of the code itself, as this can be revised later if necessary. The inviolability of the rule of law should always come before a political document such as the code. However, WADA's emphasis on legal justice may have important consequences. What if it is discovered that a drug such as THG has no performance-enhancing effect at all? In this case the reference to legal justice not only sounds hollow, it also confronts WADA with a serious problem of credibility, because they have knowingly used the principle of legal justice as a cloak of secrecy. We can only have confidence in WADA and Brian Mikkelsen when they assure us that the THG case is based on solid scientific foundations and is not 'pure politics'.

Anti Doping Danmark had this comment for the changed wording of the code:

> Following the discovery that the Balco lab in San Francisco had developed the designer-steroid THG, WADA (the world's anti-doping agency) have decided to change the doping list to the effect that this designer-steroid is now defined as an illegal drug. Therefore WADA published a revised doping list on 26 March this year (2004). In this list WADA argue that the term 'analogue drugs', as this appeared in the former doping list, can be interpreted too narrowly. In order to take new designer-steroids into consideration in future, and in order to raise charges quickly, it is important for the agency that this kind of drug falls within the definition of illegal drugs. Hence, WADA has chosen to change the definition of 'analogue drugs' from 'drugs with a similar chemical structure AND similar pharmacological effect' to 'drugs with a similar chemical structure OR similar pharmacological effect'. [43]

Initially it may appear that ADD's emphasis on the insignificant change in language is meant to help the inattentive reader. However, there is more to it than that:

> This may just look like a small change of language, but if you consider the consequences in this choice of words, you will discover that this is not the case. This slight change will fundamentally alter the premise for what can be considered doping, and which drugs will be placed on the doping list. ... The consequence of WADA's change is that the number of drugs falling within the new definition will increase significantly. Among other things, it means that a range of plant steroids and the body's own cholesterol are now placed on the doping list, which sends unclear signals to the athletes about which drugs are legal and which drugs are included in the doping list. [44]

The confused signals to athletes are not the only objection raised by Anti Doping Danmark. Far more serious is this comment:

> When the THG case started in the autumn of 2003, Anti Doping Danmark (ADD) offered to carry out investigations to establish whether THG does in fact have any performance-enhancing effect. But WADA was not interested. Now WADA and the American anti-doping agency (USADA) are waiting for the conclusion of the court cases against a range of athletes as well as Victor Conte, the man behind the Balco laboratory. In order to sentence the people accused, WADA and USADA must be able to prove that the accused are in

breach of the doping rules. In ADD's opinion, USADA and WADA may have problems proving that THG has any performance-enhancing effect. It would appear that WADA have acknowledged that they were unable to follow their own rules and have therefore chosen to change the rules, so that the court case can still be won. [45]

Only the future will show whether Anti Doping Danmark are right in saying that WADA do not have any documentation to prove that THG is performance-enhancing. But if WADA do not have the documentation they claim to possess, Rasmus Damsgaard and Bengt Saltin have not only been right in the criticism they have raised; they have also raised critical doubts about the credibility of WADA. In this regard, Rasmus Damsgaard expresses his opinion as follows:

> As THG only fulfils one of three criteria and thus cannot be considered a doping drug, WADA, who at the time had already charged several athletes with its use, chose in March 2004 – four months after publishing the names of these athletes – to change the text in the list of illegal drugs under anabolic androgynous steroids: 'analogues' and 'mimetics' in sections S4 and S5 have been deleted and replaced by 'other substances with a similar chemical structure OR similar biological effect(s)' [46]

He furthermore sums up his view of the matter in these words:

> It will never be proven whether THG is performance-enhancing and/or injurious to health. In other words, WADA's list contains drugs about which no experts know anything, but about which anti-doping politicians have a certain opinion. Do I need to mention that the change in the list was implemented without consulting the members of WADA's own medical committee, who are internationally handpicked and esteemed experts in their fields? [47]

There is no doubt that athletes caught with THG in their bodies in future will receive a sentence. There is probably no doubt either that around 350 athletes who tested positive for THG during the American championships are simply waiting to receive a sentence when the court case against Balco has been concluded. When this day arrives, it will be possible to judge whether the THG scandal really was a scandal, or whether it is WADA that should be vilified for failing to produce the promised documentation. Bengt Saltin thinks it is 'pure politics'. The question is whether Dwain Chambers will take the same view if it is found out that THG is not performance-enhancing and thus should not have been put on the list of doping substances. The changed wording of the code that has enabled THG to be added to the doping list does not alter the fact that Chambers and all the other 'named and shamed' athletes would, in such a case, be victims of what can be considered as moral panic. While the fight against doping has proved to be a quest for an imaginary evil in terms of its extent, time will tell whether the THG scandal is an imaginary evil too.

Notes

[1] This paper, including all quotations, has been translated from the Danish original by Mette Bollerup Doyle.
[2] Ministry of Culture, *Doping i Danmark – En hvidbog* (Common Code 1999), p. 5.
[3] Ibid., p. 209.
[4] Anti Doping Danmark, *Evaluering 2000–2003* (2003), p. 7.
[5] Ibid., p. 4.
[6] The approximate conversion rate is £1 equals 11 kroner. Therefore the 2003 budget for ADD was £1m.
[7] Anti Doping Danmark, *Årsberetning 2001*.
[8] Ibid.
[9] Anti Doping Danmark, *Årsberetning 2002*.
[10] Ibid.
[11] 'IOC: vi kan vinde kampen mod doping', *Berlingske Tidende*, 21 Dec. 2004.
[12] Ministry of Culture, *Doping i Danmark – En hvidbog*, p. 10.
[13] 'Myten om den dopede elite', *Politiken*, 7 April 2002.
[14] Ibid.
[15] Ibid.
[16] Pierre Bourdieu, *Sur le télévision* 1996. On Television and Journalism, translated by Priscilla Packhurst Ferguson, London, 1998.
[17] Anti Doping Danmark, *Årsberetning 2002*, p. 6.
[18] Anti Doping Danmark, *Årsberetning 2001*.
[19] Anti Doping Danmark, *Årsberetning 2002*.
[20] *Why is it illegal to use doping*. Presentations and discussion, Anti Doping Danmark Conference of Ideas, 7 Sept. 2001.
[21] Ivan Waddington, *Sport, health and drugs: a critical sociological perspective* (London, 2000), p. 111.
[22] Ulrich Beck, *Risikogesellschaft. Auf dem Weg in eine andere Moderne* (Frankfurt am Main, 1986); all excerpts translated from the Danish version, *Risikosamfundet – på vej mod en ny modernitet* (Copenhagen, 1997), pp. 98–9.
[23] 'Amerikansk doping-chok', *Ekstra Bladet*, 18 Oct. 2003.
[24] 'Skyggen af sprøjten', *Berlingske Tidende*, 28 Oct. 2003.
[25] 'Doping: Advokat kræver svar om THG', *Jyllands Posten*, 29 Oct. 2003.
[26] 'Doping: Mystik om dopingsag', *Jyllands Posten*, 28 Oct. 2003.
[27] 'Saltin sår tvivl om THG-doping', *Berlingske Tidende*, 23 Oct. 2003
[28] The news agency Ritzau, here translated from 'USA er havnet i dopingens centrum', *Dagbladet Holstebro-Struer*, 4 Aug. 2004.
[29] Ibid.
[30] 'Saltin sår tvivl om THG-doping'.
[31] 'Doping: Dopingmuren vakler igen', *Jyllands Posten*, 24 Oct. 2003.

[32]   'Øget mistanke om gigantisk dopingskandale', *De Bergske Blade*, 30 Oct. 2003.
[33]   'Ministeren kræver dokumentation', *Politiken*, 8 Nov. 2003.
[34]   'Doping: DIF går til WADA om THG', *Berlingske Tidende*, 29 Oct. 2003.
[35]   'Minister kræver dokumentation'.
[36]   'Doping: Danmark alene med skepsis', *Politiken*, 20 Nov. 2003.
[37]   'Saltin banket på plads', *Berlingske Tidende,* 26 Nov. 2003.
[38]   Minutes of WADA Foundation Board Meeting, 21 Nov. 2003, Montreal, Canada.
[39]   'Ren politik', *Berlingske Tidende,* 26 Nov. 2003.
[40]   'Kulturminister Brian Mikkelsen: THG er doping', *Berlingske Tidende*, 22 Nov. 2003.
[41]   'FBI raids BALCO chief's home – agents seek clues to IDs of Chronicle sources in scandal', *San Francisco Chronicle*, 27 Jan. 2005.
[42]   Press release from WADA, 26 March 2004.
[43]   Press release from Anti Doping Danmark, 1 April 2004.
[44]   Ibid.
[45]   Ibid.
[46]   Email correspondence with Rasmus Damsgaard, cited with his permission.
[47]   Ibid.

Index